EARLY CHILDHOOD EDUCATION SERIES

Leslie R. Williams, Editor
Millie Almy, Senior Advisor

Advisory Board: Barbara T. Bowman, Harriet Cuffaro, Celia Genishi, Alice Sterling Honig, Elizabeth Jones, Gwen Morgan, David Weikart

Promoting
Social and Moral Development
in Young Children

CREATIVE APPROACHES FOR THE CLASSROOM

Carolyn Pope Edwards
with Patricia G. Ramsey

Foreword by
Lawrence Kohlberg

Teachers College, Columbia University
New York and London

Published by Teachers College Press, 1234 Amsterdam Avenue, New York, N.Y. 10027

Library of Congress Cataloging in Publication Data

Edwards, Carolyn P.
  Promoting social and moral development in young children.

  (Early childhood education series)
  Bibliography: p.
  Includes index.
  1. Child development—United States.   2. Education, Preschool—United States.   3. Constructivism (Education) —United States.   I. Ramsey, Patricia.   II. Title. III. Series.
LB1115.E37   1986   372′.21   86-14449

ISBN 0-8077-2831-4
ISBN 0-8077-2820-9 (pbk.)

Manufactured in the United States of America

91 90 89 88 87 86 1 2 3 4 5 6

Contents

Foreword by *Lawrence Kohlberg*   vii
Acknowledgments   ix
Introduction   xi

PART I: BASIC PRINCIPLES

1 The Nature of Children's Social Knowledge   **3**
A Theoretical Base: The Work of Jean Piaget   5
Key Psychological Assumptions About Knowledge and
    Its Development   8
Key Philosophical Premises About Education
    and Teaching   15

2 Conducting Thinking Games   **21**
Thinking Games: What Are They?   22
Guidelines for Conducting Thinking Games   25

PART II: DOMAINS OF SOCIAL KNOWLEDGE

3 Children's First Social Categories: Age Groups   **37**
The Development of Children's Understanding of Age   38
Children's Age-Group Categories   45
Suggested Books for Children   55

4 "Boys and Girls": Gender and Sex-Role Awareness   **58**
Developing Gender Identity   59
Acquiring a Sex-Role Identity   66
Suggested Books for Children   75

5 Racial and Cultural Categories, by Patricia G. Ramsey   **78**
Children's Responses to Racial Differences   79

Children's Awareness of Cultural Differences   90
Stereotypes and Overgeneralizations   96
Suggested Books for Children   97

6   The Ties That Bind: Family and Friendship   102
Friendship and Family: What Are They?   103
The Development of Family and Kinship Concepts   104
The Development of Friendship Concepts   116
Suggested Books for Children   122

7   Understanding Society   126
The Development of Economic Concepts   127
The Development of Occupational Concepts   138
Suggested Books for Children   145

8   Becoming Moral   148
Defining Morality and the Teacher's Role   149
Moral-Decision Task One: Interpreting a Social
    Situation   151
Moral-Decision Task Two: Deciding What Is Right and
    Wrong   160
A Sample Moral Discussion: "The Circus Parade"   174
Suggested Books for Children   177

Appendix: Summary of Developmental Changes in
    Social Knowledge During the Early Childhood Years   182
Notes   187
References   193
About the Authors   207
Index   209

Foreword

Carolyn Edwards, the author of this book, is an outstanding researcher of the social development of children who brings to her work not only the sensitivity of a psychologist, but also that of an anthropologist who has looked in depth at children in variety of cultures. One of the foremost scholars in the cross-cultural study of social development, she is a researcher whose work is independent, integrated, and original. Her understanding of the development of social knowledge in young children is grounded in her research, in which she has utilized both clinical interviews and intensive observation of children's interaction in the classroom. While this work was the springboard for her book, her advice to educators on promoting social knowledge in the early childhood classroom is also based on a thorough understanding of a number of theories of social development (my own included), an integration of the core insights of each theory, and an awareness of both the realities of the classroom and the problems that early childhood educators face. However, this book is not only psychologically sound and extremely useful for teachers; it is also written in a clear and engaging style that will capture the attention of any reader.

I perhaps should add a word about Dr. Edwards's purpose—communicating to teachers ways of promoting the development of social knowledge. Since the time of John Dewey, early childhood educators have intuitively felt that assisting the child's development through cognitive, social, and moral stages should be an important aim of education. As this book makes clear, pursuing this path does not mean requiring the child to do artificial tasks, training him or her, or force-feeding development. Rather, the activities that are suggested appeal to the spontaneous interests of the child, making these thinking exercises an enjoyable and enriching experience for the children.

In many of my own writings I have elaborated, in a much more theoretical way, the philosophical and psychological-research support for the kind of activities that Carolyn Edwards recommends, and this work, as well as the extensive research carried on in the last ten years in the field of child development, is carefully reflected in Dr. Edwards's book. Much of her approach, however, remains unique to her, for it arises from her own research and observation.

I heartily recommend this book to any early childhood educator: Teachers with extensive backgrounds in the classroom will welcome its many practical suggestions, while the educator new to development theories as they relate to the early childhood classroom will find it an excellent introduction to theory as well as a knowledgeable guide to practice.

LAWRENCE KOHLBERG,
Harvard University

Acknowledgments

This project was supported by a Mina Shaughnessy Scholarship (from the Fund for the Improvement of Postsecondary Education and the Carnegie Corporation), which provided me time in 1983–84 to reflect on my "learnings through practice" as director of the Early Childhood Education Laboratory School at the University of Massachusetts.

I am indebted to the distinguished scholars with whom I have worked. Lawrence Kohlberg, Elliot Turiel, and Kurt Fischer, my teachers at Harvard University, influenced the views of social-cognitive development and moral education presented in this book. Irving Sigel, Rodney Cocking, and Carol Copple at Educational Testing Service and George Forman at the University of Massachusetts introduced me to a powerful approach to constructivist preschool education. Finally, though this book mainly concerns adults and children in *this* society, it grows out of a larger concern with culture, socialization, and schooling I have acquired from anthropologists Beatrice and John Whiting of Harvard University.

The staff and students at the Laboratory School have been important colleagues in this project. Patricia Ramsey, now at Mount Holyoke College, has creatively applied social-cognitive theory to multicultural education. Mary Ellin Logue, now at Westbrook College, originated some of the most effective "thinking games," coauthored conference presentations and journal articles, helped find out about children's family and friendship concepts, and collected valuable interviews with children. Anna Russell has spent countless hours with me discussing the importance of Piaget for teacher education. All of the student teachers and graduate teaching assistants at the Laboratory School from 1980 to 1985 contributed by convincing me that social-cognitive theory is an excellent entry point into the constructivist perspective, helping develop the thinking games, and collecting interviews and observations. Colleagues in the University Child Care System did the same. I especially thank Carolyn Clark, Thomas Driscoll, Kinter MacKenzie, Naz Mohamed, and Elise Seraydarian.

Many people improved this book by criticizing the manuscript at various stages: Marjorie Davies, Alison Dayno, Richard Edwards, Kathleen Hughes, Dorothy Lange, Mary Ellin Logue, Roberta Navon, Georgia Pope-Rolewski, Anna Russell, Marcy Sala, Edward Tronick, Lynn Warren, and Leslie Williams, Early Childhood Education Series Editor for Teachers College Press. Eleanor Thuemmel, administrative assistant at the Laboratory School, gave unstintingly of time and effort throughout the project.

Finally, many children in the greater Amherst area provided what I regard as the real essence of this book: the examples of children's reasoning that illustrate the theory and give it life. Samuel and George Thomas Edwards, now aged seven and four, inspired most of my best insights, and to them this book is dedicated.

Introduction

Teachers who work in contemporary early education settings have many reasons to ask serious questions about children's social and moral development.

In the first place, the tasks of managing a group and assisting children to learn seem to be becoming ever more complex. Young children are even less prone than older ones to leave their troubles at home when they arrive at school or center. Many of the most worrisome problems of American society directly affect young children: the high divorce rate, dissent about men's and women's roles, the continuing evil of racism and discrimination, the cultural and moral confusion caused by the magnitude of the new immigrant groups entering the country, the gap between generations (especially between the elderly and the young), and the lack of societal consensus about moral issues and values. All these problems affect young children by causing emotional stress in their personal lives and by making ever more difficult their task of forming stable and constructive ideas about people, society, and moral right and wrong. Can teachers and caregivers help children deal with these stresses and better understand their world—both what "is" and what "ought to be"?

Another pressure that early educators are feeling concerns "preparing children for school." Many parents and community leaders are urging early educators to put a focus on readiness skills so that children will enter first grade set to go on reading, writing, and arithmetic. Does this mean that teachers and caregivers of young children should abandon their traditional emphasis on the "social-emotional" area— that they should give up their central concern with fostering children's self-confidence and ability to get along with others?

This book is intended to address both of these educational concerns. Its central premise is that teachers and caregivers today need to recognize and respond to the special ways that *children* form working models of their social world. Young children's general intellectual drive is powered by their ideas about themselves and the people around them, and when they are allowed to use initiative in reasoning about social and moral issues, they begin to learn autonomously in all areas. Teachers can best run a classroom that prepares children intellectually while also fostering social development if they appreciate how children construct knowledge about themselves, others, society, and morality. They can best address children's emotional needs and get them ready for first grade not by emphasizing readiness skills but rather by centering their attention on children's general, self-motivated quest to learn about their social world and how it works.

This book explains young children's intellectual development, especially their acquisition of social and moral knowledge. It is intended to give a deeper account than is typical of books for teachers, in order that teachers can operate with firmer knowledge about this important subject matter. Chapter 1 introduces the theoretical framework. Because it summarizes the key psychological concepts and philosophical assumptions of the book, some readers may wish to study it last rather than first to crystallize their understanding. Chapter 2 presents practical guidelines for conducting social/moral discussions with children and can be used as a reference when the reader goes about trying out thinking games. The real heart of the book is the six chapters (3 to 8) that comprise Part II. They focus on different content areas: age identity and roles; gender identity and sex roles; racial and cultural categories; concepts of family and friendship; societal institutions; and moral decision making. These chapters are self-contained and can be read in any order.

The chart in the Appendix summarizes the key points about all these changes in the early childhood years. It reviews what children's own basic concerns or questions are at each age level, as well as what their newly emerging social understandings are. Examples of children's ideas at each age level are given to illustrate the kinds of statements that children at each level tend to make.

To be a teacher requires a continual search for answers concerning children, teaching, and oneself as a professional. This search involves a deep personal dimension that can never be ignored. Teachers must and should engage in continual self-examination as they strive to bridge theory and practice in their own unique ways. This book grew out of our fascination with children's reasoning and our desire to find out more about ourselves; it is our best "answer for now" to the question of how teachers and young children should respond to each other's attempts to make sense of their shared human world.

Part I

BASIC
PRINCIPLES

CHAPTER 1

The Nature of
Children's Social Knowledge

Young children work actively to acquire knowledge. But *how* do they acquire knowledge? And how can adults, whether teachers or parents, assist them in this process?

This book explores how children acquire knowledge about society, social relationships, and morality—what we call the social world. The focus is on children between the ages of two and six, and the purpose is to explain children's social knowledge: what it is and where it comes from.

In all cultural communities worldwide, the years from two to six are a time of rapid changes in the development of social and moral knowledge. Everywhere, children are born into an involving and demanding human environment, and although their intellectual skills are limited and immature, they want and need to make sense of *who* people are, *what* they do, and *why* they do it.

Young children use interaction to comprehend people's identities, predict behavior, and gain a sense of competence and control in social interaction. This is a difficult task, but it is critical to children's well-being. Even infants, we now know, are not socially isolated; they participate in social networks that include most or all of the people who nurture and respond to them. One noted pediatrician believes that infants are the focus of family reciprocity.[1] Certainly by preschool age, most youngsters recognize and interact with a whole cast of characters who populate their familiar community settings—for example, relatives' homes, parents' workplaces, neighborhood play areas, retail shops, and so forth. For many American children, teachers[2] are also significant figures and may be the adults outside the immediate family with whom they spend the most time and have the closest relationship. Simply by being born into the human family, then, young children are challenged to understand self, others, social and moral relations, and societal institutions.

3

Adults must help children to gain social and moral knowledge and become more aware of one another's feelings.

All this basic knowledge, gained through interaction, we can define as *social cognition*.[3] Key parts of it are systems for identifying and classifying self and others; for making inferences about people's thoughts, feelings, and intentions; for understanding institutions such as the family and the government; and for learning about rules and values that define right and wrong. Social-cognitive knowledge is never just a random assemblage of facts and rules; it is organized, structured knowledge. "Understanding others is not merely a matter of learning more about people in some quantitative sense; it is organizing what one knows into systems of meaning or belief" (Shantz, 1975, p. 266).

Social knowledge provides a basis for all communication and interaction, for all learning and problem solving, at home and school. Social knowledge is central to children's adaptation to objects and events, as well as to people. Without social knowledge, children could not even recognize themselves or others, orient themselves in a group, use learning materials in a socialized way, or correct and improve their skills through comparison with others. All educational theories begin with the assumption that learning takes place in a social context. The teacher must know about children's social cognition as a way of understanding what happens in the classroom.

Children's early social knowledge, as we shall see, differs strikingly from adults' ways of knowing, yet it serves their purposes well. Teachers must understand the special nature of children's social knowledge in order to plan a curriculum that best supports development. In addition, such understanding provides a firm basis for an approach to guidance and authority that best recruits children's cooperation.

Throughout this book, we will review recent progress in research on children's social cognition. Much of the research is not well known to teachers, yet it has many implications and applications. The research literature has expanded rapidly in recent years, and though major controversies remain, the findings represent a rich resource for early childhood educators. It is possible to use the research both in curriculum planning and in responding to guidance and disciplinary situations. In fact, we believe that the social-cognitive research supports a coherent approach to teaching that promotes the child's autonomy and mature interdependence with others in all areas of learning and development.

A THEORETICAL BASE: THE WORK OF JEAN PIAGET

Every teacher proceeds with a set of conscious or unconscious guiding assumptions. These theoretical principles include assumptions about *what children know* and *how knowledge develops*. In addition, they involve a set of assumptions about *the purpose of education* and *the practice of teaching*. The approach presented in this book derives both its psychological and its educational assumptions from the theory of Jean Piaget.

Piaget (1896–1980) was a Swiss psychologist who considered himself to be a biologist and philosopher as much as a psychologist. He created a branch of study called genetic epistemology. Epistemology is the science of the nature and grounds of knowledge, and the term "genetic" denotes a developmental progression from level to level. We believe that Piaget presented the best account of how the minds of children develop. Piaget's theory leads, not to a specific rigid and defined curriculum, but rather to a flexible approach to understanding and working with children that can be adapted to any age group and learning setting.

Piaget's theory is based on a central idea that all knowledge is *contructed*. In Piaget's own words, "To present an adequate notion of learning one first must explain how the subject manages to construct and invent, not merely how he repeats and copies" (1983, p. 112).

Everything we know, including even how to reason logically, is the product of our activity. We construct knowledge as we observe and act upon objects, communicate and interact with people, and try to make sense of discrepancies in our experience. Other people and our cultural heritage guide the direction of our thinking, of course. The knowledge that we construct bears a relationship or resemblance to that of others around us. Yet we do not receive knowledge passively; the process of constructing knowledge is best described as *guided reinvention* (Fischer & Bullock, 1984). The role of the teacher is that of guide, facilitator, and problem-stimulator.

This view contrasts markedly with the traditional assumption of American behaviorist psychology that knowledge is *culturally transmitted*. In that familiar model, which underlies much of American education, the mind is viewed as a learning device adapted for building up associations between environmental inputs (called stimuli and reinforcements) and behavioral outputs (called responses). Teaching involves gaining control of the environmental events in a way that causes desirable behavioral outcomes. Teachers instruct or shape children's behavior so that the children gradually build up competencies and accumulate information and skills.

The behaviorist model is now beginning to fade from influence in its extreme form. Still, one of its most basic ideas, the emphasis on "socialization," remains deeply rooted in our thinking because it is part of the system of common American childrearing beliefs. That is to say, American adults—whether parents or teachers—commonly and easily assume that children get all or most of their ideas "from outside." We leap easily to the idea that children express notions that they have "picked up somewhere" or "heard from someone," rather than supposing that children mostly construct their own notions about things.

While the socialization model remains part of the common parlance, the Piagetian perspective has become increasingly familiar to early childhood educators. This change is largely due to the efforts of American educators who have worked to explain Piagetian theory to teachers and explore the theory's implications for educational practice.[4] To date, the major practical impact of Piaget's theory on the American classroom has probably been in terms of curriculum activities in science and mathematics. These are the domains of concept development most focused upon by Piaget.

Moore (1979) summed up Piaget's influence on early childhood curriculum in this way: "Most current early childhood curriculums include activities that challenge children to observe the properties and functions of objects, note likenesses and differences among objects, organize objects and events into classes and concepts, order things on the basis of time or size, and describe the relation of objects or things to each other" (p. 54).

Yet some of Piaget's most widely known writings, especially those based on his early work, did discuss children's social and moral reasoning. These writings include *The Language and Thought of the Child* (1923/1960), *Judgment and Reasoning in the Child* (1924/1976), and *The Moral Judgment of the Child* (1932/1948). They have provided the seeds for the newly blossoming field of social cognition, though much of the research represents a major extension and elaboration of Piaget's work.

We believe that the whole domain of social-cognitive research should serve as a starting point for a more holistic Piagetian approach to education. Educators, including Piagetians, have not yet gone far enough in considering the implications of children's social knowledge for supporting their development. Our approach focuses on social knowledge because it is central to the self of the adult as teacher and to the self of the child as learner. It is central to the adult because an appreciation of children's social knowledge offers the most potential for transforming the teacher's relation to the child and to the process of education. It is central to the child because when a teacher moves away from an instructional and directive role and allows the child to construct knowledge freely, the child gets the biggest possible boost in becoming a self-initiated thinker and discoverer. When both adults and children use initiative in thinking about social and moral issues, they begin to construct knowledge autonomously in all domains.

The type of freedom that we are advocating, however, must be sharply distinguished from a freedom that sets no limits or standards.

That kind of "permissive" or "laissez-faire" approach is based on an assumption that all children's ideas and actions are equally good—or at least that adults cannot judge which are more adequate and which less adequate. Our approach, in contrast, postulates that some of children's ideas are developmentally more adequate than others, but that teacher-led "instructing" is not an effective way of moving children from less mature ideas to more mature ones. Instead, teachers must find ways of implementing their curriculum that do not obstruct the processes of knowledge development they are seeking to support.

KEY PSYCHOLOGICAL ASSUMPTIONS
ABOUT KNOWLEDGE AND ITS DEVELOPMENT

Both the Piagetian perspective and the approach to young children's social knowledge that we develop in this book are based on four assumptions about knowledge and its development. These are conceived of as scientific assumptions. They cannot be "proved" by scientific evidence, but they are "supported" by evidence. The meaning and importance of the four assumptions will become clearer later in this book, as we discuss the different categories of social knowledge. But it is useful here to state them directly, before trying to apply them.

1. Development follows a predictable sequence.   Central to Piaget's theory is the idea that cognitive development proceeds through a sequence. Piaget's earlier writings emphasized a sequence of *stages*, with each stage characterized by a different kind of psychological structure for organizing perceptions, actions, and representations. The stage concept involves a hierarchy from simpler to more complex and the idea that a child must pass through each stage before going on to the next. Each step in the sequence is an improvement, in the sense that the kind of thinking it represents is more inclusive, differentiated, and powerful (that is, able to resolve more problems). In Piaget's view, children may develop through the stages at different rates, and anyone may stop developing at any point, but when development does occur, it always follows the same invariant sequence.

Development, in this theory, involves a process of continuous transformation and reorganization of earlier patterns into more mature patterns of thinking. While the process of change is continuous and gradual, the results are discontinuous. Children's concepts of justice, for example, typically evolve over time in a smooth and gradual way.

Yet the ideas of kindergartners are qualitatively different from the ideas of older children: kindergarten children typically think that the only fair solution to a dispute is for everyone to get exactly equal shares, while older children understand that considerations of special need and merit need to be figured in.

Errors and uncertainties are a natural and necessary part of development. Errors (oversimplifications or contradictory ideas) are inherent in all stages but the last. Errors of a given kind are normal for a child at each stage. For example, young infants are usually unperturbed when people disappear from sight; they do not realize that people are permanent objects "out there"; to them, only what is visible exists.

Errors and uncertainties are necessary and valuable because they create the mental tension that motivates growth and change. Because the "right" kind of errors and uncertainties are essential to development, the teacher's role should not be to try to root out and correct children's errors, but rather to implement learning encounters that let children work on the problems that naturally interest them. This perspective challenges one of the most common assumptions of teachers—that they should try to "correct" children's errors right away. Instead, teachers should create learning encounters that amplify the problems and uncertainties in children's own thinking. These encounters will capture children's interest because they correspond to the issues on which children themselves are spontaneously working at their stage of development.

How many stages of development are there? Piaget (1983) posited three principal periods of development: (1) the sensorimotor period, (2) the representative period (containing preoperational and concrete operational subperiods), and (3) a period of propositional or formal operations. These three periods correspond roughly to infancy, childhood, and adolescence. Piaget believed that these stages of cognitive development are made possible by spurts in neurological development, that is, the physical maturation of the brain.

The existence of these broad stages—in fact the whole stage concept itself—has proved controversial. Some psychologists have disputed the idea of an invariant sequence or that development occurs in broad waves. The controversy has caused some Piagetian researchers to adopt "modified" stage theories, with weaker assumptions about the nature of stages. These revisions retain the ideas of sequence, of transformation and reorganization, and of qualititative change, but they drop other assumptions.

For example, William Damon (whose work we shall examine in

depth in Chapter 8) disputes the idea of "stages in the strong sense" and speaks instead of *levels*. Damon has proposed sequences for the development of concepts of friendship, justice, authority, and social regulation. He does not believe in stages in the strong sense because his evidence suggests that children occasionally regress in level from one testing time to the next; moreover, children often show inconsistent levels of performance across different tasks measuring knowledge of a concept (Damon, 1983a).

Another theorist, Kurt Fischer (1980), has presented a major revision of Piaget's stage system that includes ten hierarchical cognitive "skill" levels, organized into three tiers. We have found his system to be extremely useful because it presents the most detailed explanation of the changes that take place within the early childhood years. The "sensorimotor" tier (typical of infancy) consists of skills composed of sensorimotor sets, that is, sensory perceptions and motoric actions on objects, events, or people in the world. The "representational" tier (typical of early and middle childhood) consists of skills composed of representations, that is, concepts by which children can think of objects, events, and people independently of looking or acting on them. The "abstract" tier (typical of adolescence and adulthood) consists of skills composed of abstractions, that is, concepts that apply to broad categories of objects, events, or people, such as "justice" and "beauty." Abstract concepts can be analyzed or compared apart from the particular instances to which they apply.

Fischer believes that the 10 skill levels underlie all thinking, no matter what its subject matter. However, Fischer feels the idea of stages is misleading because it implies that children will tend to use one level of thinking across all subject areas. In fact, says Fischer, children are never at the same skill level for all subject areas; development always proceeds unevenly. Children do have one highest level of which they are capable at a given point in time, and as their brains mature, their highest level increases. During the early childhood period, the years from two to six that are the focus of this book, children typically develop cognitive skills from Levels 4 through 6 in the representational tier. First (Level 4) they can understand and use images, words, hand signs, or other symbols as simple labels. Later (Level 5) they can relate two representations and think about how things covary, for example, in terms of cause and effect. Later still (Level 6) they can combine representations into systems and think systematically about how several dimensions of variation are interrelated.

In later chapters, we will refer to both Damon's and Fischer's ideas in greater depth. Like them, we assume that development does occur in orderly sequences, and in order to place ourselves on the strongest ground in terms of the empirical evidence, we too will speak in terms of levels rather than stages.

2. Knowledge is organized, or "structured." The idea of structure is obviously key to Piaget's theory. Structure characterizes intelligence because from the start of life, people tend to organize their cognitions and behavior into patterned units (Piaget called them schemes; Fischer calls them skills). At first these structures are simple and crude, for example, the sucking reflex in infancy. Over time, the structures come under more voluntary control and become more abstract, for example, the concept of self as different from others (a structure emerging in late infancy) or the concepts of "good" and "bad" (structures emerging in early childhood). A structure itself cannot be seen, of course; what we see are instances of behavior that exemplify the structure.

How general or broad are structures? Here again Piaget and some (but not all) of the neo-Piagetians disagree. Piaget believed in very broad structures—the stages. Lawrence Kohlberg, one of the major social-cognitive theorists whose work we will discuss, also believes in very general structures. Kohlberg has created a six-stage theory of moral-judgment development, and he believes that a person tends to have one dominant stage that he or she uses when making moral judgments about issues as diverse as keeping promises, obeying parents, and helping people in need. While Kohlberg believes that a person may also employ reasoning at one or two stages adjacent to the main stage, he denies that a person can use all of the moral stages simultaneously.

Other social-cognitive theorists believe in much more limited structures. Elliot Turiel, for example, divides the structures of moral reasoning into two separate domains, one including knowledge about justice and human welfare, and the other including knowledge about social conventions that regulate or order society, such as dress codes, sex roles, and rules of etiquette.

Kurt Fischer is extreme in terms of arguing for specific or limited structures (called skills). Fischer believes that a child is never at the same cognitive level across all skills because even small alterations in the context of behavior change the skill being used. Skills develop in complexity as they are stimulated by environmental challenge; skills challenged most frequently will typically be at the highest level of which the child is capable. Skills are constructed and reconstructed as the child acts on the environment, and when stimulated by challenge, the child combines and differentiates skills from one level to form skills at the next higher level. Movement from one level to the next for every skill occurs in many micro-steps, rather than in large, sudden surges (Fischer, 1980).

Which theorist is correct? In our opinion, the question remains open. Probably structures or stages as broad as Piaget first envisioned them do not exist, but whether structures broader than Fischer's skills may be found, we do not know.

From the practitioner's point of view, the debate is interesting but perhaps not of critical importance. Whether structures are broad or narrow, we can still say that children's thinking is organized or structured and consists of networks of ideas. Whether their structures are broad or narrow, they will be confused by a teaching method that seeks to correct their errors and replace their ideas with isolated bits of adult wisdom. As Kamii and DeVries (1978) so aptly put it, "Such teaching confuses the child because it is in opposition to his spontaneous beliefs, and it thus contributes to the development of attitudes that stifle the construction of his own knowledge" (p. 36).

3. Development takes place through interaction between child and environment.   Development is not the result of maturation unfolding from within the child. Nor is it the result of a simple copying of the environment outside the child. Rather, it is the result of interaction between child and environment, regulated by the child. Children construct knowledge for themselves and ultimately are responsible for what they know.

Following Piaget, we can identify ways in which people use their experience and logical capacities to construct new knowledge. One is called *empirical abstraction*, the other *reflexive abstraction*.[5] It is important to clarify these processes because they explain the role of the environment in the development of social knowledge. They explain how children construct their own knowledge yet are "guided" in their "reinventions" by other people and the wisdom of their cultural heritage.

Empirical abstraction produces knowledge about the observables. By "observables" we mean all the characteristics of objects, events, or people that a child is capable of noticing. This includes how they appear, how they respond to the child's activity, and (very important in the case of social knowledge) how they are classified or described by other people, especially by people who are authority figures. Information is drawn from observation of objects, events, or people, or it is gained through activity, interaction, or communication with them.

Empirical abstraction never involves a pure taking in of other people's words or physical facts. Rather, it always involves a filtering of the information in terms of the child's previous knowledge or preconceptions. Children notice only certain things about objects, events, and people; they "hear" only some of the things that are said to them. On the basis of their current state of knowledge, they empirically abstract some observations from all the potentially observable qualities that are flowing by them or being presented to them through their activity, interaction, and communication with others.

Imagine the situation of a young boy (aged about four) beginning to notice features of social life related to gender differences. If the child should notice the way in which gender labels are used, he might think, "Some people are called 'boys' and some are called 'girls.' People call me 'boy.'" This involves observing how people are classified in his language. Or if he should participate in gender-stereotyped play at his school, he might abstract the idea, "Boys play rougher with me and like to be wild!" This involves observing how boys versus girls respond to him in peer interaction. Should he be an attentive watcher of the television show "Mr. Rogers' Neighborhood," the child might conclude, "Mr. Rogers says that a boy is a boy from the beginning, and a girl is a girl from the beginning. That must be an important rule to remember about boys and girls." This involves committing to memory (and perhaps only partially understanding) an adult pronouncement. Or, should he try out on his grandmother an idea that turns out to be shocking to her, he might think to himself, "I told my grandmother that I want to be a Mommy when I grow up, and she made a very strange face. I must have said something bad." This involves forming a conclusion on the basis of one person's response to him in an emotionally charged incident. All these examples illustrate common ways in which young children empirically abstract social knowledge. Though adults typically assume that children attend mostly to people's words, in fact children are active and acute observers of people's facial expressions, behavior, dress, and anything else that they consider significant.

Reflexive abstraction goes beyond empirical abstraction. It produces knowledge indirectly from experience by intellectual reflection on the experience. Reflexive abstraction involves the application of logical thinking to experience, "logical thinking" here meaning the kind of cognitive structures set forth in Fischer's skill levels. Thus, the logic a child brings to bear on experience itself becomes more powerful as he or she matures. At every age, however, reflexive abstraction involves a mental coordination of relationships that are present in

experience but not directly "visible." This kind of abstraction produces knowledge about the underlying nature of reality. Reflexive
abstraction, even more than empirical abstraction, reveals the constructive nature of human intelligence.

Some examples of reflexive abstraction may be given for the situation of the four-year-old reflecting upon sex differences. The boy
might realize that the fact of "boyness" logically excludes the fact of
"girlness"; "If you're a boy, you can't be a girl!" Or he might infer the
logically corresponding nature of the categories of boyhood and man-
hood; "If you're a boy, you have to grow up to be a man." Or the boy
might (incorrectly) infer that job and kinship roles are exclusive categories and conclude (as we once heard the three-year-old son of a
female pediatrician say), "Mommies can't be doctors."

Reflexive abstraction in the case of social and moral knowledge
often involves a particular kind of cognitive coordination, the coordination of social perspectives. Piaget (1923) showed that young children's cognitive structures place severe limits on their ability to coordinate the perspectives of self and others. For example, in understanding
how things look to another, a child must take the other's role on spatial
relations. In understanding how things are *understood* by another, a
child must infer what the other is thinking, feeling, or intending. When
children (or adults) fail to take the role or perspective of others adequately, they exhibit what Piaget called *egocentrism*. Egocentrism
involves assuming that the other thinks, feels, or wants what the self
does, or it involves a failure to coordinate perspectives and instead to
just focus or center on one perspective in a problem. With time, a child
becomes more able to coordinate perspectives through reflexive abstraction. For example, he or she constructs knowledge of justice
through realizing that one must coordinate the claims of everyone in a
dispute about fairness. Similarly, a child constructs an understanding
of kinship through constructing one system that coordinates the perspectives of all the kinfolk toward one another simultaneously.

**4. Social development involves a spiraling increase of knowl-
edge of self and knowledge of others.**   Throughout life, new knowledge about the self illuminates one's understanding of others, and vice
versa, new knowledge about others is quickly transformed into understanding of the self. Neither progresses without the other.

This insight comes from the theory of James Mark Baldwin, an
American psychologist influential at the turn of the century and read
closely by Piaget. Baldwin (1899/1973) wrote, "My sense of myself
grows by imitation of you, and my sense of yourself grows in terms of

my sense of myself" (p. 9). This is the dialectic of personal growth. Discoveries made about others are quickly applied to one's sense of oneself, and insights into oneself are projected outwards to see what light they shed on the actions of others. Thus, the development of social knowledge equally involves self-study and learning about others (Lewis & Brooks-Gunn, 1979a, 1979b).

KEY PHILOSOPHICAL PREMISES ABOUT EDUCATION AND TEACHING

Our approach to the development of social knowledge also depends on some key assumptions about the purpose of education and the practice of teaching. These assumptions are conceived of as philosophical premises about the best ways to apply the developmental perspective in actual work with young children.

1. Development is the aim of education. "Development as the Aim of Education" was the title of a landmark paper published in 1972 by Lawrence Kohlberg and Rochelle Meyer. This paper sets forth a way to translate constructivist developmental theory into educational practice.

Development is the aim of education not simply because children do develop but because development is good. Development is not just any type of change; it is change toward greater differentiation, inclusiveness, and powerfulness of ideas. It involves progress toward more advanced or mature forms of reasoning, judgment, and action. The goals of development are not imposed from outside but set by internal criteria that are provided by the mind itself as it grows in its powers.

Adults who facilitate development are those who hold mature intellectual and moral ideals and who both defend them in the classroom and project them effectively to children. Education ideally involves the support of intellectual and moral values that correspond to developmentally more mature levels of reasoning. Such values include *scientific standards* of truth, based on ideals of impartiality and respect for evidence. They also include *democratic standards* of justice, based on concern for human well-being and respect for rights of each individual.

Such a projection of intellectual and democratic values, however, is not the same thing as the "transmission" or "socialization" of values involved in behaviorist psychology. We are not speaking of the teacher arbitrarily imposing his or her own (adult) standards of truth and

Young children are eager to discuss social and moral issues when problems are presented at their level of understanding.

justice. Instead, the teacher's goal should be to try to discover and support those forms of inquiry, discussion, and democratic decision making that are appropriate given the experience and age of the children involved. When children are actively involved in the processes of critically examining ideas, evaluating proposed solutions, and formulating classroom rules, they feel that the values come from within themselves, not that they are imposed from without. Their cooperation and commitment are enlisted on behalf of those values, as understood by them.

2. Education involves elaboration and extension of children's competence, not its acceleration.   The goal of education should be to support and facilitate development and help children to develop appropriate competencies.

Acceleration, in contrast, involves making demands on children for which they do not have the necessary cognitive prerequisites. For example, two-month-olds are not cognitively ready to talk, two-year-olds to read, and four-year-olds to do formal arithmetic. Pushing or hurrying children to accomplish such tasks is intellectually useless and emotionally stressful to them. "In the blind rush to accelerate growth, overexpectancy can be a form of oppression. The child may experience the adult's desire to push him into adults' ways of thoughts as a lack of respect for what he is" (Hooper & DeFrain, 1980, p. 160).

What are the types of learning for which young children are cognitively ready or prepared? The entire period of early childhood is normally one of rapid development of representational skills, and teachers should have a central objective of fostering this process. Young children show tremendous expansion of their abilities to use and manipulate signs and symbols (such as words, pictures, sign language, and sculpture). This *representational competence*, as Irving Sigel has called it,[6] provides the basis for all of the thinking we consider "human"—reconstructing the past, anticipating and planning for the future, understanding and performing creatively in science, technology, the visual arts, music, and almost all other endeavors. The development of representational competence can be seen in all of the areas of social concepts that we will explore: age, sex, and ethnic categories; family and friendship connections; societal institutions; and moral and conventional values.

The goal of an early education program should be to facilitate the development of representational competence in two ways. The first is by *extending or broadening the range* of children's knowledge, curiosity, and concern into new content areas. The second is by *elaborating or deepening the kinds of questions* that children are able to ask about the underlying nature of physical and social reality.

People sometimes ask whether such education is necessary if children develop representational competence naturally. While children in all cultural communities do normally develop representational competence, they do not necessarily develop equal scope or elaboration of their knowledge. Cultural differences exist in how much emphasis is placed on particular modes of symbolic expression, for example, on music, dance, visual arts, dramatic arts, literature, or technological invention. Awareness of such cultural emphases may be important to teachers who work with a particular cultural community and wish to enhance competence by starting from children's strengths. Socioeconomic status differences also exist in some aspects of representational competence (especially verbal analytic skills) within stratified societies such as our own. The skills of representational competence preparatory to literacy have traditionally been more emphasized by the middle and upper classes in their childrearing practices.

Given the importance of symbolic skills, including literacy, for sheer survival in American society (not to mention for achievement in most occupations and endeavors), we assume that it is valuable to enhance and enrich the representational competence of young children in all American educational settings—valuable for children of all cultural backgrounds and socioeconomic classes.

3. Educational settings and activities should have the objective of promoting "constructive experience." Young children learn through play. George Forman has coined the term "constructive play" to describe all play that leads to an increase in skill or competence. Such play is intrinsically pleasurable and rewarding to the child because it enhances his or her sense of mastery and creativity.

We assume that constructive play is just as important for the development of social knowledge as it is for the development of physical knowledge, if the meaning of "play" is taken very broadly. To take into account all the experiences that stimulate the construction of social and moral knowledge, we have to include various kinds of "playful" and "sociable" experiences that promote constructive interaction or conversation with others.

A main objective of teachers should be to plan and arrange such constructive experiences. As Eleanor Duckworth (1972) has said, "Children can raise the right question for themselves when the setting is right" (p. 113). This book will present many examples of activities and experiences that may help children to raise their own "right" questions about the social world. Activities as diverse as washing dolls of different skin color, listening to a group of men and women nurses speak about their work, visiting an infant/toddler center to play with the babies, and going about a school with a tape recorder to interview people about their families—all have in common that they may stimulate questions about the social categories of race, gender, age, and kinship. Experienced teachers, of course, will know of countless other activities and experiences that fulfill the same objectives.

Beyond initiating such constructive experiences, the teacher can enrich the constructive content of play by "entering the children's world" in a stimulating way. We assume that it is an important part of the teacher's role to observe closely children's activity, then enter at critical moments. At appropriate moments, teachers can gently challenge children's thinking (without interfering with the self-regulated nature of their activity) by introducing new materials or even rearranging what is there, by making pointed observations in a subtle way, or by posing direct or indirect questions (Forman & Hill, 1980; Forman & Kuschner, 1983).

4. Teachers guide a process of inquiry when talking effectively with children about social and moral ideas. That adults know more than children about social and moral issues is obviously true. But not only do adults possess more correct facts and more complete knowledge of the rules and conventions, they also have a qualitatively different vision of social and moral reality.

The gap between adults' and children's visions of reality is so great that it may be no exaggeration to state that neither side can fully understand the dimensions of the other's experience. Adults cannot fully comprehend children's interpretations, and children cannot fully comprehend adults' interpretations—no matter how hard adults struggle to simplify their ideas or how hard children try to understand what they are told. When adults explain their vision of reality and children listen, a seeming meeting of minds occurs, but underneath the two sides may have gone their separate ways.

Consider the following instance of miscommunication, or "missed communication." At a day care center early one morning, Christopher, age four, watched another boy, Peter, come in the door. As Peter began to struggle out of his snowsuit and say a few last words to his mother, Christopher charged over, shouting, "Peter, be my friend! Will you be my friend?" Peter, startled and still preoccupied with his own activity, said, "No," firmly and turned away. Christopher began to cry softly. A teacher came to comfort him and said, "Christopher, we are *all* friends here. *Everyone* is your friend here."

What happened in this incident? What did Christopher make of the teacher's remarks? Empathizing with his distress, she tried to comfort him with words that would have comforted her had she been in his situation. She based her words on an understanding of friendship appropriate to an adult or older child but totally unrelated to that of the young child. As will be discussed in Chapter 6, young children's definition of friendship is concrete and tied to the immediate present; friends are people who are playing together, look alike, or like each other "right now." Peter and Christopher shared this concept; Peter said he did not want to be a friend because he wanted to do something else right then (remove his snowsuit and say goodbye to his mother). How could it comfort Christopher to be told, "We are *all* friends"? Christopher could see for himself that not everyone was playing together. Obviously, everyone was *not* friends. A more comforting remark to him might have been, "Maybe Peter will want to play with you in a few minutes when he is not so busy."

A communication strategy of open-ended dialogue has the most potential for promoting effective communication, a true meeting of minds, between adults and children. Such a strategy, called the clinical method by Piaget and guided inquiry by Sigel and colleagues, requires adults to change their goals in communication. Rather than instructing, explaining, and correcting, teachers can talk with children in ways that stimulate children to do their own thinking. This conversation, however brief, can be called inquiry because it involves a sustained focus on a problem in an attempt to solve it through thinking. Such inquiry does not bring a child to the "truth" in terms of the adult's understanding of the true nature of reality. However, it does allow the child to move toward "truth" in terms of a best temporary solution, given the child's current knowledge and level of cognitive development. The dialogue allows teachers an opportunity to enter children's world and gain a better understanding of children's reality. It allows children to think in a more focused way, listen to the contrast between the ideas of themselves and others, and perhaps become aware of the errors, gaps, or inconsistencies in their reasoning.

The next chapter will consider *how* social inquiry can be effectively conducted with young children.

CHAPTER 2

Conducting
Thinking Games

Young children need to talk with adults to develop their social ideas and moral values. But what kind of talk is best? And when should it take place? Any early childhood setting presents many opportunities for adults and children to talk together about social and moral issues. Conversation can help children to organize their thinking about questions that are interesting to *them*. It gives teachers the kind of concrete information that they need in order to understand children's developmental needs and communicate effectively in guidance and disciplinary situations.

Dialogue about social and moral issues can arise spontaneously or as part of planned activities. The spontaneous conversations are of tremendous significance because they play such a critical role in shaping children's understanding of their ongoing experience. Adults—whether teachers or relatives—*do* talk with young children continually about social and moral topics. They define their roles as transmitters of social and moral information and values. When they step back from the instructional aspect of those roles, ask children genuine questions, and listen carefully to children's perspectives, adults engage in true dialogue with children. While no one kind of talk is "best" in an absolute sense, dialogue is unique in allowing adults and children to understand each other's perspective. It builds bridges that pave the way to mutual and ongoing respect between adults and young children.

To illustrate how fascinating and revealing this spontaneous dialogue can be, many quotations are presented throughout the chapters that follow. The dialogue excerpts come from observations conducted in all types of early childhood settings, and they cover a wide range of issues. They illustrate typical questions, comments, and responses of children and show how teachers can turn spontaneous moments into opportunities for focused conversation (or inquiry, as Sigel calls it). Such conversation reveals the underlying structure of children's social reasoning. The quotations illustrate key points of the theoretical description and also will remind readers of similar conversations of their own. Of course, personal experience is the most effective organizer of a teacher's theoretical knowledge.

In addition, the chapters that follow suggest many activities for preschool and kindergarten groups. Experienced teachers will recognize some of them as traditional social studies experiences, designed to enrich children's informational base about social roles, their community, the world of work, and so on. Other activities will seem newer, however. They are called thinking games, and they engage children in focused dialogue about social and moral issues. They are an adaptation to the early childhood curriculum of an approach to social and moral education that has proved highly successful with older children.[1] Thinking games are certainly not a necessary part of a curriculum that promotes social development. A teacher may prefer to rely simply on naturally arising opportunities for dialogue. Yet they can add a valuable dimension to children's classroom experience, and they give teachers a way to organize and focus children's attention on social and moral issues. Their purpose is not to transmit adult values or factual knowledge. Rather, they present intellectually challenging problems in a context that allows a relaxed, reflective, and in-depth discussion. They have four main objectives:

1. Children become aware of a broader range of social and moral problems and questions concerning them.
2. Children become aware that social and moral problems are thinking problems that require a stand and intellectual justification.
3. Children learn that in the classroom, people listen and respect the thinking of others (though they may disagree).
4. Children are given experiences that let them notice gaps or discrepancies in their own thinking, or discrepancies between their ideas and the ideas of others.

This chapter describes what thinking games are and procedures for carrying them out. Two complete accounts of how the activities worked in preschool classrooms are included in Chapters 4 and 8.

THINKING GAMES: WHAT ARE THEY?

Two related types of thinking games work well with young children. The "dramatic skit" is a large group activity for 10 to 15 preschoolers or a whole class of kindergarten children. The "interview" involves a teacher and a small group of one to five children. The advantage of the skit format is that it is exciting and commands children's interest in the subject matter. It allows a whole group to hear one another's ideas about a social or moral problem. The advantage of the interview format is that it allows teachers to probe a few children's ideas with greater depth and flexibility. This can be important when exploring concepts such as divorce, racial identity, and the cause of physical handicaps, where it might be useful to know more about the thoughts and feelings of particular children. Both skits and interviews provide teachers with the opportunity to hone their communication skills. These skills are directly transferable to spontaneous situations, for example, in talking with children in conflict situations or in dealing with behavioral problems.

Whether skit or interview format is used, the thinking game is a story-situation presented to children for discussion. The story always sets up, or poses, a social-cognitive problem. The children are then invited to take a stand and discuss what the solution should be. The thinking game lets the children see the story-situation as a cognitive conflict that requires resolution. A teacher then invites them to state and justify different solutions and also asks a set of related "probing questions" intended to provoke closer consideration of the underlying moral or social problems posed by the game.

For example, a thinking game focused on authority and obedience presents a character who promises her mother that she will clean up her bedroom. As the girl goes to work, she is interrupted by her friend running in from outside to say that a circus is passing by that very minute. Just as the story child is about to dash outside, her mother returns to remind her that first she must clean up her room. The conflict has now been posed, and the children are asked to consider what the story character should do next, run outside or clean up her room, and why. They are also asked whether it is fair of the mother to require the girl to clean up and miss the circus, and why; whether it would be wrong of the girl to sneak out, and why; what the mother should do if the girl does sneak out, and why; and what it is about mothers that gives them the right to tell children to clean up their rooms.

A thinking game about kinship concepts revolves around an old man figure (e.g., grandfather doll) who hears some wonderful news and wishes to share it with his "brother." The problem for the children is to select the "brother" out of a set of figures varying in age—a baby, a little boy, a young man, and an old man. Probing questions concern

Thinking-game interviews are small-group activities that let teachers and children talk in depth about a social or moral issue.

whether adults can ever be brothers, what happens to boy brothers when they get old, the definition of "brother," and the way in which people become brothers.

Ideas for thinking games can come from research literature or real episodes in the classroom. One procedure is to use real and hypothetical stories alternately. Real stories rivet children's attention and allow them to reflect on personally meaningful episodes. Hypothetical stories allow more risk taking and let children think about the issues in a more detached way. Anyone can invent thinking games. The ones presented in this book were developed in collaboration with preschool teachers or adapted from situations or questions used by psychologists. They have been extensively pretested with children aged three to six in preschools, day care centers, and kindergartens. Their formats can, of course, be modified but are specified in the following chapters as an aid to teachers new at Piagetian interviewing.

GUIDELINES FOR CONDUCTING THINKING GAMES

What Is Needed

When a thinking game is conducted as a skit, the action of the story must be dramatic enough to capture the attention of a large group of children. The characters should be portrayed by real people (teachers and aides) or large puppets. In addition, a few props are sometimes required, and these can be normal school or household items. The "stage" can be any section of the classroom cleared for action or, if puppets are used, a puppet theater.

When the interview format is used, the dramatic scale of the story can be small because only a few children are watching. A teacher can dramatize the story using any kind of figures—dollhouse people, puppets, cardboard figures, and so forth. We have found that dollhouse people purchased at a good toy store capture children's attention and are realistic, sturdy, and fun for children to handle and manipulate. The few simple props required can be found around the classroom or made. The setting for the interview is a quiet place. Teacher and children can sit together at a table or on the floor.

Preparing the Children

The activity is prepared by having children sit in a large semicircle (for a skit) or in a quiet area (for an interview). The children are told, "Today we are going to have a thinking game. First you will see a story, then I will ask you to tell me *what you think should happen next.*"

When skits are incorporated as a regular part of the curriculum, it is effective to set aside a "special time" for them. At one school, for example, they were conducted as the final activity on Wednesdays. Many parents came early on those days to watch the skit before picking up their children. The parents in the observation booth discussed the skit's objective with the teacher present; parents enjoyed talking about why the children gave the kinds of answers they did. They claimed that the skits gave them insight into their children's behavior at home.

Acting Out the Story-Situation

The time required to present the story-situation is brief, perhaps a minute. The story action must be presented in a simple, sharp, crisp, and dramatic way. Young children become confused or forget the key elements if the story is not conveyed clearly. Bold drama, including a heightening or exaggeration of the emotions involved in the story, helps enlist children's attention and suggests to them that social/moral problems are exciting. Teachers who are present but not participating in the action can react appropriately to the plot line (showing surprise, sympathy, sadness, puzzlement, etc.) to help key younger children to the meaning of the story.

Asking Initial and Follow-up Questions

Following the story-situation, a teacher leads a discussion. It cannot last long, perhaps about five to ten minutes, depending on the age and experience of the children. There are two phases of questions—initial and follow-up. Initial strategies introduce the issue and develop awareness. Follow-up strategies focus in depth on elements of the discussion important for inducing developmental change. Teachers of young children will find that the initial questions are more important and that they occupy the bulk of the discussion time.

INITIAL STRATEGIES

1. Lead-off question. The story-situation culminates in a problem or dilemma. The lead-off question frames this dilemma for the children in a direct, concrete way. The lead-off question thus highlights the central issue and starts the dialogue. A specific *choice* is put to the children that invites them to take a stand on the issue. The choice can involve pointing to one story character versus another, deciding what action the central character should take, selecting an appropriate object (say, a gift) for a story character, deciding what item of clothing is important to put on (or take off) a story character, or any other concrete choice. Framing the essence of the social or moral issue in this way allows children to participate no matter what their level of verbal skill.

The discussion tends to be most lively when the group opinion is *divided* on the initial question. Some children urge one solution, others disagree. The disagreement between the children in the group mirrors on an external plane the cognitive conflict felt within each child and helps the children reflect upon both sides of the issue. The thinking game must involve a *genuine* problem—genuine, that is, to the children present. If the problem is either too easy or too advanced, children will disengage or give glib answers. A thinking game is seen to

A thinking game has worked when it causes children to reflect deeply and ask new questions about their experience.

be effective when children follow the story-situation with close attention, eagerly put forward their solutions, and listen attentively to one another's answers.

   2. The "why" question.   Children who take a stand on the initial question should be asked to justify their choices. They are asked, "Why do you think so?" Of course, not all young children will be able to answer that question. Teachers should remember that even in stating a choice, children feel that they are participating. Young children find it difficult to articulate their reasoning and justify their choices.

Sometimes a long, thoughtful silence indicates that children are engaged in the problem. When children leave the activity still pondering the problem—and talk to their parents or teachers about it later—then the thinking game has surely achieved its objective.

> TEACHER: What do you think Anna should do?
> AMY: She is supposed to clean up her mess, so she can see the parade.
> TEACHER: Why should she do that?
> AMY: [No answer].
> ETHAN: After nap she should see the parade.

3. Clarifying the story-situation. When children are trying to "escape" the dilemma through a solution that avoids the original dimensions of the problem or through a "magical" solution, the teacher can reemphasize the original conflict or complicate the circumstances of the story to focus the children on the central problem.

> CHILD: *All* of the dolls are his brothers.
> TEACHER: Let's say this [old man] doll has only *one* brother. Which one of these dolls here do you think is his brother?
> CHILD: That one. [Points to little boy doll.]

4. Raising personal examples. Questions that encourage children to relate the problem to their own experience, that personalize the situation, help children make sense of the issues being discussed.

> TEACHER [during a thinking game on friendship]: Do you have a best friend, Sean?
> SEAN: I have all little kids.
> TEACHER: How did they get to be your friends?
> SEAN: 'Cause I just keep making more and more friends!
> LILLIAN: By playing.

FOLLOW-UP QUESTIONING STRATEGIES

1. Clarifying probes. Inviting children to explain their terms or consider what circumstances are included or excluded in their answers will help them to clarify their ideas.

> CHILD: You have to do what your mother says.

TEACHER: Is there ever a time when you don't have to?
CHILD: Yes, if there's an emergency.

2. Issue probes. Questions in this category ask children to explore a particular key issue for the type of social/moral problem being discussed. Key issues in the moral domain, for instance, include authority and obedience, justice, punishment, and the value of life.

TEACHER: Do mothers *have a right* to be obeyed?
CHILD [nods]: Because they're big.

3. Role-taking questions. Stimulating perspective taking by children will help them to consider the thoughts, feelings, and needs of others. Social and moral development cannot take place without increasing role-taking capacities. Development of kinship concepts, for example, depends on increased capacity to take the perspectives of each family member toward the others in the system.

TEACHER: Suppose this [old man] doll was your grandpa.
CHILD: I *do* have a grandpa. And a grandma.
TEACHER: Your grandpa wants to telephone his brother. Ring! Ring! Which doll is his brother?
CHILD: I think it's this one. [Points to second old man doll.]

GUIDELINES FOR FORMULATING AND USING QUESTIONS

Both initial and follow-up questions should be planned ahead of time. As teachers gain more experience, they become able to lead discussions more spontaneously and flexibly. Effective questions adhere to four guidelines developed by Edwards, Logue, and Russell (1983).

1. Questions should be short and clear. Questions that are too complex or too abstract confuse and overwhelm young children. On one occasion a teacher showed a child a magazine picture of two babies lying together in a double carriage. She posed two short, clear questions before she got into trouble.

TEACHER: Do you think these babies are friends?
CHILD: Yes.
TEACHER: Why do you think so?

CHILD: Because they're babies.
TEACHER: Is it that babies are always friends?
CHILD: [No answer]
TEACHER: All babies are all friends, all the time?
CHILD: They're big.

The teacher's first question was well framed, and the child explained her answer to it when she said, "Because they're babies." (That is, they are the *same*.) The teacher's next two questions were extremely confusing, however, and the child decided that she must have said something wrong. She retracted her original answer: "They're big," she then said.

2. Questions should probe the underlying structure of the children's reasoning.   Sometimes teachers conclude too quickly that they understand what children are saying. They assume that children mean one thing when in reality they mean something quite different. Teachers can avoid this error by probing the children's ideas until the underlying structure is revealed. This requires an intuitive understanding by teachers of what those structures "sound like" for a given age group. In the following observation, the teacher almost jumped to the conclusion that the child did understand the "genital basis" of gender. However, she wisely probed the child's underlying structure and discovered that the child actually had quite a different concept.

TEACHER: How can we find out if this [doll] is a boy or a girl?
CHILD: We can tell if we undress it.
TEACHER [nods, almost goes on, then pauses]: What would undressing show?
CHILD: We could look at the hair. If she has long hair, it's a girl. [The child removes the hat to see for herself.]

3. Questions should be framed in a neutral way.   Rhetorical or leading questions limit children's freedom to give the answers that they think are right. In the following, the teacher's first question is framed in a neutral way, but her second question clearly demands one "right" answer.

TEACHER: If we didn't have a rule about hitting, then would she be allowed to hit?

CHILD: No, you can't hit kids in school.
TEACHER: You shouldn't hit anyone, anyway, right?
CHILD: Right.

4. Questions should allow ample time for reflection. It is almost impossible to go too slowly in a social or moral discussion with young children. Silence between questions provides the necessary time for reflection. A pause or a restatement of part of the child's response in question form often encourages the child to elaborate his or her answer.

CHILD: She should pick up.
TEACHER [pauses]: She should pick up?
CHILD: Yes, it's pick-up time, and you gotta pick up when it's pick-up time.

Moderating the Discussion

In conducting the discussion, teachers usually follow the procedure of calling on children who raise their hands, particularly when the group is large. Having a second adult sit in the midst of the audience can be helpful because this second adult can spot children bursting to speak and quietly find out what they want to say. The second adult can then help guide the leader with such comments as, "George has something to share," "Sae Won has been listening carefully," "Joy says that boys don't wear makeup; did you hear that?" and so forth. It is of course desirable to hear from as many children as possible; teachers may occasionally wish to solicit opinions from silent children.

Genuine interest by the discussion leader in the children's ideas will lead to appropriate responses to those ideas. Often, the discussion leader can clarify each child's answer by repeating some of the key phrases. The teacher should not evaluate children's answers, because reinforcements such as "Good answer" or "Correct" cause children to think that the teacher is fishing for one "right answer." Instead, the teacher can encourage critical thought by means of any of the following:

- Giving close attention to children as they speak
- Allowing children time to compose and/or change their answers
- Commenting, "That's an interesting idea"
- Commenting, "I wonder why you think that"

- Commenting, "Jack says [repeats his idea]. Does anyone else have another idea?"
- Suggesting an alternative idea: "One time another child told me [explains idea]. What do you think of that idea?"
- Responding with even a simple, "Hmmm, I see"

Concluding the Activity

Teachers should end the discussion by summarizing what the children have said and perhaps also thanking the children for their thoughtful participation. Here is an example:

> Some of you thought this [little boy] doll was the brother because he is a boy. Others thought this [old man] doll was the brother because he is old-looking like the first man. So some of you think that brothers have to be children, and some of you think that two old men can be brothers if they have been together a long, long time. That's very interesting! Thank you for thinking about these hard questions. If you have any more ideas later, I would enjoy hearing about them.

Sometimes teachers feel that such a nonevaluative summary does not do justice to a child whose ideas are more mature than the rest of the group's. For example, on one occasion most of the group confidently asserted that the boy doll was the brother. One girl tentatively suggested that the old man doll was the brother "because they used to be boys together when they were little," but she was drowned out by the rest of the group. The teacher attempted to encourage her line of reasoning in two ways. First, she carefully included the girl's comments in the closing summary. Second, she later continued the discussion with the child and explained to her why her idea was a good one.

Follow-up Activities

Thinking games have most impact if they are prepared for, or followed up by, related activities. For example, a skit on age roles may be part of a thematic unit on the bodily self, including activities in which children weigh and measure themselves, interview adults and children and chart their ages, learn how to tell the age of trees, compare the growth cycles or life spans of different plants and animals, and so forth.

Another effective technique is to follow up a thinking game with a repeat presentation a week or so later—perhaps with modification of a few minor details to make it seem slightly new. Young children enjoy tackling the same problem more than once, and the elaboration of their answers seems to increase dramatically from the first presentation to the second.

Part II

DOMAINS OF
SOCIAL
KNOWLEDGE

CHAPTER 3

Children's
First Social Categories:
Age Groups

AUBURN (age 4:5)[1] [stands pensively at the water table, using a funnel to fill a jar with water]: I have to practice for when I become a teenager.
TEACHER: When will that be, I wonder?
AUBURN: I don't know.
TEACHER: Am I a teenager? [Actually she is 20.]
AUBURN [pauses]: Yes.
TEACHER: Tell me, when will you be a teenager?
AUBURN [reflects for a moment]: Maybe when I'm seven.

How to make sense of the immense, diverse social world around them is a problem facing all young children. They need to understand people and social interaction in order to gain predictable responses from others. Even infants seek contact and affection from many people—father, brothers and sisters, close neighbors and kin, babysitters, and special teachers—in addition to their mothers. Certainly by preschool age, most children are part of a social network and interact daily with a large cast of characters in a variety of settings.

Adults make order of the social world by classifying people in terms of nationality, place of residence, ethnicity, occupation, social class, religion, and so on. For young children, however, those category systems are too abstract (Furth, 1980). Young children must rely on categories related to more concrete and visible cues. Thus, *familiarity*, *age*, *gender*, and *race* may be the first attributes that children employ to make social distinctions (Lewis & Feiring, 1979).

Distinctions between people based on age/size seem to be noticeable to children from the very start of life. In research studies, babies have been found to respond to unfamiliar babies and children in a way that is quite different from the way they respond to unfamiliar adults. They are friendly, curious, and playful with the babies and children but are much more wary and shy with adults (Brooks & Lewis, 1976; Field, 1979; Fogel, 1979). Clearly they can tell age groups apart, and the differences have meaning to them. Many children notice and discriminate between three main groups ("babies," "children," and "grown-ups") even before they learn to distinguish between the two genders. Certainly throughout early childhood, children use age categories as one of their most important ways to think about differences between people. Age differences are fascinating to young children because they correspond so clearly to competence, power, and authority.

THE DEVELOPMENT OF CHILDREN'S UNDERSTANDING OF AGE

Although the behavior of infants and young children indicates that they can categorize people into age groups on the basis of looks, nevertheless they cannot yet realistically distinguish people as younger versus older or apply the yardstick of chronological age. Before about age 10, children are notoriously inaccurate in assessing other people's age in years. They respond sensitively to age/size differences without really understanding what age is. This concept must be constructed.[2]

MATTHEW (age 4:7) [to teacher]: You know, you look like my friend, Mr. Griswold.
TEACHER (age 60): I do? How do I look like Mr. Griswold?
MATTHEW: You have, well, crinkles on your face.
TEACHER: How old do you think I am, Matthew?
MATTHEW [pauses, looks intently]: I don't know. You can't be 100, because my grandfather is 100, and he's dead.
TEACHER: No, I guess I'm not 100 then. How old do you suppose?
MATTHEW: I guess you must be . . . 36.

Constructing an understanding of age is a cognitively complex task because it requires the child to construct a linear, quantitative scale based on increasing "years of life." Just as young children cannot deal with length, weight, volume, time, or monetary value in terms of exact quantities, so they cannot deal quantitatively with years of life. There are many steps to mastering the concept of chronological age, and they require many years of development.

Very young children do not even think of age as measuring anything; they just think of it as a kind of label, like their name—"I'm Joell, I'm two." In our culture, this age label must seem like some kind of badge of importance, because children are asked about it so often and because it "causes" such wonderful events, birthdays. Young children often believe that their age somehow *is* their birthday. One child, Elena, awoke crying on the morning following her third birthday. "I'm not three anymore," she sobbed to her parents. It takes children time to understand that their birthday merely *marks* or *signifies* changes in their age. Stuart, aged four, was on the verge of this concept. Two days after his birthday, he sadly told his teacher, "My birthday is gone already. Nothing is left but I am older" (Stone, 1966, pp. 4–5).

Children next develop the understanding that age measures something, or rather, that age has to do with "more" or "less" of something. Children become interested in *comparative* ages—who is older, who is younger. Of course, they cannot yet correctly rank by age a large set of people. Nor can they rank by size a set of graduated sticks. Both kinds of ranking, or "serial ordering," are beyond preschool children because they cannot master the multiple comparisons involved. What they can do is consider which of two or three people is the older one.

Young children then may attach what seems to adults to be absurd importance to comparative age. For example, children may believe that age differences—even those of a week or two—tell them who knows more about everything. Children may insult someone younger than themselves as "knowing less," while according unrealistic respect to the opinions of older children. This pattern may be disturbing to teachers because it puts some children down at the expense of others, but it is usually more offensive to the adults than to the children involved and is a passing phase.

When considering which of two people is the older one, the judgments of children younger than age five or six are strongly influenced by differences in "bigness," especially differences in standing height. Young children confuse, or actually fuse, age and physical size.

JAMES (age 4:0) [stands face-to-face with his best friend, Susan, who is one month younger but half a head taller than he is]: I'm taller than you are. See! [He uses his hand to compare their heights, tilting his hand upward as it goes from his head to hers.] When you're older than someone, you're taller than someone.

SUSAN (age 3:11): [nods slightly and says nothing, seemingly impressed by James's conviction.]

Children are sure that age has to do with "bigness," something they can see themselves, because "time since birth" is much too abstract to hold onto. Adults reinforce this concrete association between size and age when they use the word "big" in conversations with young children about age. However, the adults are mainly just following the children's thinking, not causing it.

MOTHER: Sam, who are the youngest people?
SAM (age 3:11): Babies.
MOTHER: Who is next oldest?
SAM: Toddlers.
MOTHER: Who comes next?
SAM: Big boys.
MOTHER: Who comes next?
SAM: Grown-ups.
MOTHER: And what's after grown-ups?
SAM: *Giants!*

The fact that children confuse age and size has a practical impact on their behavior with peers. Children tend to treat other children according to their size. For instance, they accord respect to bigger children but take the lead with smaller children. Usually, this works well, because size does correlate with maturity, especially in a mixed-age classroom.

Sometimes, however, problems arise when a child's physical size is greatly discrepant from his maturity level. At one preschool, children had difficulty finding a successful way to interact with a boy named Nicholas, who was extremely tall and stocky though only a young three-year-old. Nicholas particularly wanted to be part of a group of older boys, aged four and five, but these children rejected him. In fact, they were much harder on Nicholas than they were on other three-year-olds. They made such remarks as, "He talks funny," "He doesn't know how to do anything," "He drools." Some of the teachers were distressed, because Nicholas was just a sweet little three-year-old from their point of view.

These teachers could not understand why the older boys were so "mean" to little Nicholas. Finally, they realized that the children did not, cognitively *could* not, see Nicholas as just a younger child. They saw him as a big boy, like themselves, and therefore expected him to know better than to grab toys and such. The teachers then understood why telling the older boys that Nicholas was only three did not solve the problem. The children would seem to accept that information when told it, but actually they would immediately "forget" it because it did not fit their own cognitive structures. Thus, an entirely different kind of solution had to be found to the problem. The teachers found a way to arrange some special individual time between Nicholas and Sean, the leader of the older boys, and these two then developed a friendlier relationship that carried over to the large group.

Perhaps the first crack in children's solid fusion of age with size comes at about age four or five, when children begin to realize that certain adults—those with gray hair, baldness, facial wrinkles, and, usually, glasses—are called "old people" or grandparents. They begin to realize that "old people" are a distinct group, but they use only surface cues to describe and classify them, and the cues represent an idiosyncratic collection of physical and behavioral features that have caught their attention. Lillian Phenice (1981) found that when asked to tell what they knew about old people, preschoolers gave such descriptions as the following:

> They get big as the sky; they have a stick to walk with; sometimes they have lots of wrinkles; they wear more clothes to keep warm; sometimes they don't have a car because they can't drive; their veins show; they have white hair; they don't look new. . . .
>
> Some could die. They put mail in the mail box. They get sick and they take medicine. They break a leg and go to the hospital. They wash hands before dinner and use soap. (p. 94)

Young children try to make sense of how some adults can be much older than others without being taller. This is extremely confusing to them. They try to understand how it is that a person stops growing bigger and stronger at a certain point. They wonder if that means he or she also stops getting older. For instance, Anthony (age 4:4) asked his teacher, "How old were you when you stopped having birthdays?" Another day he asked, "When are you going to stop getting older?"

Even when young children seem to understand and accept adult explanations about the independence of age and growth, they may not really have given up their own intuitive beliefs. Sam (age 4:1) became indignant when his teacher told him about an artist, Michaelangelo, who lived to age 89. "No," he protested, "He could not be 89. Then he would be bigger and stronger than Superman!" The number 89 was just too big to be associated with anyone smaller and weaker than Superman.

Children tend to be misled by height cues at least until age seven, and often until age ten. A first-grade teacher, aged 55, brought her two adult sons to class with her one day. The children thought that her tall son, aged 33, was her father and that her short son, aged 29, was her husband. While these first-graders realized that age has to do with years of life, they still were confused by height cues. They had not yet fully constructed the notion that years of life is the *essential* and *defining* characteristic of age.

Classroom Activities on Aging and Age Differences

How can teachers help young children construct their ideas about age? While adults cannot speed up the processes of cognitive maturation that underlie the understanding of the concept of age, nor should they want to, they can orient young children to consider age as an "interesting problem." They can provide children with rich opportunities to make concrete observations about age differences and aging processes. These experiences will not push the children ahead in inappropriate ways, but will stimulate them to do their own thinking and wondering. At times teachers may call children's attention to puzzling discrepancies, such as a puppy who is obviously much bigger than an old dog of a different breed: "How can that be?"

There are many specific activities teachers can conduct with preschool and young grade-school children. The major objective is to provide concrete experiences with processes of growth and aging and opportunities for comparing living things in terms of their relative age, height, and weight. Some examples include the following:

1. *The growth of plants and animals may be studied in the classroom*, with the help of fast-growing bean plants, baby mice, and so forth. Children may discuss, describe, and record the changes in height or weight observed. Teachers can point out interesting discrepancies, such as two plants that sprout at the same time but end up very different in height.

2. *Kindergarten children can consider the aging process in relationship to "time since birth."* Teachers can prominently display birthday charts with each child's and teacher's birthday. A "tooth chart" can note the dates on which children lose teeth.

3. *Children may learn about the typical life spans and transformational changes of different plants and animals*, large and small. They

can count rings on tree stumps, compare the teeth of young and old horses, examine feathers of baby and mature birds, study the life cycles of insects, and so forth.

4. *Children may do a unit entitled "Ourselves,"* in which they study their dreams, likes and dislikes, and bodily selves. To add a life-span perspective, teachers, children, and any other well-known figures in the school can bring in photographs of themselves as infants and toddlers to compare with current snapshots.

5. *Children can use scales, yardsticks, and tape measures to construct a chart of their height, weight, and age.* Teachers should call children's attention to interesting discrepancies and allow them to discuss their explanations.

Here is an example of one such discussion provoked by this activity. It began when the teacher pointed to Jenny's and Evy's respective height marks on the height chart.

TEACHER: Jenny is five and she is down here. Evy is four and she is up here. Why?

JENNY (age 5:3): It's because I'm not five and a half yet.

DAE-SUN (age 4:6): There's something wrong with it. Maybe your eyes are too small, so you can't see right. The five shouldn't be down low.

LAURA (age 4:7): I know what the problem is. People grow in different ways. Some grow short, some grow fast and tall like me.

6. *Children in a small or large group can be engaged in a thinking-game skit focused on the problem of age and size.* The thinking game creates a cognitive problem by putting these two cues into conflict with each other: the shorter figure looks (to adults) much older than the taller one. This activity has been found to arouse great interest in young children of all backgrounds. Children at ages three and four usually select the taller figure as the older one, though they sometimes seem troubled or perplexed by their choice. Children aged five to six often make the correct choice, though they cannot always explain their reasoning.

On one occasion when this skit was used, Sean (age 5:4) disagreed with the rest of the group and stoutly asserted that the shorter teacher was the older one. Asked why he thought so, he lapsed into thought. Finally he said, "Because—because—because she has crumbly cheeks." The teachers felt that they had witnessed development taking place right before their very eyes. When asked how old the two people were, Sean guessed that short Anna (age 60) was 25 and that tall Carolyn (age 17) was 23. Sean was able to construct the independence of age and height, but he still had not yet mastered the quantitative scale of chronological age. Sean's answers were more mature than the rest of his group's, yet during the skit the teacher leading the discussion did not evaluate his answer as right and the other children's as wrong. Instead, after the skit she took Sean aside and told him that he "really understood about who was older." She thus confirmed his line of reasoning without disconfirming that of the other children.

A Thinking Game on Height and Age: "Birthday Party"

CHARACTERS: Two adults, where Adult 1 is noticeably shorter but older-looking, and Adult 2 is noticeably taller but younger-looking.

MATERIALS: Two simulated birthday cakes, one containing many candles (ten or twelve) and one just a few (three or four).

ACTION

ADULT 1 [standing up]: Guess what, today is my birthday!

ADULT 2 [also standing]: It is? Imagine that! It's my birthday, too! I love birthdays. Oh look, here come our cakes! There is one for you, and one for me.

TEACHER: [to children in group]: I have two birthday cakes for my two birthday friends. This one has more candles on it because it is for the older person. This one has fewer candles on it because it is for the younger person. Here, take a good look. [Shows cakes.]

DISCUSSION QUESTIONS

- Which birthday friend should get the cake with more candles? Why?
- How do you know that ——— [whomever children picked] is older?
- How old do you think ——— [Adult 1] is? Why? How old do you think ——— [Adult 2] is? Why?
- [After arranging for the two adults to *sit down*] Now who do you think is the older friend, and who is the younger one?

SUGGESTED VARIATIONS: The thinking game may be elaborated by having a postal carrier bring in a package for "the grandparent here." The children are asked to select the adult that "looks like" a grandparent. If they pick the elderly character (after having given him or her the cake with fewer candles), the children may be asked: "How can he/she be a grandparent when his/her birthday cake only has just a few candles?"

For older children, another variation is to substitute photo albums for the cakes—one "big and fat for the person who has lived a long, long time" and one "small and thin for the person who has just lived a short time." The discussion is the same.

An activity on age presents a conflict between "years of life" and "bigness." The children are asked, "Who should get the birthday cake with a lot of candles, and who the cake with just a few?"

CHILDREN'S AGE-GROUP CATEGORIES

Young children have not mastered the complex concepts that underlie an understanding of chronological age and the aging process. Yet they are sensitive to age/size differences because they correspond so visibly to differences in competence and authority. Rather than precisely ranking people along the quantitative scale of "time since birth," young children simply divide people into *age-group categories*.

Children use age-group categories as an early, shared, and structured system to classify the social world (Edwards, 1984). The advantage is that they can use the labels without needing to know much about chronological age.

Children as young as two years old can label people, real or represented, from the entire life span. Research has found that children aged two to five typically use three types of labels:

1. Age-group terms (especially "baby," "child," "kid," "adult," "grown-up")
2. Sex/age-group terms (especially "girl," "boy," "woman," "lady," "man," "old woman," "old man")
3. Kinship terms (especially "sister," "brother," "mother," "father," "grandmother," "grandfather")

What is noteworthy about this list is that there is no term for adolescents, or "teenagers." Before age five or six, most children merge everyone past puberty into one big category of "grown-ups." They may distinguish elderly from middle-aged adults, but they seem satisfied to classify adolescents with "parents." They also seem to treat adolescents with the same respect that they do adults, and they seem unaware that adolescents are in a transitional phase between childhood and adulthood.

By age three or four, children can not only label but also *sort* photographs of faces into age categories. According to the preschool way of dividing up the life span, "babies" are in an entirely different category from "little children." Young children often think that "child" terms (such as "kid," "girl," "boy," "sister," and "brother") cannot even be applied to babies.

TEACHER: Do you have a sister, Seth?
SETH (age 4): No, we have a baby. She'll be my sister when she's big enough to play with me.

KRISTINA (age 4:11): [Announces that her mother has had a baby.] Her name is Amanda.
TEACHER: So you have a sister!
KRISTINA: No, she's still just a baby.

Preschoolers set the boundary between "babies" and "little children" at about two years, between "little children" and "big children" at six years, between "children" and "parents" at fourteen years, and between "parents" and "grandparents" at approximately fifty years. By far the most difficult part of the activity for them is distinguishing "parents" (young adults) from "grandparents" (old adults). Children aged two to three cannot make this distinction consistently or realistically, but older preschoolers usually do realistically distinguish middle-aged from elderly adults.

When adults face this task, they differ from preschoolers in putting the boundary between "little children" and "big children" at 13, and between "big children" and "parents" at 18–20 (Lewis, 1980). Thus, adults are more discriminating in considering adulthood: they segment off the adolescents. Young children are more discriminating in considering childhood: they distinguish preschool from school-aged children. Each group is more subtly attuned to distinctions closer to the age of the self.

Young children's age categories differ from those of adults in more ways than just their boundaries. They also differ in their conceptual relationship to the underlying dimension of chronological age. Adults, but not young children, understand that age categories are just a convenient set of labels imposed rather arbitrarily on the life span. Young children aged three to four think that age categories are absolute divisions. To them, a "baby" is someone absolutely different from a "little child." Similarly, a "grandparent" is a completely different kind of grown-up from a "parent," and a given grown-up falls into either one category or the other.

This kind of static thinking does not work well for young children when they try to contemplate people getting older, that is, moving from one category to the next. Then children are led to problems generated by the contradictions within their thought system. Such internal disequilibrium is a major source of social-cognitive change. Here are some examples of spontaneous moments of disequilibrium:

EDWARD (age 5:1) [lying in bed, nearly asleep, suddenly pops up and runs to his mother]: It seems so strange that you're a little toddler, you're two, and then magically you turn into a big kid on your birthday when you're three.

DANIEL (age 3) [driving with his father past his sister's elementary school]: That's the Jackson Street School.
FATHER: Yes, that's right.
DANIEL: I'll go there when I'm big like Rudy, right?
FATHER: Yes, you will.
DANIEL [troubled]: When I go there, will I still be Daniel?

Another example comes from an autobiography by a Navaho elder:

By the time I was seven and eight years of age, when I began to know things, I used to think about the children, large and small, and boys of different sizes up to a tall man. I used to look at children who were smaller than I was and think they were that small all the time, and I thought that I would be the same size always, and that men too were always that same size. I used to wish I were that tall. It worried me when I looked at myself and thought, "I'm a small boy. I won't grow up to be like these tall men." (Dyk, 1938/1966, p. 44)

In all of these examples, the young children ponder cognitive problems that arise from thinking about *themselves* in relation to the age-group system. Young children do not just classify other people into categories, they also classify themselves. They wonder about how they will cross the boundary from one age group to another. They develop strong opinions about their own age group, and these identifications are not always completely realistic. Edwards (1984) found that preschool boys aged three to four tend to identify themselves as "big children," in spite of the fact that they say the boundary between "little" and "big" children is at age five or six. In contrast, three-year-old girls typically identify themselves as "little children."

The boys and girls may have confused differences between people that have to do with *age* with differences that have to do with *gender*. They have noticed that adult men are generally taller than women; therefore, they decide that boys must be big, whereas girls can be little.

RICHARD (age 4:5): Girls are medium-sized, and boys are big. You're medium-sized and I'm big.
FEMALE TEACHER: You're bigger than me?
RICHARD: Yeah, you're medium-sized.
TEACHER [incredulous]: You're taller than I am?
RICHARD: Yup.

SAM (age 4:3): We're medium-sized.
MOTHER: We're medium-sized?
SAM: Yeah, Geordie [age 1] is small. Dad is big. You and I are medium-sized. Dads are bigger than moms.

The tendency of three- and four-year-olds to fuse together age, gender, and size may account for some interesting differences in behavior between boys and girls. One difference between boys and girls that some teachers observe is boys' greater fascination with superheroes (Paley, 1984). Boys' superhero play is strongly reinforced by the media, which present mostly masculine superhero characters, but it also relates to boys' early identifications. In their striving through fantasy to become big and powerful, like adult men, they indicate an underlying cognitive confusion about the relationship of gender and size. "If men are big," they seem to reason, "then boys must be big, too."

Another difference between young girls and boys that teachers have noticed—and researchers have documented[3]—is girls' greater attraction to infants and toddlers. Studies of children in many cultural communities have found that overall, girls are more nurturant to younger children than are boys. Girls more willingly take responsibility for infants and toddlers, and they are less aggressive toward them. What causes this sex difference? Modeling of parental roles is surely important, but children's self-concepts may again reinforce the societal pressures. That is, boys may try to avoid associating with "little children" because they want so desperately to be "big." Girls too want to appear mature and "grown-up," but for them adulthood does not have so much to do with sheer "bigness" as it does for boys.

Age Groups and Behavioral Roles

Children use age-group categories because they are functional for them. They employ the categories to divide up the social world into groups that make sense in terms of people's differential competence, interests, and authority. Young children attach to the age categories a complete system of behavioral expectations. These expectations can be termed *age roles*, and they are found in children as young as age two.[4]

GEORGE (age 2:3): Babies drink bottles, big boys drink cups.
TEACHER: What do grown-ups drink?
GEORGE: They drink coffee.

Children attach "high-power" social functions to adults: giving help, commanding, and disciplining. They attach the reciprocal "low-power" functions to children: asking, demanding, obeying.

Furthermore, young children think that work is what adults do and play what children do. According to this stereotyped way of thinking, adults cannot play and children cannot work.

TEACHER: Can *mommies* play with tractors? [She is curious about
the child's gender roles.]
WHITNEY (age 4:7): No, they don't play!
TEACHER: Do *daddies* play with tractors?
WHITNEY: No, they don't play. Big people *ride* tractors. [She
answers in terms of age roles, more salient to her.]

Edwards and Lewis (1979) found how attracted young children are
to what they call "big children," that is, the seven-to-ten-year-old
group. Young children accord "big children" with a special status and
all the best qualities of both adults and children. They think that older
children are good partners both for play and for help-giving. They
demonstrate this attraction in real-life situations, too, for example,
when an older sibling visits the class or when an upper-grader comes in
to tutor a lower-grader. The younger children work hard to stay near
the new older child and accept much more dominance and bossing
than they might from a peer or an adult.

It seems unfortunate that in our modern, age-graded American
society, not all young children receive consistent opportunities to play
with and learn from older children. In other societies, the two age
groups have more regular interaction, especially in traditional, rural
communities, such as are found in Asia, Africa, and Latin America.
There, where family sizes are large, mothers routinely assign their
children household, economic, and child care chores. The attraction
between big and little children seems mutual in those societies. While
the seven-to-ten-year-olds may not see the three-to-six-year-olds as
their most preferred playmates, nevertheless they often enjoy teaching, commanding, showing affection, teasing, and roughhousing with
them. The older children exercise a natural dominance or power over
the younger ones that we should not see as unequal and unfair, but
rather understand as part of the way young children learn about cross-
age relationships.[5]

In fact, in many societies the dominance relation between older
and younger children is much more formal and explicit than in our
own. For example, in Italy the elder sibling was called the *grande* and
traditionally had certain defined rights and duties (Edwards, 1985a).
He or she was expected to be responsible for the younger sibling and
to yield things the little one wanted, such as toys or treats. The younger
sibling, the *piccolo*, was expected to respect his or her older sibling.
These traditional Italian age roles limited children's freedom in certain
ways, but they also smoothed sibling relations by setting clear expectations. In contrast, in American society, age roles are not well defined,

and sibling relationships, as portrayed in children's books, are often rivalrous and tense.

In contrast to their attraction to "big children," preschool children all too often have negative or impoverished images of both "old people" and "babies." Many have little idea about what kinds of things they could do *with* or *for* elderly people. Similarly, many young children are not sure how to relate to infants and toddlers. They do not see this age group as a good source of help or comfort, but neither do they see it as good for playing with. They select only same-age peers and "big children" as playmates. Edwards and Lewis found this to be more true of white middle-class children than of black working-class children (all of whom lived in New Jersey). Black culture has traditionally valued large families and the care of younger children by older children.

Perhaps many young American children today need more real-life experiences with senior citizens and with infants and toddlers[6]. Concrete experiences might help children develop more detailed and extended images of the kinds of things that they can do with these age groups. Because modern family life is deficient for many children in these kind of contacts, schools and day care centers could help fill the gap. Not only will teachers thereby be assisting young children in learning reciprocity and nurturant behavior, they will also be stimulating children to develop more rich and detailed concepts of their social world.

Classroom Activities on Age Groups

Age categories give a strong and stable conceptual system from the age of two onward. This system is more important and central to young children than to adults, who have more mature concepts for understanding age differences and the aging process.

Teachers can work with children to clarify and elaborate their age-group thinking. The activities also sharpen and extend the teachers' understanding of this most important aspect of children's social knowledge.

The major objectives of age-group activities are to give children experience with labeling and classifying people of all ages (to extend their vocabulary and ability to draw distinctions); to let children reflect on their own age-group identity, that is, their position in the social system; and to let children consider the relationship between age groups and behavioral roles (in order to integrate a first, age-appropriate picture of their social universe).

1. *The material environment of the preschool classroom can be enriched to provide "data" for children thinking about age groups and roles.* Some examples include the following:
  • Wooden family sets (available from major toy companies) can enhance block play.
  • A wooden dollhouse can be equipped with a set of flexible dolls (attractive dolls representing all the age groups from infancy to old age are available at good toy stores).
  • Wall displays can be prepared using photographs or posters to show either a group of people of the same age (e.g., teenagers) or the life span from infancy to old age.

2. *Children aged one to two can be stimulated to think in a simple way about their relationship to different age groups.* The teacher may tape photographs of the faces of either known or unknown people to a set of four or five play telephones. As a young child "talks" on the phone to each person depicted—perhaps a baby, older brother, and grandfather—the child will naturally make changes in the way he or she talks and what he or she talks about. Beyond preparing the activity, the teacher need take no active role.

3. *Children aged three and above can discuss and compare what younger and older family members can and cannot do.* They can be invited to describe problems and happy experiences with people of different ages.

4. *Children aged three and above can extend their concrete knowledge of other age groups through field trips and classroom visits.* Elderly people can participate in classroom activities as special guests or regular assistants, and children can visit a senior citizen center. Children can learn more about infant behavior and care by visiting an infant/toddler center or having a parent and infant visit their class. If possible, children should participate in holding, changing, feeding, and playing with the babies; they will also want to talk about themselves as babies.

5. *Children aged three and above can label or sort photographs or pictures representing different age groups.* How many pictures are used depends on children's age and attention spans: three-to-four-year-olds can usually deal with about 10 pictures, five-to-six-year-olds with 20. Pictures of familiar and unfamiliar people can be used, representing the entire life span.

To discover children's spontaneous labels, the teacher can point to each picture in turn and say, "What do you call this one?" It is helpful to begin with an infant picture because almost all children can produce the label "baby."

To explore children's age categories, the teacher can provide boxes and ask children to sort the pictures. Three-year-olds can usually deal with three categories: "babies," "children," and "grown-ups." Older children can handle a more complex task, such as first sorting pictures into "children" versus "grown-ups," then re-sorting the children into "little kids" and "big kids" and the adults into "young adults" and "old adults" (or "parents" and "grandparents").

6. *Children aged three and above can sort magazine pictures into piles and then make books about "babies," "little children," "big children," and "grown-ups."* Children can discuss each others' books as a group and talk about how people look different, what different age groups can do and like to do, and so forth.

7. *Children aged three and above can engage in a thinking-game interview on age roles.* The interview encourages children to map *behavioral roles*—giving help, showing, playing, needing food, roughhousing, and hugging—onto age-group categories (adapted from Edwards and Lewis, 1979).

A Thinking Game on Age Roles: "Whom Should This Doll Ask?"

MATERIALS: A set of family dolls (wooden, paper, or whatever is available), including grandparents, parents, big children, little children, and a baby. Band-Aid, scrap of cloth, tiny toy (e.g., matchbox truck), tiny ball, tiny brown bag tied up (with raisins inside).

ACTION: The teacher sits with the children and tells them: "This doll [picking up a little child figure] is named ———" [perhaps using the name of one of the children present]. Then the teacher acts out with that doll a little series of story-situations, as outlined in the discussion that follows. After each, she asks the child to "look carefully" and "choose the best person" to fulfill the required social role.

DISCUSSION QUESTIONS
- The doll runs along, falls, and cuts his knee. Then he sees someone who can *help* him and wash and bandage the cut. Who would that one be? Why?
- The doll finds a new toy, one that he has never seen before. Then he sees someone who can *show* him how to use it. Who would that one be? Why?
- The doll has been playing ball a long time all by himself. Then he sees someone who can *play* with him. Who would that one be? Why?

An activity on age roles invites children to think about the different ways they relate to each age group in society.

- The doll has a big bag of fruit, juice, and other good things to eat. Then he sees someone who *needs* some of it. Who would that one be? Why?
- The doll feels full of energy. Then he sees someone who can *run, chase, fight, and wrestle* with him. Who would that one be? Why?
- The doll feels like hugging someone. Then he sees someone that he would like to *hug* or maybe give a *kiss* to. Who would that one be? Why?

SUGGESTIONS: Children may enjoy handling the dolls themselves and acting out the roles as they go along. The teacher should not comment on the rightness or wrongness of their answers; after all, the questions have no right answers. If the children in a small group disagree on an item (pick different choices), they can be asked to explain their reasoning to each other. If the children all agree on an answer, the teacher may introduce some cognitive conflict, perhaps by some such comment as, "One time another child made the *baby* help this hurt boy. The baby patted the hurt spot, then crawled off to get a Band-Aid, like this [demonstrating]. What do you think of that idea?"

8. *Children aged four to five and above can engage in a thinking-game interview on age roles,* adapted from Youniss (1980). This problem stimulates children to think about the variety of ways in which a person of one age can perform a particular behavioral role with a partner of a different age.

A Thinking Game on Age Roles: "How Many Kinds of Kindness?"

MATERIALS: A set of family dolls, of any type.

DISCUSSION QUESTIONS: The teacher takes any pair of dolls differing in age group (e.g., a grandfather and a boy child). He or she asks, "What could he [grandfather] do that would be *kind* to him [child]? Can you show me? . . . Can you show me something else he could do that would be kind to this boy? Can you show me another way? . . ." When the child has no more ideas, the teacher repeats with another pair of dolls. He or she may do this about four to six times, with the "kind one" sometimes being the older member of the pair and sometimes being the younger one.

The procedure can be used with any set of behavioral roles, including being kind, helpful, fun, generous, showing affection, starting a conflict, stopping a conflict, and so forth.

SUGGESTED BOOKS FOR CHILDREN

Some of the following selections discuss the process of growing older as it takes place during the childhood years and also as it occurs during old age. Other selections focus on the nature of age roles. Because so many children's storybooks portray the competitive side of sibling relations, the following selections were chosen to depict positive or balanced images of cross-age caring and play.

Alexander, M. *I'll Be the Horse If You'll Play with Me*. New York: Dial, 1975. This book for younger children portrays a girl's relations with her big and little brothers. She learns, to her surprise, that a toddler can be a very good playmate.

Aliki. *The Two of Them*. New York: Greenwillow, 1979. This book puts a grandparent/grandchild relationship into long-term perspective, showing changes in both people over time.

Bottner, Barbara. *Big Boss! Little Boss!* New York: Pantheon, 1978. Stories about five- and seven-year-old sisters portray the girls' contrasting roles and perspectives.

Byars, Betsy. *Go and Hush the Baby*. New York: Viking, 1971. An elder brother entertains and puts to sleep the crying baby while their mother finishes her tasks.

Clifton, Lucille. *My Brother Fine with Me*. New York: Holt, Rinehart & Winston, 1975. This book portrays an eight-year-old sister who looks after her five-year-old brother while their parents are at work.

dePaola, Tomie. *Nana Upstairs and Nana Downstairs*. New York: Putnam, 1973. This book portrays a young boy's love for his grandmother, who is old, and his great-grandmother, who is very old and eventually dies.

—— . *Now One Foot, Now the Other.* New York: Putnam, 1981. This book describes how the life cycles of old and young intermesh: a grandfather teaches his grandchild to walk, then after a stroke, the same help is reciprocated.

Farber, Norma. *How Does It Feel to Be Old?* New York: Dutton, 1979. A very old, vital woman describes what she likes and what she misses in her old age. A complex subject is presented well for older children.

Garelick, May. *What's Inside: The Story of an Egg That Hatched.* New York: Scholastic, 1968. Photographs detail the process of hatching and growth of a duck. The text poses questions that stimulate children to think about what kind of bird might be coming out of the egg.

Hazen, Nancy. *Grownups Cry Too; Los Adultos Tambien Lloran.* Chapel Hill, N.C.: Lollipop Power, 1973. This book explores different reasons why people cry and explains that the adult role does not preclude crying. (In English and Spanish)

Herzig, Alison Cragin, & Mali, Jane Lawrence. *Oh, Boy! Babies!* Boston: Little, Brown, 1980. Illustrated with striking photographs, this nonfiction book describes what happened at a boys' primary school when a teacher started a course in baby care. The text must be simplified for young listeners.

Kellogg, Steven. *Much Bigger Than Martin.* New York: Dial, 1976. This book centers on sibling rivalry but also clearly portrays the different competencies of older and younger children and indicates that while growth is continuous, it cannot take place suddenly.

Krasilovsky, Phyllis. *The Very Little Boy.* New York: Doubleday, 1962. This book for younger children illustrates the continuous nature of growth.

Little Sisters of the Grassland. Peking: Foreign Languages Press, 1973 (distributed by China Books & Periodicals, 125 Fifth Avenue, New York, N.Y. 10003). Two young sisters exhibit extraordinary bravery and bring their commune's sheep through a fierce blizzard. The relationship of the sisters is remarkable; the elder is a good leader, the younger helps her steadfastly.

Manley, Deborah. *Bigger and Smaller.* Windemere, Fla.: Ray Rourke, 1981. A book for toddlers compares the sizes and capabilities of small, medium, and big boys in a family.

McCloskey, Robert. *One Morning in Maine.* New York: Penguin (Puffin), 1971. Sal loses her first tooth and learns about the process of maturation in herself and other things around her. This book portrays a supportive older/younger relationship.

Scott, Ann Herbert. *Sam.* New York: McGraw-Hill, 1967. Sam goes from one person to the next in his busy family as he seeks to be included in someone's activity. Age roles are a main issue: what is the right job for Sam?

Seguin-Fontes, Marthe. *A Wedding Book.* New York: Larousse, 1983. This "Thinking Cap Story" uses a photographer at a wedding to stimulate young children to think about social categories, including age.

Selsam, Millicent E. *How Puppies Grow*. New York: Scholastic, 1971. Photographs explain the growth and development of a litter of puppies.

Stinson, Kathy. *Big or Little?* Toronto: Annick Press, 1983. Sometimes a preschool child feels big and competent, sometimes small and young.

Watson, J. W., Switzer, R. E., & Hirschberg, J. C. *Look at Me Now!* Racine, Wisc.: Golden, 1971. This book portrays what a two-year-old can do and contains a good note for parents on the development of self.

Williams, Barbara. *Someday, Said Mitchell*. New York: Dutton, 1976. Mitchell wants to help his mother but has the idea (common to young children) that only big people have the power to help. His mother tells him ways that little people can be just the right size to help.

Zagone, Theresa. *No Nap for Me*. New York: Dutton, 1978. On her fourth birthday, Fay decides she is now suddenly different, but her body (growing up more gradually) sends her another message.

CHAPTER 4

"Boys and Girls": Gender and Sex-Role Awareness

TEACHER: Lisa, are you a girl or a boy?
LISA (age 3): I'm a girl, but when I'm four, I'll be a boy.

"Man," "woman," "boy," "girl"—these seemingly simple terms are actually complex and difficult symbols laden with historical, cultural, and individual meaning.

As we adults go about our daily lives, each of us assumes that every human being has a biological sex and is either a male or a female. Each of us has noticed that males and females are likely to behave in somewhat different ways—wear certain clothes, speak and move in certain ways, prefer certain activities, work in certain jobs. We assume that some of these things are necessary and biologically based (child-bearing, for example), while the others are culturally learned and variable. Many adults believe further that males *should* want to do some or all of the "masculine" things, and females *should* want to do "feminine" things.

But these adult ideas and values of ours are not objective and incontrovertible. They reflect our cultural heritage, family upbringing, and individual perspective. Their content is to some degree shared but to a great degree variable. Especially in the United States, a culturally pluralistic and rapidly changing society, values related to sex roles and preferences are not a matter of social consensus.

How then can teachers help young children to acquire gender awareness and knowledge about sex roles? The years from two to seven are a sensitive and dynamic period for the development of this knowledge, but what part can and should teachers play?

Two principles should guide teachers as they work to support children's development:

1. *No one single answer, right for all times and places, defines what masculine and feminine roles must be.* Sex roles, like all other social rules, are related to the most basic goals and world-views shared by a people. American society is pluralistic but has come to accept as a unifying moral principle the goal of maximizing individual potential. Teachers represent the overarching values of the whole rather than the particular values of any one subgroup. Therefore, teachers act in accordance with the moral foundation of American society if they respect children's own choices and yet help children to explore options in terms of their own talents. "The wide range of potential options available to one should be available to all and should not be denied to a child on the basis of what sex he or she happens to have been born" (Brooks-Gunn & Matthews, 1979, p. 8).

2. *The task of constructing gender awareness and sex-role knowledge belongs ultimately to the child.* Adults can support and guide children, but in the end children themselves are responsible for what they know and believe. Therefore, in order to best facilitate children's self-regulated growth, teachers need sound and comprehensive information about how children develop.

This chapter will review recent research findings on young children's development of gender and sex-role knowledge.

DEVELOPING GENDER IDENTITY

Identity—one's sense of self—is composed of many kinds of knowledge about who one is. Age, racial group, cultural identity, body image, self-esteem, and skills and weaknesses are aspects of total self-identity. In addition, gender identity, sexual identity, and sex-role identity are three related aspects of knowledge about the self.

Gender identity refers to an individual's biological sex. A person is born either male or female. (In rare cases where a newborn's sex is unclear, the newborn is usually labeled male or female and reared accordingly.) *Sexual identity* refers to a person's sexual orientation. A person may be heterosexual, homosexual, bisexual, or asexual. *Sex-role identity* refers to a person's preference for activities that are labeled by society as "masculine" and "feminine." It requires knowledge about socially defined roles and a choosing of a masculine, feminine, or androgynous (combination) behavioral style.

Of the three aspects, sexual identity remains most hidden from teachers and mysterious to researchers. Gender and sex-role identity formation, more visible and better understood, will be our focus.

Children have acquired *gender identity* when they understand that they are and always will be male or female. Gender identity is central to children's self-definition because it allows them to classify themselves and everyone around them into two basic groups. Although gender identity would seem a simple concept, actually children take several years to construct it in full. Three distinct steps are involved: (1) learning to label people by gender, (2) understanding the permanence of gender, and (3) understanding the "genital basis" of gender. This sequence has been validated in cultures from around the world. Everywhere, children's development is gradual and continuous through the three steps.

The first step in constructing a gender identity is learning to use words that label people as male or female. American children must learn noun terms ("boy," "girl," "man," "woman") and pronoun terms ("he," "she," "his," "hers").

Research has found that most children master gender labels by age two and a half or three.[1] Children usually master the nouns before the pronouns and correctly apply labels to others before consistently labeling themselves as a "girl" or "boy." By age three or four, children are certain about their own gender; they have formed one of the most stable self-categorizations that they will make in their lifetimes.

When very young children first use gender labels, however, they do so in a simplistic way. They treat each label (e.g., "girl") as if it were independent and not related to its opposite ("boy"). In other words, when they call someone a girl, they do not mean a girl as opposed to a boy. To them, the label is just a word, like a name, that applies to a person. They may even say that an ambiguous looking person is "a boy *and* a girl." At age two to three, they can only control one symbolic representation at a time; they cannot coordinate symbols into systems (Fischer, 1980).

What clues do young children use when they apply gender labels? Hair length and clothing are the features young children use most. Children under about age four usually look only at the hair or faces of naked dolls when asked to label them (even when the dolls are "anatomically complete"). The following incident occurred in a day care center where boys and girls shared one bathroom and were fully familiar with the differences between male and female genitals.

TIFFANY and CONOR (age 4) are washing naked anatomically complete dolls with sponges and water.

CONOR: My doll is a boy.
TIFFANY: My doll is a girl.
TEACHER: How do you know?
CONOR: My doll is named David so he must be a boy.
TIFFANY [pauses and looks at both dolls]: They don't have any clothes on. [Studies their faces intently.] My doll is a girl because she has lipstick and mascara on. See!

In fact, children under age four can label the gender of paper dolls more easily when the dolls are clothed than when the dolls are naked. This is true even for children whose parents have been very open about nakedness. Why? Children under age four can focus on only one dimension of a problem at a time, and hair length and clothing are more visible than genitals in a "clothed society" such as ours. In effect, young children often "forget" about genitals.

The second step in constructing gender identity is gender permanence—knowing that people remain male or female throughout their lives. Usually at about the age of four, children begin to correctly answer questions such as, "When you grow up, will you be a man or a woman?" and "When you were born, were you a boy baby or a girl baby?" This is the age at which children become able to coordinate *two* symbolic representations at a time. Children now realize that terms like "woman" and "man" (and "mommy" and "daddy") are opposites—mutually exclusive categories.

BOB (age 4) to strange woman on elevator: Are you a mommy?
WOMAN: No, I'm not. [She has no children.]
BOB: Oh. You're a daddy.

They realize that the terms "woman" and "girl" (and "man" and "boy") are related in a different kind of way. Because all of the adults tell them so, they come to understand that "baby girls" become "big girls," "big girls" become "women," and the same for boys. They accept that gender is permanent.

The final step in constructing gender identity involves understanding that gender is defined by anatomy, not by hair, clothes, toy preferences, or other correlated but irrelevant characteristics. The problem for young children in understanding the genital basis of gender is coordinating *many* representations into a single complex system. Four-year-olds know about the anatomical differences between the sexes, but they do not understand that genitals are the one defining feature of gender. They tend to answer incorrectly such questions as, "If Sandra cuts her hair very short, then will she be a boy or a girl?" or "If John wears dresses and plays with dolls, then will he be a girl or boy?" They are heavily swayed by hair, clothing, and behavioral cues and think that these irrelevant features identify gender. Before the age of six or seven, and sometimes even later, children "forget" about genitals when focusing on other aspects of gender differences.

Classroom Activities on Gender Identity

Gender identity is a central issue for young children and one about which they are strongly motivated to ask questions and gather information. Teachers can assist children's development by honestly answering their questions and by planning activities that stimulate the children's thinking. The activities also provide teachers with rich information about children's classification and problem-solving abilities.

1. *Children as young as two years can begin to label male and female figures, including themselves.* This activity requires a set of magazine pictures or photographs representing all ages. With photographs, both familiar and unfamiliar people can be included. The teacher points to each picture and asks, "Is this a *boy* or a *girl*?" (Or, "Is this a *man* or a *woman*?" or "Is this a *he* or a *she*?") Or the teacher can ask the child to classify the figures into two boxes, one for "girls" and one for "boys."

2. *The material environment of the preschool classroom can be enriched to provide "data" for children thinking about gender identity.* Suggested materials include
   • Dressing-undressing puzzles (available from major toy companies)
   • Anatomically complete sister and brother dolls (available from the major toy companies)
   • Art books portraying nude human beings.

3. *Children aged three and above can use magazine pictures to construct books or montages entitled "Girls of All Ages" and "Boys of All Ages."* The teacher should include some pictures that may provoke discussion, such as a man with long hair, a woman bus driver, or a girl playing football.

4. *Children aged four and above can engage in a thinking-game interview on gender identity.* This activity encourages children to

consider the relationship (or nonrelationship) of physical attributes, behavioral activities, and psychological traits to gender.

A Thinking Game on Gender Identity: "Jack and Jill"

MATERIALS: The teacher needs to prepare, on separate sheets of paper, line drawings of a girl and a boy—identical except for their genitals. Their hair can be ambiguously short. The teacher also needs to make cutouts of a "boy's haircut" and a "girl's haircut" that can be laid on the heads and a "boy's shirt and pants" and a "girl's dress" that fit the bodies. (The clothes can be made of semitransparent paper that only partially obscures the genitals.) Finally, two or three paper cutouts of toys that the group will tend to recognize as "boy toys" or "girl toys" (e.g., football, police hat, Barbie doll, tea set) can be made.

DISCUSSION QUESTIONS: Using the materials, the teacher performs transformations on the figures to see if the children think a figure is still a boy or girl even after the change. The questions need not follow a set order; a sample list is included below. Each question should be followed by ample time for reflection and discussion, and the teacher should not correct children's answers or answer the questions himself or herself.

- If Jack really wants to be a girl, then can he be a girl? Why?
- When Jill becomes a grown-up, could she be a daddy? Why?
- When Jack was born, could he have been a baby girl? Why?
- Could Jill stop having that [pointing to girl's vagina] and start having that [pointing to boy's penis]? Why?
- If Jack wears a dress, like this, would he be a girl? Why?
- If Jill has a boy haircut, like this, would she be a boy? Why?
- If Jack plays with a Barbie doll, like this, would he be a girl? Why?
- If Jill plays football, like this, would she be a boy? Why?
- If Jack is gentle to babies, would he be a girl? Why?
- If Jill is a rough fighter, would she be a boy? Why?

5. *Children aged three and above can engage in a thinking-game skit focused on identifying gender.* The skit allows children to actively explore the possible clues.

A Thinking Game on Gender Identity: "Big Doll"

MATERIALS: A large doll, dressed in sex-neutral clothes and with a hat covering its hair.

ACTION: Big doll is dramatically "led in" by a teacher, who says, "This is my friend, Big Doll. I wonder if all of you can figure out whether my friend is a boy or a girl."

DISCUSSION QUESTIONS
- Is Big Doll a boy or a girl? Why do you think so?
- Is there any way to tell for sure whether Big Doll is a boy or a girl?
- [If children suggest undressing, ask] What would undressing show?

- What could we do with Big Doll to tell for sure if it is a boy or a girl? Would anyone like to come and try it?
- I guess Big Doll is a —— [whatever children say]. If Big Doll wanted to, could he/she turn into a —— [the opposite]? Why?
- When Big Doll grows up, will he/she be a mother or a father?
- If he/she really wanted to, could he/she be a —— [the opposite of whatever most of the children answer]? Why?

A Sample Discussion on Gender Identity: "Big Doll"

The following observation illustrates the process of discussing gender identity with young children. The discussion took place in a preschool classroom in Amherst, Massachusetts. The discussion leader was student teacher Maryjo Beane. Her questioning strategies appear in brackets. It is interesting to note that although the teacher never corrected Maggie's ideas, Maggie revised and developed them several times.

TEACHER: Is Big Doll a boy or a girl? [*Lead-off question*]
KATE (age 4:10): A boy.
TEACHER: Why do you think so? [*Why question*]
KATE: Boys have that kind of shoes.
TEACHER: What do you think, Maggie?
MAGGIE (age 3:11): A boy.
TEACHER: Why, Maggie? [*Why question*]
MAGGIE: Because of his brown shoes. And his hat.
KURT (age 5:1): Boys have that kind of sweatshirt.
TEACHER: Can anyone think of a way to find out for sure whether Big Doll is a boy or a girl? Another way besides the clothes? [*Issue probe*]
CRISTEN (age 3:8): Because his face is a boy.
MAGGIE: He has blue eyes and I have blue eyes.
TEACHER: So do you still think my friend is a boy, Maggie? [*Encourages communication; seeks to understand her perspective*]
MAGGIE: No, I think he's a girl now. He should wear shorts.
TEACHER: Maggie, if this is a girl, can it change and become a boy? [*Issue probe*]
MAGGIE: No. It will be a mommy.
TEACHER: Why do you think so? [*Why question*]
MAGGIE: Because—I know. You have to take off his clothes. [Maggie went up to see for herself and unzipped not the pants, but the sweatshirt!] He is a boy!

During an activity on gender identity, Aisha has an idea about how to find out "for sure" whether Big Doll is a boy or a girl—she removes its hat!

TEACHER: That's a boy. Now why do you think it's a boy? [*Encourages communication*]

MAGGIE: I want to take off his pants. [The whole group begins to giggle and laugh. Several children rush up to participate in stripping off all of the doll's clothes.] It's a girl.

TEACHER: How do you know, Maggie? [*Why question*]

MAGGIE: [No answer]

TEACHER: Jeff, what did you find? [*Why question*]

JEFF (age 3:5): It's a boy.

TEACHER: Jeff, did you see a penis? [*Issue probe*]

JEFF: Right there. See? This is where it would be. [In fact, there were no genitals on the doll.]

TEACHER: Sarah, is this a boy or a girl? [*Refocuses on conflict*]

SARAH (age 4:10): Boy *and* girl.

TEACHER: Annamaria, what do you think? [*Refocuses*]

ANNAMARIA (age 4:1): It's a girl. Because it doesn't have anything long.

TEACHER: Thank you, everyone. Those were interesting ideas. Some of you looked at Big Doll's hair or clothes to see if it is a boy or a girl, and some of you took off the clothes to find out by looking at Big Doll's body. [*Summarizes*]

ACQUIRING A SEX-ROLE IDENTITY

FRANK (age 3) [appears puzzled by a man in a television show who is singing falsetto]: Is that man a mommy?

JUDY (almost 4) [plays with a new robot toy she has just been given and comments to her father]: I'll have to lose this Go-bot because girls don't play with Go-bots.

During the same years that children are constructing gender identity, they are also coming to form a sex-role identity. The sex roles in their cultural community, the socialization practices of their family, and their own personal style form the basis of their sex-role identity. First, from watching television, reading books, and observing the people around them, children develop *sex-role knowledge,* or sex-role stereotypes. Second, children begin to value what they consider to be sex-appropriate behaviors; they form *sex-role preferences.*

These processes begin early. Children only two to three years old already have some simple and concrete sex-role knowledge. Kuhn, Nash, and Brucken (1978) found that boys and girls aged two to three agree that little girls like to do the following: play with dolls, help mother, cook dinner, clean house, talk a lot, never hit, and say, "I need some help." They agree that boys like to play with cars, help father, build things, and say, "I can hit you."

Furthermore, already by age two for boys and age four for girls, children prefer for themselves or peers the sex-typed toys designated by adults as for their gender. At age three to four, children may reject opposite-sex toys with such explanations as, "Boys don't like that, " or "Girls don't want that" (Eisenberg, Murray, & Hite, 1982).

How do young children acquire the knowledge and preferences that form the basis of their sex-role identity? What part can or should teachers play in the process? Research on sex-role development indicates two findings. First, cognitive maturation controls the sequence of steps in sex-role development. Second, society influences the content of sex-role knowledge. Children's sex-role stereotypes have been found to be directly affected by the films, television shows, and commercials they watch, the books they hear, the way in which teachers label activities and use or avoid sexist language, and their parents' attitudes, work roles, and involvement in child care.[2]

Steps in Acquiring Sex-Role Knowledge

Sex roles are essentially social rules for "appropriate" masculine and feminine behavior. They are a type of *social convention*. Sex roles prescribe what is standard or allowable for males and females in terms of clothing, hair styles, speech patterns, toy choices, occupational roles, and a multitude of other behaviors. In some societies, sex roles are highly prescribed and rigid. In American society, there is a good deal of disagreement among subgroups and individuals about many social conventions, including sex roles.

Social conventions evolve and change in every society through the slow, informal process of shifting public opinion. Sex roles represent the majority's conception of the "done thing," and the main consequence of violation is social disapproval or ridicule.

Developing concepts of conventional rules, including sex roles, has been found to involve a predictable sequence of steps.[3]

Young children aged two to three use the terms "boy" and "girl" as simple category labels. They attach concrete associations to each label, such as "hairbands" and "barrettes" with "girl," but they feel no moral compulsion about the associations. If they notice events that violate their expectancies, they are surprised or amused, but they are not indignant or offended.

At about age four, children begin to construct the idea that "girls" and "girl things" are somehow opposite to "boys" and "boy things." Still, they feel no sense of necessity about what boys and girls *must* do, other than what they *want* to do. Children do not yet see rules as a system outside the self to which the self must or should conform. Rather, they think that they follow rules because they "like to" or "want to." In fact, they tend to adhere only to certain sex-typed behaviors that have caught their imagination. For instance, Jacqueline (age 4) insisted on wearing dresses to school even though her own mother typically wore slacks. Once Jacqueline's dress got wet and the teacher found her some spare overalls to put on. Jacqueline threw the overalls across the room and screamed in rage, "No, I *won't* wear them. I *have* to wear dresses."

Children aged four to five also may try to enforce certain sex roles on other children, but their concern with "rules" is clearly influenced by their personal and immediate desires. Children use the rules to get something they want; they do not enforce the rules because they care about upholding right and wrong. For example, Nick (age 4) came into the housekeeping area where Heather was sitting on a bench pretending to drive her car. Nick asked to play, and Heather told him, "Okay, you can be the daddy. Get in the car." Nick paused for a moment, then said, "But daddies *drive*." Nick's teacher later told his mother this incident, and she laughed and said, "But in our family I do almost all of the driving!"

To cite another example, Gerry (age 4) was playing doctor using a real stethoscope when Anna asked if she could have it. Gerry refused, saying, "Only men can be doctors. Women have to be nurses." A teacher commented, "Colin's father is a nurse and he is a man." Gerry then told Anna that she could have the next turn with the stethoscope. The teacher concluded that the real issue for Gerry was not sex roles but rather who could have the stethoscope.

At age six or seven, children usually move to a new level of understanding. Because they can cognitively construct a representational system, they form ideas about what is masculine and feminine based on the regularities seen out there in the world. Now children regard the "rules out there" with genuine, but exaggerated, respect. They assume that just because the rules are there, they must *always* be right. They cannot conceive of a rule that allows exceptions or a rule that is followed only some of the time.

The early school years are a period of extremely rigid sex-role stereotyping in children. Children aged six to eight often overstate sex roles and overconform to them because they cannot understand that exceptions to the general rules are possible or reasonable. They frequently prefer same-sex playgroups; in fact, sex-segregated playgroups are considered one of the "hallmarks of middle childhood" (Maccoby, 1985). Accompanying the sex segregation there is often a certain amount of behavior that excludes or derogates the opposite sex. Children may even misperceive facts that go against their stereotypes. In one study, children aged five to six were shown videotapes of a female doctor and a male nurse. The majority of children reported that they had seen a male doctor and a female nurse. A quarter of them reported that they had seen two doctors, and only one-fifth accurately described what they had really seen (Cordua, McGraw, & Drabman, 1979).

These sex-role stereotypes can severely limit children's concepts of what they themselves can do or be when they grow up. Beuf (1974) asked three-to-six-year-olds living in Philadelphia what they wanted to be when they grew up and what they would want to be if they were the opposite sex. She quotes one little girl as saying with a sigh, "When I grow up I want to fly like a bird. But I'll never do it because I'm not a boy." A similar idea was expressed by a boy who said when asked what he would be if he were a girl, "A girl? Oh, if I were a girl I'd have to grow up to be nothing."

Later childhood brings with it greater cognitive maturity and sex-role flexibility. Older children can better tolerate diversity and appreciate the complexities of reality. For instance, children aged ten to twelve have been found to be much more flexible than younger children (aged six to eight) about whether men and women can and do hold various occupational roles (Garrett, Ein, & Tremaine, 1977). Later childhood also brings with it a lessening of sex-segregated and exclusionary behavior, as well as a gradually deepening understanding of the general function of social conventions. American children begin to believe that these rules standardize and coordinate interaction in society but are different from "moral rules" that define principles of justice and virtue.

Interestingly, according to theorist Elliot Turiel, children go through alternating developmental periods of "affirming" versus "negating" the conventional system. During affirmation phases (typically ages 6–7, 10–11, and 14–16), children generally believe that people *should* follow conventional rules. During negation phases (typically ages 8–9, 12–13, and 17–18), children generally believe that people *need not* follow conventional rules (Turiel, 1983). These phases explain why many children go through cycles in their general willingness to conform to parental and school rules.

What are the implications for teachers of the stages of sex-role development? The main point is that it is the task of teachers to provide children with access to accurate, complete, and digestible information about societal reality, but it is the task of children to make sense of that information in constructing their own sex-role identity.

Differences Between Boys and Girls in Sex-Role Preferences

The general course of sex-role development is identical for both sexes. Boys and girls first construct descriptive knowledge that gradually develops into prescriptive rules. Both go through phases of affirming and negating conventional rules.

In spite of these basic similarities, American teachers and researchers have long been aware that preschool boys are typically more rigidly committed to sex roles than are girls. Boys more consistently choose and prefer sex-typed toys and activities, and their preferences accelerate more strongly with age throughout early childhood. In preschool classroom play, boys criticize other children for "cross-sex" play more than girls do (Lamb & Roopnarine, 1979).

Why does this happen, and what is the implication for teachers? Teachers can play a more effective educational role with both sexes if they understand how the environment influences boys versus girls in the development of their sex-role identity (Edelbrock & Sugawara, 1978).

Children develop many of their ideas about sex roles from observation. Girls in Western society have traditionally had an advantage over boys in terms of the amount of intimate, daily contact they have with *adult role models.* In both home and school settings, women do the bulk of the caregiving and teaching and are physically and emotionally available to children. In contrast, men are often less available as role models for boys. Therefore, boys, more than girls, are forced to use other sources of information to construct a sex-role identity.

Peer role models seem to be more salient and influential for young boys than for young girls. Boys turn more toward other children to get information about their sex role. Thus, boys strive for masculinity through choosing "boys' ways" of dressing and playing, and rejecting "girls' ways." Girls feel more latitude about toys, clothes, and games because they feel that femininity is based on "*womens'* ways." They are most rigid about sex roles when imitating *adult* roles—caring for babies, going to the office, managing the farm, or whatever is typical of the women they see around them.

Teachers can go a long way in helping children build up their direct experience about the work and behavior of adult men and women. Young children profit from direct and concrete experience, the kind that is provided by adults' visiting their school to tell them about the work they do or by visits out into the community. Contact with adult role models can help children construct more substantial and accurate knowledge about their social world.

Teachers can also guide children in their contacts with media, especially books. American social critics have demonstrated that the majority of children's books and television shows (and also television commercials pitched at children) present sex-role images that are much more stereotyped than the realities of contemporary life. Researchers who have examined children's literature, for example, have consistently found that the most widely read books—including those

winning the prestigious Caldecott Medal—portray males and females
in a distorted and oversimplified manner.

> Most of the characters are males. When females do appear they are
> passive, dependent, ineffectual individuals who are usually serving the
> males or being rescued by them. Women are rarely found outside the
> home; no women are shown in a job or profession in the Caldecott winners
> [1941–71], and their role is clearly presented as that of wife and mother.
> (Flerx, Fidler, & Rogers, 1976, p. 999)

Though some books reinforce traditional sex-role stereotypes, others can be used to counteract them. Many recently published books for
young children present nontraditional images of male and female
behavior. "Reverse-stereotyped" books and television shows have
been found to influence children's sex-role concepts, especially when
their message is made explicitly (Davidson, Yasuna, & Tower, 1979).
That is, their impact is greatest when the visual images are accompa-
nied by verbal description, such as, "John is a man who likes to cook."

Nevertheless, teachers should exercise some caution and also consider children's likes and dislikes when selecting books and classroom
materials. Some children may (at least at first) reject experiences that
present nontraditional sex roles. Kropp and Halverson (1983) found
that preschoolers had definite preferences in storybooks. Four books
were read to children, and the girls liked them in the following order
(going from best to least liked): *Debbie and Her Dolls, William's Doll,
A Train for Jane, Peter's Train Set.* Boys liked them in the exact opposite
order. Both sexes liked best the book about their own sex doing a
traditionally sex-typed activity. They liked least the book about the
opposite sex doing a traditionally sex-typed activity. Books about
the same or opposite sex doing a cross-sex activity were ranked in the
middle.

Children's preferences are fluid, however, and a book rejected on
one day may be sought after on another. Books and discussion can
help children to understand sex roles in their homes, as well as in the
larger society. In one day care classroom, a teacher read Marge
Blaine's book, *The Terrible Thing That Happened at Our House.* The
father in this story begins to do household tasks such as cooking,
cleaning, and laundry when his wife resumes her career. Ricky (age 4)
listened attentively, then began to tell the other children, "That father
in the story is not a *real* father. My mom goes to work and she never
lets my dad do any of those things." Several weeks later, Ricky asked

his teacher to read him the book again. In the meantime, his mother's job had moved to a farther location and Ricky was being cared for primarily by his father. Now after hearing the story, Ricky declared that he liked the book because "that dad is just like my dad!"

Rather than presenting books of only one type, teachers should have the goal of *opening up options* to children. Teachers can take care to provide books that present a multiplicity of images to children. Teachers can encourage children to think and talk about the subject of what "men and women and boys and girls like to do." The diversity of opinions and preferences within the group of children will be sure to stimulate children to think more deeply about sex roles. In the context of the discussion, teachers too can state their opinions and beliefs and encourage all children to reason at their own highest level about what sex roles in society are and should be.

Classroom Activities on Sex Roles

In conclusion, the task of constructing a sex-role identity clearly belongs to the child. Yet teachers can support children's development by stimulating their thinking and providing them with a sense of the broad options for males and females in a pluralistic, democratic society.[4]

1. *The material environment of the classroom can be enriched to provide data for children thinking about sex roles.* To increase children's awareness of nontraditional options, a variety of materials can be used, including the following:
- Male Nurturing Puzzles, Nonsexist Career Puzzles, and Community Workers (available from major toy companies)
- Play Scenes Lotto (available from Milton Bradley) presents nonsexist images, including handicapped youngsters
- Prints, photographs, posters, and felt-board displays can be hung portraying the variety of occupations held by men and women. They present more diverse and attention-catching information when they are frequently changed. Young children readily notice and comment upon them and discuss them with teachers and one another.

2. *Children aged three and above can draw and discuss pictures of "some things mothers and fathers do to help at home."*

3. *Children aged two and above can take field trips to observe people doing jobs that are not sex-stereotyped.* The teacher can take photographs and later make a display, with the children dictating the text.

4. *Children aged four and above can engage in a group discussion about what they would like to be when they grow up.* The teacher can write their answers on a large sheet of paper in two columns, Boys and Girls, and then read the answers back to see if any conclusions can be drawn. Children can discuss if boys could do girls' jobs and vice versa. Then they can be invited to change their choices or add additional fantasies.

5. *Children aged four to five and above can be asked to name "good things for girls to do when they grow up" and "good things for boys to do when they grow up."* The teacher can write down their answers and then read them off, discussing with the children whether the lists have any items in common or are completely different. The children can discuss whether activities in one list could also be in the other.

6. *Children aged five to six can discuss the sex stereotypes in books.* Each child can be asked to bring a favorite book to the circle. Children can discuss what a "main character" is and then name the main characters in their books. The teacher can keep a count of males and females on the board. The children can also discuss the kinds of activities the main characters do and whether the opposite sex could do those things. The teacher can talk about "unreal ways" that men and women are sometimes portrayed in books, television, and movies.

7. *Children aged about four and above can engage in a thinking-game interview about sex roles,* adapted from Damon (1977). This story-situation encourages children to consider the rightness and necessity of certain traditionally sex-typed behaviors. The specific content of the story can be varied to focus on any behaviors of interest.

A Thinking Game on Child Sex Roles: "George's Dolls"

MATERIALS: Any kind of dolls or figures to represent a young boy, his parents, and his "toys," including truck, ball, doll.

CHARACTERS: Using the materials, the teacher enacts a story about a boy, George, who likes to play with dolls. His parents tell him that little boys shouldn't play with dolls, that only girls should. They give him a lot of toys "for boys." But George would still rather play with dolls.

DISCUSSION QUESTIONS

- Why do people tell George not to play with dolls? Is that right?
- Is there a rule that boys shouldn't play with dolls? Who makes that rule?
- What should George do, play with dolls, or not?
- What will happen to George if he keeps playing with dolls?
- Is it fair for George's parents to tell him not to play with dolls? Why (or why not)?
- Is it fair if George's sister, Michelle, gets to play with dolls all she wants, but George doesn't?
- What if George wanted to wear a dress to school? Can he do that? Why (or why not)? Why can girls wear dresses to school but boys can't? Is that fair?
- Do people tell you that you should act a certain way because you are a girl/ boy? What do they say? What do you think about it?

8. *Children aged four and above can engage in a thinking-game skit on adult sex roles.* The skit allows children to consider whether a man and woman should be given certain objects according to the general sex norms of society or the division of labor in their own family. Young children cannot coordinate general norms versus specific facts, but they can be tugged in one direction or the other according to which one is more salient to them. The disagreement heard between children in a group stimulates their reasoning because it mirrors on an external plane the cognitive conflict that each child feels intuitively. Many preschool children "solve" the conflict by insisting that each gift should be given to both mother and father ("They both want it!"). Others distort the facts of the story to fit their preconceptions ("Give the clipboard to the father. He goes to work"). Others simply contradict themselves, focusing now on one true fact they know, now on another ("Fathers don't need sewing kits because they don't sew. [Pause] My father sews. He fixed my button").

A Thinking Game on Adult Sex Roles: "A Box Full of Presents"

CHARACTERS: Mother, father, postal carrier.

MATERIALS: Apron, iron, clipboard (or briefcase), sewing kit, hammer.

ACTION: The narrator explains that in this family, the mother goes off to work at the office, while the father stays home to cook, wash laundry, and take care of the baby. The parents are seen greeting each other at the end of the day and reviewing all their activities. Then the postal carrier enters carrying a large box and says to the audience, "I have a large box of presents for the mother and the father. You children have to help me decide who should get each present. Look what I have."

An activity on adult sex roles involves a mother who works at the office while the father cares for the baby at home.

DISCUSSION QUESTIONS: For each item, the teacher asks the following:
- What is this? What is it for?
- Who should get this, the father who takes care of the house and the baby, or the mother who goes to work at the office?
- Who needs this thing most, the mother or the father? Why?

SUGGESTED BOOKS FOR CHILDREN

This list includes some books that focus on gender identity. Teachers might read and discuss them with an individual child or small group for whom gender identity is a pressing issue; parent communication should be a critical part of this process.

The list also includes books that focus implicitly or explicitly on sex roles. Because so much of children's literature presents stereotyped sex-role images, books were selected that present alternatives. The books listed here focus on child protagonists; related books focused on adult sex roles are provided in Chapter 7.

Berenstain, Stan, & Berenstain, Jan. *He Bear, She Bear*. New York: Random House, 1974.   This book uses humor and rhyme to make the point that boys and girls can choose from the same array of occupations when they grow up.

Blaine, Marge. *The Terrible Thing That Happened at Our House*. New York: Parents' Magazine Press, 1975.   A young girl feels as if her world has caved in when her mother resumes her career. Her family together work out satisfying solutions.

Cohen, Miriam. *The New Teacher*. New York: Macmillan, 1972.   This book portrays a group of racially mixed children at an urban school whose activities are not sex-stereotyped.

de Paola, Tomie. *Oliver Button Is a Sissy*. New York: Harcourt Brace Jovanovich, 1979.   Oliver is ridiculed because he does not like to do the things boys usually do, but eventually the boys realize that they like him because of, not in spite of, his tap-dancing skills.

Hopkins, Lee B. *Girls Can Too!* New York: Franklin Watts, 1972.   This is a book of poems about the different things that girls can think, do, and feel.

Klein, Norma. *Girls Can Be Anything*. New York: Dutton, 1973.   A kindergarten boy tells his good friend that she can't be a doctor, pilot, or President because she is a girl. She does not like hearing that, and her questioning leads to discovery and learning for both.

————. *A Train for Jane*. New York: Feminist Press, 1974.   Jane finally gets the train she wants for Christmas after her family tries unsuccessfully to convince her that girls' toys would be more fun.

Merriam, Eve. *Boys and Girls, Girls and Boys*. New York: Holt, Rinehart & Winston, 1972.   Boy/girl friendship pairs are depicted sharing similar interests, activities, and ambitions.

Rich, Gibson. *Fire Girl*. Old Westbury, N.Y.: Feminist Press, 1972.   Brave, determined Brenda ignores social disapproval and convinces her town's fire department that they need her as an apprentice helper.

Skorpen, Liesel M. *Mandy's Grandmother*. New York: Dial, 1975.   Mandy is such a tomboy that at first she shocks her visiting grandmother. Soon they find rich common ground for a close relationship.

Waxman, Stephanie. *What Is a Girl? What Is a Boy?* Culver City, Calif.: Peace, 1976.   Arresting photographs illustrate this simple and clear discussion of gender identity.

Wilt, Joy. *You're Either One or the Other*. Waco, Tex.: Educational Products, 1980. Line drawings illustrate this discussion (for older children) of gender identity.

Wolde, G. *Tommy and Sarah Dress Up*. Boston: Houghton Mifflin, 1972. Two young children enjoy dressing up and wearing both masculine and feminine clothing.

Zolotow, Charlotte. *William's Doll*. New York: Harper & Row, 1972. William wants a doll, even though the males in his family disapprove. At last his grandmother gets him one and explains to his father why William needs it.

CHAPTER 5

Racial and Cultural Categories

PATRICIA G. RAMSEY

NAOMI (white, age 4) [looking at a photograph of Chinese-American child and a photograph of a black child]: These are both Chinese.
TEACHER: Are they both the same?
NAOMI: Yes, except this one [photograph of the Chinese-American child] is only a little Chinese, and that one [photograph of the black child] is a lot Chinese.

Parents and teachers often assume that children do not notice racial and cultural differences. Because they fear that they will convey or foster prejudiced attitudes, adults often avoid any mention or discussion about these differences. Many express the wish to keep children in a state of "color-blind" innocence.

However, numerous studies have shown that young children notice skin-color differences by the age of three or four[1]. There is even some suggestion that infants notice different physical characteristics (Thurman & Lewis, 1979). One white parent reported that when her three-month-old son met his black babysitter for the first time, he showed a startle reaction that was not evident in his initial encounters with white strangers.

Although it has been less systematically studied, children's awareness of cultural differences is often evident in their comments about unfamiliar types of clothing, foods, and life-styles. Children, of course, do not conceptualize these differences as "cultural"; rather, they simply construct associations between various visible attributes. For instance, when Afro-American and Euro-American children look at pictures of Asian people, they frequently mention "those stick things that you eat with." They do not have a concept of cultural or national categories, but they have learned to associate certain physical characteristics with particular social conventions. Children also react when their expectations are violated by different cultural conventions. At a Saint Patrick's Day parade, a four-year-old child expressed his astonishment about "those men in skirts" at the sight of the kilted members of a local Irish-American society.

In short, children notice concrete manifestations of racial and cultural differences and often struggle to understand them in the context of their existing social categories. However, unlike their exposure to differences in age, kinship, and gender, children's contact with other racial and cultural groups varies widely in terms of frequency and attitudinal context. As a result, teachers first need to become familiar with the affective and informational content of the children's ideas. As the following sections show, children sometimes draw erroneous conclusions that can lead to negative reactions to physical characteristics and life-styles different from their own. Teachers can use thinking games to encourage children to talk about their reactions, questions, and assumptions.

The following sections describe some of the ways in which children think about racial and cultural differences. These discussions reflect findings of many studies, as well as classroom observations. Many of the specific examples are drawn from extensive interviews that I have conducted with preschool and kindergarten children in a variety of communities. Some of the children lived in multiracial and multicultural communities; others had very little contact with other groups. The interviews included several tasks in which children sorted, described, and ranked photographs of Afro-American, Asian-American, and Euro-American children. Activities that reflect these findings and that may serve as a guide for teachers in talking with children about racial and cultural categories are also included.

CHILDREN'S RESPONSES TO RACIAL DIFFERENCES

Perceptual Salience of Racial Differences

By the age of three or four, young children can identify, label, and match people according to different racial characteristics (Katz, 1976, 1983; Williams & Morland, 1976). Most studies have compared children's reactions to black and white stimulus objects such as puppets, pictures, dolls, and photographs. In general, these studies have found that children are most likely to notice skin-color differences. Since color is an early visual category for children and a concept stressed in most preschool programs, it is not surprising that skin color is more salient than hair or facial features.

Some children appear to associate skin-color variations with the colors they are learning to name in school as opposed to the socially defined categories of "black" and "white." When they hear the word "black" used in conjunction with Afro-Americans, both white and black children frequently point out (with some indignation), "Her/his/my skin is not black! It's brown!" Likewise, young children often describe Caucasian skin as pink, orange, or tan as opposed to white.

However, when looking at photographs of Asian-American children, both black and white children express some confusion. They often say, "The face is different," but are at a loss to describe the nature of that difference. They sometimes apply social categories but do not seem to understand them in the ways that adults do. In some recent interviews, children who lived in a virtually all-white community often put Afro-American and Asian-American people into the same category, although they seemed to realize that the two groups were not exactly the same.

RONNIE (age 4:7): Well, they are both black, but this one [Chinese-American child] is blackish and that one [black child] is real black.

A few children in this group identified the Asian children as white, yet noticed some differences.

ROGER (age 4:9): He's white like me but looks asleep.

The black children in a racially mixed community usually grouped Asian and white children together because "they all have light skin." However, they sometimes mentioned other features that suggested that they realized some discrepancies in these groupings.

TARA (black, age 5:2) [looking at a photograph of a Chinese-American child]: She's white, but her eyes are like lines and mine are like balls.

DANNY (black, age 4:8) [looking at a photograph of a Korean-American child]: He's white, but his hair is real flat; mine is standing up hair.

In short, children perceive racial differences in many ways. What they notice and how they categorize others may in part depend on the amount of contact they have had with other groups and their own racial membership. To prepare effective activities, teachers need to learn how the children in their particular classroom perceive these differences and what categories they are using to organize social information.

Racial Permanence

Children do not have a clear understanding that racial characteristics are permanent until they are about seven or eight years old.[2] As with gender constancy, children pass through several stages of understanding before their concepts of racial permanency are stable. Just as young children believe that gender identity is determined by such irrelevant factors as clothes and hairstyle (as described in Chapter 4), they also develop ideas about racial identity that are often contradictory and inconsistent. Furthermore, many young children have only limited contact with racially different others and few opportunities to test their assumptions about the nature and permanency of racial differences. Children also see evidence that skin color does change with exposure to the sun, and many assume that this is the cause of all skin-color variations.

ALTHEA (black, age 4): I wish those white kids would hurry up and get their suntans so that they'd be nice and brown like me.
TEACHER: Does everybody get to become brown?
ALTHEA: Yes, but first they have to get their suntans.

TOMMY (white, age 4:5) [looking at a photograph of a black boy]: I guess he must have stayed out in the sun too long.
TEACHER: Does everyone who stays out in the sun too long change like that?
TOMMY: Yeah. You gotta be careful. He must have forgot his suntan lotion!
TEACHER: Would you change like that if you stayed out in the sun.
TOMMY: No!

Perhaps because whites are the majority in this society, most of the children interviewed believed that all people were originally white and that some later became black through tanning, dyeing, or painting.

JERRY (black, age 4:9): I think that the doctor dyed me brown.
TEACHER: Could you change back?
JERRY: Yeah, but I'd have to really pull my skin off like this [tugs at his skin] and the blood might spill out.

TERRY (white, age 3:9) [looking at photos of black children]: They sure got painted up!
TEACHER: How did that happen?
TERRY: I don't know, but it better be off by Christmas!

The widespread assumption that skin usually changes from light to dark may be further supported by the fact that most of children's experiences with color involve this transition. Paint is usually applied to light or white paper, cooking often involves a darkening of color, and food color is added to play-dough, water, or paste.

Another source of confusion is that racial distinctions are not always clear. The fact that all skin colors are on a continuum of light to dark brown may contribute to children's assumptions that some people are in a transitional stage between one color and another. Variations of skin color on individuals also supports the idea that people change.

MONICA (white, age 4:3) [holding up a photograph of a black girl next to a freckle on the (white) teacher's arm]: You're getting brown like her, but she's already brown all over.
GERALDINE (black, age 4:1) [holding out the palm of her hand]: See, my hand is still pink.

Racially Related Preferences

In numerous studies of children's playmate choices and selections of dolls, puppets, and anonymous peers, children have expressed varying degrees of same-race preference.[3] Preschool children exhibit this preference less than do older children, however, and preschoolers who express same-race preference in an interview often select cross-race playmates. In one interview, a white child was vehement about his dislike of "black people." Yet when he selected his friends from the photographs of his classmates, he chose several Afro-American children. When asked about this apparent contradiction, he adamantly referred to his friends as "brown, not black!" He appeared to be seeing the social category of "black" as completely separate from his observed characteristic of "brown." He kept these two categories distinct to reconcile his otherwise contradictory feelings that "black people are bad" and "I like my friends with brown skin."

Same-race preference often emerges when children are asked to select dolls, puppets, or photographs that represent potential friends. Although they usually give nonracial reasons for their choices, it does appear that race exerts some influence on their selections. Same-race preference is also suggested by the roles that children assign same- and cross-race dolls (Porter, 1971). For example, white children may give positive roles to white dolls, negative roles to black ones. Recently, a white parent expressed to me her concern that her daughter, who had had no contact with any black people, invariably assigned negative roles to her black dolls. The mother felt she had not conveyed racist attitudes to her daughter, and she wondered where they came from.

In my discussions with children, both black and white children frequently expressed aversion to darker skin. When asked why they did not like particular children, they often said that they did not like the colors black and brown. Although Williams and Morland (1976) have claimed that this aversion to black and brown derives from a universal fear of darkness, it is also true that dark colors are associated with fearful or bad events in our culture. For example, in most classrooms, dark colors are used only at Halloween, often on scary figures such as witches and goblins. Thus, whether or not avoidance of dark colors is in part based on fear of the dark, it is certainly accentuated by children's social experiences in American society.

Cross-Racial Recognition

Children (and adults) often have a more difficult time in distinguishing individuals and interpreting facial expressions among cross-race than among same-race peers. In the interviews, children misidentified photographs of their cross-race classmates more often than they misidentified those of same-race classmates. White children with little cross-race social experience frequently confused the gender of Chinese-American children. Likewise, facial expressions of cross-race peers were often misinterpreted. When photographs of a smiling black boy and a smiling white boy were presented to white children, several of the respondents described the black child as "mad"; they did not make similar errors when looking at unfamiliar white peers.

Young children, who tend to center on single pieces of information, may not be able to simultaneously process racial differences and other identifying information. As children become more familiar with the range of racial diversity, they may become adept at perceiving more subtle distinguishing characteristics.

Classroom Activities on Racial Awareness

With the following activities, teachers can encourage children to express their ideas about racial differences and to question some of their misperceptions. Because of their concern about eliminating prejudice, teachers may be tempted to quickly correct misinformation or challenge negative reactions about other racial groups. However, as with the thinking games on other subjects, the goal is to help children to reflect on their assumptions, not to suppress them. In communities where children do not have the opportunity to interact with diverse groups, the following activities may also make other groups seem more familiar, less distant.

1. *Children as young as three years of age can engage in activities with photographs and dolls that represent different racial groups.* Children can be asked: "Which people are the same?" "Which people are different?" "Who could be in the same family?" To see what characteristics children notice spontaneously, they can be instructed to simply "put the people together that go together." The frequency with which children use racial groupings is an indication of how prominent race is vis-à-vis other traits in their perceptions of others. For young children, it is recommended that teachers present only three or four photographs at a time. Factors such as gender, facial expressions, age, and clothing can be varied in the sorting activities to see which ones are more or less prominent than race.

2. *Children four years of age and older can use the photographs in guessing games.* In another series of activities, children can guess which picture a peer is thinking of from verbal clues. Both the clues and the readiness with which they are understood reveal some information about which characteristics particular children find most meaningful.

3. *Jigsaw puzzles of faces made from photographs cut in identical pieces can stimulate children's awareness of what characteristics constitute different types of faces.* Teachers can observe children's efforts to reconstruct faces representing diverse groups and see from their

patterns of selection which characteristics are prominent. Puzzles can
be constructed to be appropriate for children of different ages.

SARA (white, age 4:6): Eye goes with eye, lips with lips [as she
incorrectly puts together pieces from two different faces].

TEACHER [after Sara has finished moving pieces]: What can you tell
me about that person [pointing to one "completed" puzzle]?

SARA [looking puzzled as she gazes at the figure]: They don't
match. [She quickly reassembles the two puzzles correctly.]

Because she was initially concentrating on the particular features of
eyes and lips, Sara did not at first notice that there were two different
faces. It was only when she saw the puzzles as wholes that she realized
that there were ways that the faces did not match.

Teachers can also present "completed" puzzles with racially incon-
gruent features and see what comments the children make about these
discrepancies.

4. *Skin-color charts can help children four years of age and older
see skin-tone variations as a continuum rather than as polarities.* In one
multiracial kindergarten, children were teasing each other by the name
of "Old Black ——— [child's name]." The teacher introduced a skin-
color chart that included white and black and numerous shades of
brown. After everyone in the class matched their skin to the chart, they
discovered that everyone was a shade of brown, only the classroom
rabbit was white, and no one was black. The name-calling stopped
immediately.

5. *Small dolls, puppets, and photographs can be used to stimulate
children's thinking about shared racial features in families.* Teachers
can present children with small dolls, puppets, or photographs and ask
them to form families. In this process, children can articulate which
properties they assume must be common and which ones they assume
are not. This activity could be incorporated into ones focusing on
children's understanding of kinship (see Chapter 6).

The following responses occurred when children were looking at a
photograph of a black family (father, mother, and daughter) and a
series of photographs of Asian, black, and white children. They were
asked to select the children who could be part of the family. Their
answers demonstrate the different ways in which children organize the
same information.

ELLEN (white, age 4:7) [selecting the girls of all three groups]: Only
these can go 'cause they are all sisters. One, two, three, four [in-
cluding the original daughter].

TEACHER: Could these children be part of the family [pointing to the boys]?
ELLEN: No, silly! They're boys!

JAMES (white, age 4:3) [selecting photographs of white and black children, both boys and girls]: These could be the brothers.
TEACHER: [pointing to the Asian children]: Could these children be part of the family?
JAMES: No, they are the Indian boys.

SUSAN (white, age 5:7): [Selects black boys and girls.]
TEACHER: What makes those children part of the family?
SUSAN: They are black and the family is black.
TEACHER: Could these others [white and Asian] be part of the family?
SUSAN: No, they are white.

6. *Projects can be designed to challenge the idea that things always change from light to dark.* Teachers can provide children with light chalk or crayons to use on dark paper. In a series of winter solstice activities, teachers and children can experiment with many ways of making paper, clay, paint, and wood change from dark to light. It is important that, as teachers introduce children to this kind of transformation, they do not suggest in any way that lightness is preferable to darkness.

7. *Washing hands and dolls can be used as a time to dispel the assumption that darker skin is dirty.* Children often confuse darker skin color with dirt; it is important that teachers try to counteract this assumption, as it is often expressed in conjunction with derogatory statements about dark skin colors.

    JAMES (white, age 4:6) [watching a black classmate wash her hands as they were both cleaning up from finger painting]: She's gonna have to wash her hands real hard to get all that brown off.

In this case, the teacher did not respond at the immediate moment. Instead she planned the following "Bath-Time" activity to challenge James's assumptions.

A Thinking Game on Racial Permanence: "Bath-Time for the Babies"

CHARACTERS: A babysitter (played by a teacher).
MATERIALS: A conspicuously "dirty" white doll (covered with washable paint),

a clean black doll, a container of soapy water that is just large enough for one doll, paper towels.

ACTION: The two dolls are shown to the children. The babysitter says, "It is time for the babies' baths, but there is only enough water for one bath." He or she then asks the children, "Which baby needs a bath the most?" After the children have selected the doll that needs the bath the most, the babysitter washes the doll. If the group of children is small, they can also assist in the washing. During the washing, the teacher can have children describe what changes they see. After the first baby is washed, the babysitter decides that there is still enough water for the second baby to be bathed. During this bath, the teacher asks children how the changes are different from those that occurred in the earlier washing.

When this activity was tried in several classrooms, the children's responses reflected an increasing understanding that racial characteristics are permanent.

The three-year-olds could not agree on which baby needed the bath the most. Some said that the painted doll did; others said that the "one that is all-over brown really needs the bath." However, all firmly expected the black doll to become lighter through washing. When no visible change appeared after several minutes of vigorous scrubbing, the children confirmed their expectations by pointing to soap bubbles or small imperfections in the plastic as indications that the doll was indeed changing color. When the doll was at last removed from the bath (with no visible change), the children seemed puzzled but still expressed confidence that it would eventually change.

The four-year-olds agreed that the white doll needed the bath the most. After they finished washing it, they washed the black doll. As they began, the children all expressed the expectation that it would eventually become light. One child explained that "the paint's been on longer and is more dry so it will take a long time to get it white again." Unlike the three-year-olds, these children did not "see" the doll getting lighter. Instead they noticed that the water made the doll look darker. At the end they were still convinced that the doll would eventually get lighter, but they were puzzled and beginning to wonder.

The five-year-olds derided the question about who should have the bath, as it was obvious to them that the white doll was the dirty one. When the black doll was washed, they seemed to be sure that it would not change and soon lost interest. As one child said in exasperation, "It's supposed to be that way!"

8. *To understand the role that race plays in children's preferences for others, teachers can analyze their spontaneous and elicited choices.* If the classroom is racially mixed, teachers can systematically make

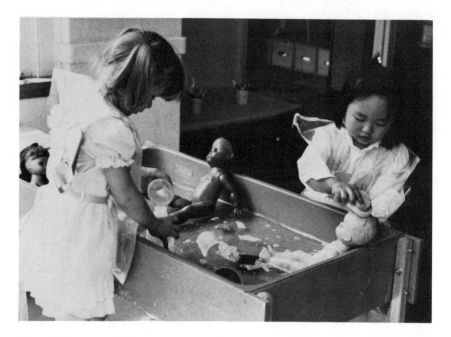

An activity on racial permanence: bathing baby dolls challenges children's assumption that dark skin color washes off.

note of the groups that form in various activities at different times of the day. These patterns may indicate which factors children are considering as they make their social decisions. If particular children are habitually clustered, whether by race, class, gender, or activity preference, teachers can encourage them to expand their circle of friends by arranging activities to appeal to more diverse groups. These shifts may cause some interesting responses from the children that will enlighten teachers about some of criteria that children use for selecting friends.

In both monoracial and multiracial classrooms, teachers can use dolls, puppets, photographs, and pictures to elicit children's preferences related to race. By having children select friends or potential playmates from these possibilities, teachers can get some idea of the extent to which race is a factor. Observations of the kinds of roles assigned to racially different puppets and dolls are also revealing.

9. *If preferences and roles seem to be racially related, teachers can challenge children's assumptions.* If children assign negative roles to black dolls, teachers could create a skit that includes a white doll and a

black doll and that shows the white doll misbehaving. Children could be asked to identify the child who is being bad.

In one kindergarten classroom, teachers heard children talking about how "Indians kill children." To challenge this assumption, teachers brought in photographs of Native Americans nurturing children in many ways. They also engaged the children in the following thinking-game interview:

A Thinking Game on Racial Preferences: "Who Is a Helper?"

MATERIALS: Puppets of a child, an angry-looking white adult, and a friendly-looking Native American adult.

ACTION: The puppet child is lost in the park. There are two grown-ups nearby.

DISCUSSION QUESTIONS: Whom should the child ask for help?

If the children do not seem to notice that the second adult is an "Indian," teachers can mention that fact and see how this influences their decision.

For each choice, teachers can ask children what made them think that the adults would be helpful or not helpful.

If children insist that the Indian would hurt children, teachers can keep elaborating on the positive aspects of the Indian to see if they can shake their convictions. For example, "The Indian person is a mother," or "The Indian person is a teacher at a school like this one."

10. *Children can use dark colors in a variety of activities.* Teachers can attempt to counteract the prevailing negative associations with dark colors by using the colors brown and black in appealing activities and the color scheme of the room and by making sure they are represented in the materials provided. In the winter solstice activities mentioned earlier, teachers and children worked with dark and light colors and shadows and lights to see the many ways that darkness and light are related and of equal value. Teachers should also monitor their own comments to be sure that the words "black" and "brown" are not used in disparaging ways. They can draw positive attention to these colors. For example, when working with the soil for the school garden, teachers can point out all the rich tones of brown.

11. *Children from infancy on can learn to see more individual differences by close contact with people from diverse racial groups.* When doing activities on gender identity in Chapter 4, children can be encouraged to see the similarities and differences among their peers. If the classroom does not have a racial mix, these activities can be based on photographs of children from other racial groups. For example, teachers can present children with a set of three photographs of children from a racial group different from their own, give the de-

picted children names, and ask the group to "learn the names." Then they can remove one photograph and let the children try to guess which one is missing.

CHILDREN'S AWARENESS OF CULTURAL DIFFERENCES

Social Conventions

As mentioned earlier, young children cannot conceptualize "culture"; however, they do notice concrete differences in languages, eating styles, foods, and clothing (Lambert & Klineberg, 1967). While they cannot be "cultural relativists" because they do not have the capacity to see social conventions from another point of view, they can learn about and enjoy many concrete manifestations of cultural diversity. If these differences are presented in positive and meaningful ways, children will find them to be an intriguing source of pleasure rather than experiencing them as violations of expectations or inexplicably strange.

In a culturally diverse environment, teachers have many opportunities to study children's reactions to cultural differences and to create experiences to help them move beyond aversive reactions. For instance, in one kindergarten, a child from India was being called "garbage head" because of the coconut oil that he had on his hair. The teacher brought in shampoos and hair tonics and had the children compare many preparations, including coconut oil. The children began to see that everyone's hair has a different smell and were able to generate a category of "stuff for your hair" that included familiar shampoos as well as the more novel coconut oil.

In a less diverse environment, teachers should introduce different cultural styles through classroom activities, guests, and community events. Different foods, unfamiliar clothing, and a variety of implements for eating, painting, and printing will all stimulate varying degrees of curiosity, aversion, and interest.

Language

Another aspect of cultural differences that relates closely to intergroup understanding is language. When there is not a shared language, meaning has to be conveyed through nonverbal means. Although language differences do impede verbal communication, they can be used to heighten awareness of facial expressions and gestures. They can also stimulate children's awareness of other points of view. As children attempt to exchange information with peers who do not speak their language, they can experience in a concrete way the idea that what is meaningful to one person is not necessarily meaningful to another.

With children who speak languages other than English, language teaching should be viewed in a reciprocal way. While these children are learning English, they can also have the chance to teach others words and phrases from their languages. If they are seen exclusively as children who cannot speak English rather than as children who *can* speak another language, then the potential for an exchange of languages is short-circuited.

Monolingual classrooms do not provide as many spontaneous occasions for these kinds of interactions. However, teachers can incorporate different languages and ways of communicating that will provide similar opportunities for children to expand their ideas about how people can understand each other.

Classroom Activities on Cultural Diversity

1. *Teachers can use photographs to learn how children perceive cultural differences.* With photographs that show people dressing, eating, and living in unfamiliar ways, teachers can stimulate children's thinking and curiosity about these differences. Children's reactions to these pictures will offer some indications as to the relative salience of these differences in their perceptions of people. Their comments may also reflect the types of categories that they apply when confronted by unfamiliar information.

GEORGE (age 4:6) [looking at a photograph of a Vietnamese man with a straw hat who is carrying a small child]: He's a hunter.

TEACHER: How can you tell?

GEORGE: He's got a knife in his back pocket [not visible in the photograph].

When confronted by an unfamiliar face and unfamiliar clothing, George mentioned a familiar role (it was the hunting season in his locale). He assimilated the image in the photograph into his image of a hunter.

2. *Activities that juxtapose the familiar and unfamiliar will help children see the similarities and differences in various ways of life.* In cooking activities, familiar foods such as eggs, rice, or beans can be prepared in numerous ways. Here the children can experience familiar

items being transformed into ones that are less familiar but that retain
some known qualities. In a multicultural environment, these experiences can be personalized and placed in a more meaningful context
through parent participation in these projects and visits to classmates'
homes. In a less diverse environment, the unfamiliar can be personalized through photographs and stories so that children can compare
"the way we cook and eat ——— [a familiar food] at school" with "the
way that Mei Ling [see suggested books] cooks and eats it at her
house."

3. *Using the format of the following thinking game, teachers can
present dilemmas that highlight the existence of different social conventions.*

A Thinking Game on Different Social Conventions: "Suppertime in Yellow Blanket Country"

MATERIALS: Dolls or puppets representing two children, Sara and Jeremy,
and their parents (teachers can experiment with using familiar or unfamiliar
names); a bowl that is an appropriate size for the dolls.

ACTION: The teacher explains: "In the Yellow Blanket Country there are no
forks, knives, or spoons. It is time for supper, and Sara and Jeremy's parents
give them their food in this bowl."

DISCUSSION QUESTIONS
  • How will Sara and Jeremy eat their supper with no forks or spoons?
  • What will their parents say if they eat with [whatever technique the
    children have suggested]?
  • What would your parents say if you ate like that?
  • Why is it that some people have knives and forks and spoons and other
    people do not?
  • Can the people in Yellow Blanket Country get knives and forks and
    spoons?

When faced with this problem, children aged three to five generated similar ideas: use one's fingers, lick up the food like a cat, use a
straw, make a scoop, and eat with your feet. One three-year-old
mentioned "sopsticks," and one four-year-old suggested that if the
children covered their fingers with the sleeves of their shirts, they
could eat with their hands and not get their fingers dirty.

When the children thought about whether or not the rules might be
different from those in their own homes, they showed some clear
developmental differences in their abilities to understand a person's
actions in a context different from theirs.

TEACHER: What would their parents say when they ate with their
hands?

JEREMY (age 3:6): Their mother say "you get a fork!"
TEACHER: But in Yellow Blanket Land there are no forks.
JEREMY: They have to get forks.

TEACHER: What would their parents say when they ate with their hands?
SARA (age 4:7): Okay.
TEACHER: What would your parents say if you ate with your hands?
SARA: We eat with our hands when we have lobster!

TEACHER: What would their parents say when they ate with their hands?
SEAN (age 5:6): That's okay.
TEACHER: What would your parents say if you ate with your hands?
SEAN: Don't get your hands dirty!
TEACHER: How come the two parents would say two different things?
SEAN: 'Cause in that place they don't have forks or spoons.

When asked about why people might not have these implements, all of the children assumed that the reason that the people did not have the familiar implements was because they "had run out" or "forgotten to buy some." Even the five-year-olds who were able to see that conventions might differ according to circumstances could not grasp the possibility that there might be absolutely no access to the implements that are familiar to them. They vigorously maintained that more could be obtained from a store.

This approach can be incorporated into all topics of the curriculum. For example, if the class is doing a project on transportation, children can consider how the Yellow Blanket People transport themselves and their goods under various circumstances (e.g., without cars, across sand, in the snow). Teachers can provide different materials that children can use in experimenting with various means of transporting objects and people on their bodies, tricycles, and invented vehicles.

4. *Children as young as three years of age can learn words from other languages.* In multilingual classrooms, there are many opportunities for children to experiment with alternative ways of communicating. In one preschool, where many different languages were spoken, the children very quickly developed ways of communicating with one

An activity on culture challenges children from different heritages to discuss whether there is a "right way" to eat food.

another using objects, gestures, and force. Because they were not as language-dependent as adults, they readily found substitutions for speech. They also began to incorporate many expressions from one another's languages. Teachers can support children's experiments with unfamiliar languages and with alternative ways of communicating by encouraging children to see "how many ways we can say ———" using different languages and various nonverbal techniques.

In monolingual classrooms, different languages can be incorporated in many activities. Many books for children (e.g., the Curious George series) have been translated into different languages. Children's interest in other languages can be stimulated by hearing the same story read in two languages either by the teachers or on recordings. As they see familiar pictures but hear different words, they can begin to relate unfamiliar vocabulary to familiar objects and events. Following the two readings, they can discuss whether both versions tell the same story. Likewise, they can learn new terms for familiar objects and consider whether the object is the same with another name. While listening to the unfamiliar language, they can also experience the state of "not understanding" that is part of the experience of people who are in unfamiliar language environments. Similar activities with other languages can be incorporated with songs, counting games, and art activities.

5. *Children in both monolingual and multilingual classrooms can learn that there are many different ways of referring to the same objects and events.* Teachers can greet children in several different languages (there are numerous translations of various greeting songs). They can point out the many different ways of saying hello, goodbye, and so forth. Young children enjoy simply saying new words and perhaps rhyming with them. Older children (aged five and above) can engage in thinking games such as the following.

A Thinking Game on Different Languages: "What Is the Right Name?"

MATERIALS: Two puppets or dolls named Mary and Rosa. A small table appropriate to the dolls or puppets.

ACTION: Mary and Rosa are looking for something to write on. Mary is looking for a "table" and Rosa for a "mesa." They see the table and they both say, "That's what we need!" Rosa says, "A mesa," and Mary says, "A table." Then they start to argue about what it is really called. Which one is right?

DISCUSSION QUESTIONS
• Who is right, Mary or Rosa?
• What is the real name of that object?
Children who are ready to do some switching of roles can consider what "mesa" means to Mary and what "table" means to Rosa.

6. *Alternatives to spoken communication can be used in both multilingual and monolingual classrooms.* Sign language, piano chords, drum beats, pantomime, and visual cues are only a few of the many alternatives to spoken directions and comments. In addition to drawing children's attention to the many possibilities of communicating, they also expose children in a very immediate way to both traditional and contemporary ways of communicating that they might not become aware of in our very verbal society of radios and telephones.

7. *The use of different languages helps children to focus on the question, "What is talking?"* As children hear and speak other languages, they may become interested in what is and is not talking. Some intriguing discussion questions include: "Do babies talk?" "Do fish talk to each other?" "Can you talk to yourself?" "Are nonsense words talking?"

STEREOTYPES AND OVERGENERALIZATIONS

As children try to understand the nature of physical and social phenomena, they frequently overgeneralize certain characteristics. Children's assumption that age and height must be correlated (as described in Chapter 3) is a good example of this phenomenon. When adults hear children overgeneralize information about racial and cultural differences, they worry that children are learning to be prejudiced. The distinction between developmentally related categorical errors and a more willful refusal to see the range of human possibilities is often unclear. However, we should not assume that children are prejudiced or deliberately using stereotypes when they make overgeneralizations. They may simply be thinking in an age-appropriate way and trying to make sense out of their limited experience with other groups.

> KIM (white, age 4:7): Chinese people eat in restaurants.
> TEACHER: All the time or just some of the time?
> KIM: All the time!
> TEACHER: What about the babies, do they eat in a restaurant?
> KIM: Yep!
> TEACHER: Where do Chinese people eat breakfast?
> KIM [sounding impatient]: In restaurants!

In this case, the child had been to a local Chinese restaurant, and, in the absence of any other information about Chinese people, she overgeneralized from her limited information.

To design appropriate ways to encourage children to reconsider some of their assumptions, teachers need to have an idea about the content of these assumptions. In the case of the child believing that all Chinese people eat in restaurants, the following ideas were suggested.

• The teacher can introduce books and photographs that portray Chinese-Americans living, eating, and washing in homes. Children can see that people can use "those stick things" (often mentioned in relationship to Chinese people) in homes as well as restaurants.

- The teacher can set up the role-play area as a restaurant so that children learn about how a restaurant functions and how it differs from a home and perhaps why it is unlikely that anybody would eat there all the time.
- Chopsticks, rice, and other things that the child noticed at the restaurant can be used in cooking and housekeeping activities so that she can see that they can exist outside of the restaurant environment.

Besides overapplying certain pieces of information, children also learn misinformation or draw erroneous conclusions. Often they misunderstand a comment or a picture or have heard some neighborhood lore. Once an incorrect connection is made, more misinformation is added.

LEO (white, age 4:5) [looking at a picture of a black girl]: That's a disease person. If you touch her, you'll die!
TEACHER: How would that happen?
LEO: If you touch a black person, you catch the disease!

Since Leo was telling many of his classmates about this theory, the teacher wanted to move quickly to challenge his ideas. We designed the following activities to help him reconsider some of his associations.

- With a series of photographs of a black doctor attending a white child, the teacher encouraged the child to explore the conflicting information that "the disease guy" was actually making the patient better.
- The teacher read stories about children getting sick and then recovering to challenge his ideas about sickness involving a permanent change.
- The teacher introduced books and pictures showing black children and adults in positive roles or engaged in appealing activities. She included several photographs of black and white children touching each other in affectionate ways.

SUGGESTED BOOKS FOR CHILDREN

The following list offers examples of different kinds of books and ways that they might be used to support the curriculum described in the previous pages. There is a dearth of good books written for young children that present authentic and contemporary images of life in other countries and in ethnic communities in this country. Thus, several books have been included that present more traditional or legendary images. While these stories are limited in terms of their current accuracy, they do introduce young children to the idea that people live in different ways.

In selecting books for this list, particular attention was paid to how easily young children could identify with the themes that were presented in order to help children focus on the similarities that transcend cultural and racial differences. When using this list and other ones, teachers should try to balance traditional images with contemporary ones.

Adoff, Arnold. *Black Is Brown Is Tan.* New York: Harper & Row, 1973.   In this story about a racially mixed family, a child muses upon the various skin colors of the family members. This book conveys the message that differences are real and enriching and do not separate people.

Anno, Mitsumasa. *Anno's Italy.* New York: William Collins, 1980.   Pictures (no text) juxtapose the elegance of Italy's classic architecture and the daily life of traditional peasants and contemporary urban dwellers. The highly detailed pictures are fascinating to children and challenge them to find familiar biblical and historical scenes as well as the lone horseman who appears in all the pictures.

Baker, Olaf. *Where the Buffalo Begin.* New York: Frederick Warne, 1981 (based on the author's text in *St. Nicholas Magazine* 42, no. 4 [1915]). This story of a traditional Plains Indian boy who dreams of finding the lake where the buffalo begin captures the wonder and excitement of this legendary search.

Baylor, Byrd. *Before You Came This Way.* New York: Dutton, 1969.   Using replicas of prehistoric Southwestern Indian pictographs, the author evokes the past lives of Native Americans. This book challenges the assumption that the Europeans "discovered" this country.

Behrens, June. *Together.* Chicago: Children's Press, 1975.   The photographs and words in this book illustrate many ways that people can be best friends. The inclusion of many cross-race dyads illustrates the fact that friendships need not be confined to one's own group.

Bemelmans, Ludwig. *Madeline.* New York: Viking, 1939/1960.   While this story takes place in an unfamiliar context, a convent school in early-twentieth-century Paris, it deals with the familiar themes of illness, visits to the hospital, and recovery.

Bernheim, Mark, & Bernheim, Evelyne. *The Drum Speaks.* New York: Harcourt Brace Jovanovich, 1971.   This African story describes a young boy's transition from his home village to school. The traditions of the village, including the importance of the drum as a means of communication, are described in positive but not romanticized terms.

Caines, Jeannette. *Abby.* New York: Harper & Row, 1973.   This story about an adopted girl coping with her aloof older brother can be used to discuss different family origins and to challenge children's assumptions that black children were originally white.

Clark, Ann Nolan. *In My Mother's House.* New York: Viking, 1941.   Written in a poetic form, this book describes the daily life of the traditional Pueblo People. It includes accounts of activities such as getting water and cooking and offers a way for children to see some unfamiliar ways of doing familiar routines.

Clifton, Lucille. *All Us Come Cross the Water.* New York: Harper & Row, 1973.   In this book, Clifton describes how slaves were brought to this country from Africa. She makes this complex history comprehensible to young children and imbues the slaves with dignity.

Clymer, Theodore. *The Travels of Atunga.* Boston: Little, Brown, 1973. Based on an old Eskimo legend, this story tells of a man's travels to different gods in order to find food for his people. It illustrates some of the adaptations that people have made to their physical environment, as well as systems of beliefs different from those familiar to most children in the United States.

Coutant, Helen. *First Snow.* New York: Knopf, 1974.   One of a very few stories written for young children about Vietnamese immigrants, it describes a family's adjustment to the climate and mores of this country. Focusing on the death of the grandmother, it introduces a few Buddhist rituals and illustrates how events familiar to many children in this country might appear magical to a child who has just arrived.

Feelings, Muriel, & Feelings, Tom. *Moja Means One.* New York: Dial, 1971.   This book teaches children to count in Swahili. The accompanying pictures illustrate some of the ways that Swahili-speaking children and adults live and work.

———. *Jambo Means Hello.* New York: Dial, 1974.   As in the previous book, this volume introduces children to Swahili words using pictures that children can easily understand.

Goldman, Louis. *Turkey: A Week in Samil's World.* New York: Crowell-Collier, 1973.   This book, along with others in the same series, *A Week in . . .* , describes the daily life of children in other countries. The routines are familiar, but the ways that they are carried out reflect particular cultures and physical environments.

Keats, Ezra Jack. *Whistle for Willie.* New York: Viking Press, 1964.   Set in an urban environment, this book describes a young black boy's efforts to master whistling so that he can call his dog. For children who have not had much contact with black peers, this book offers a meaningful way of seeing them as similar to themselves.

———. *Peter's Chair.* New York: Harper & Row, 1967.   This book offers the same opportunity using the theme of the birth of a new sibling.

Lewin, Harry. *Jafta's Father*. Minneapolis: Carolrhoda Books, 1983. *Jafta's Mother*. Minneapolis: Carolrhoda Books, 1983.   In these two books, a black South African boy describes his father and mother. While the feelings and routines are familiar, the images and metaphors reflect the culture and environment of the South Africans.

Miles, Miska. *Annie and the Old One*. Boston: Little, Brown, 1971.   A Navaho girl learns from her grandmother that people cannot interfere with the natural processes of aging and dying. This book not only introduces children to some aspects of Navaho life and their concept of time, but it also takes a reassuring approach to the topic of death.

Paek, Min. *Aekyung's Dream*. San Francisco: Children's Book Press, 1978. Written in both Korean and English, this book is the story of a Korean child adjusting to life in this country.

Perrine, Mary. *Nannabah's Friend*. Boston: Houghton Mifflin, 1970.   A Navaho girl, who is lonely when she is tending her family's sheep, finds another child to be her friend. Set in an unfamiliar setting (for most U.S. children), it deals with the familiar theme of making friends.

Reich, Hanns. *Children and Their Fathers*. New York: Hill and Wang, 1960. *Children and Their Mothers*. New York: Hill and Wang, 1964.   These photographic essays illustrate how children and their fathers and mothers enjoy each other all over the world.

Roberts, Nancy, & Roberts, Bruce. *A Week in Robert's World: The South*. New York: Crowell-Collier, 1969.   Life in the rural South is portrayed through Robert's daily activities. Photographs enable children to see Robert and his family as real people.

Steptoe, John. *Daddy Is a Monster . . . Sometimes*. New York: Lippincott, 1980.   A father's changing moods are described through a child's view. Written in Black English, the book also introduces children to a particular way of speaking.

Tsow, Ming. *A Day with Ling*. London: Hamish Hamilton, 1982.   A visit to her Chinese classmate's house enables a child to experience the blend of English and Chinese traditions in various routines.

Wallace, Ian. *Chin Chiang and the Dragon Dance*. New York: Atheneum, 1984.   Written about the annual Chinese New Year celebration, this book describes a young boy's fear of failure and way he is able to overcome it. It also portrays warm relationships between older and younger people.

Yahya, Fauzia, & Jones, Lynn. *Ali and the Camel*. Self published, 1983. Available through Claudia's Caravan, P.O. Box 1582, Alameda, Calif. 94501.   Written in Arabic and English, this book describes some events in the life of a Bedouin boy. It is a rare portrayal of this way of life.

Yarborough, Camille. *Cornrows*. New York: Coward, McCann, & Geoghegan, 1979.   While her grandmother braids her hair, a child learns the meaning and history of the different patterns of cornrows.

Yashima, Taro. *The Village Tree*. New York: Viking, 1953.   This story describes memories of summer fun in Japan.

———. *Crow Boy*. New York: Viking, 1955.   A tale of a very small Japanese boy who in the face of his classmates' scorn finds his special way of learning.

Yee, Sylvia, & Kokin, Lisa. *Got Me a Story to Tell*. San Francisco: St. John's Educational Threshold Center, 1977.   With photographs and excerpts from taped interviews, children describe in their own words their experiences of living in this society. One story is about a child in a black community. The others describe children's adjustments as they have moved from other countries, including El Salvador, Hong Kong, the Fiji Islands, and the Philippines.

Yolen, Jane. *The Seeing Stick*. New York: Crowell, 1977.   This book is about the blind daughter of a Chinese emperor who learns to see with her hands from a wise old man. Although the story does not depict contemporary China, it does illustrate that people who lived in another time and place experienced emotions that contemporary children can understand.

Zimmerman, Andrea G. *Yetta the Trickster*. New York: Seabury, 1978.   This tale, which takes place in a traditional Eastern European village, describes all the tricks that a young girl tries on the adults around her. Set in an unfamiliar time and place, it presents a theme that is appealing to young children.

CHAPTER 6

The Ties That Bind: Family and Friendship

SAM (age 3:10) [reflecting spontaneously]: You know, when people are in the same family as you, you like them but they are not your friends. Other people, who are in different families, are your friends. Like Geordie [Sam's little brother], I like him, but we're not friends. If someone is in your family, and it's a baby, mostly it's a brother.

Family and friendship ideas are a central part of young children's social cognition. Young children are deeply concerned about people's *connections* to one another. They want to know to whom they particularly "belong." Realizing that some but not all of the people that they know are special to them, they are sensitive to the existence of bonds based on association, caretaking, and affection. They think about these connections and construct their own age-appropriate ideas about them. They tend to talk spontaneously about these ideas most when they feel confused or concerned about them, for example, when bonds are threatened or change in some way. Such moments provide adults with natural windows on children's thinking.

MEGAN (age 4) [to day care teacher]: You know, my daddy is going to be *dead*. [Actually, her parents are getting divorced.]

FREDDIE (age 5) [to day care teacher]: My dad has a new brother named Paul. [Freddie's parents are separated. Paul is a man who has just moved in with Freddie's mother.]

ANNE (age 3:6) [comments to nearby teacher, while playing with dolls]: The mother is with the baby. The father is on vacation and he's never coming back. He doesn't like the kids, the mother, and the baby. [Anne's father has recently gone overseas, getting things ready for the family soon to follow.]

GREG (age 9, special-needs child) [to teacher]: You know, I used to have a sister.
TEACHER: You did?
GREG: Yeah, she used to live with my dad.
TEACHER: She doesn't anymore?
GREG: No.
TEACHER: [Pause] Are you wondering if he's still your dad, too?
GREG: Yeah. He doesn't live with me and my mom.

Young children clearly use the same family and kinship terms that adults do in talking about their social relationships, but their systems of meaning are different. It is not just that young children are confused about their relationships, it is that they define and use words differently. Adults and young children each assume that they are communicating fully with the other, but at times they may not be.

In this chapter, we will discuss young children's understanding of family, kinship, and friendship concepts as a basis for considering how adults can best talk with children about their relationships.

FRIENDSHIP AND FAMILY: WHAT ARE THEY?

Children's close relationships come mainly in two types—friendships and family relationships. To adults, these are distinct categories. Friendship can be defined as a voluntary, self-chosen relationship between people. Friendship is based on ties of liking, concern, respect, reciprocal help, common interests or goals, and so on. Thinking about the nature of friendship requires considering such issues as why people like each other, how relationships are created, how they are preserved.

Family relationships can also involve close personal bonds and reciprocal obligations, but they are defined by adults on the basis of a different kind of link, the kinship bond. Kinship connections derive from genealogical and legal connections between people: "blood," marriage, and adoption define kinship. Thinking about the nature of families, then, requires thinking about how a whole system of interrelated people is created out of kinship ties.

Young children, naturally, do not operate on the basis of explicit definitions of the terms "friendship" and "family." Their concepts are

different from adults'. In this chapter, we first explore children's
family concepts, then consider their ideas about friendship.

THE DEVELOPMENT OF FAMILY AND
KINSHIP CONCEPTS

Family and kinship relations are important in all human societies,
including our own.[1] In some parts of the world, for example, the
"traditional" cultures of Africa, Asia, and Latin America, kinship provides a main source of structure and solidarity for society. In such
places, kinship relations are more formal, set, and prescribed than in
American society. An example of such a system is seen in the following
anthropological description of an Australian aboriginal tribe. The Arun-
tas were the largest central Australian desert tribe at the time of
European contact, around 1900.

> Arunta children learn the content of kinship terms as they interact daily
> with specific people. They are informed repeatedly by adults who individ-
> uals are and how they should act toward them. A boy may be told by an
> adult, "This person is your sister; you call her (kin term), and you must look
> after her. When you get older, you must give her some of the meat you
> catch, and she will give you vegetable foods. You are not to say her name,
> but when she gets married, her husband will give you gifts. If her husband
> treats her badly, you must take her part." On another occasion, he may be
> told about a little girl walking by him, "She is your mother-in-law. You
> must not look at her face to face, or speak to her, but later when she is
> married you will send her gifts of meat. If she bears a daughter, she may
> give her to you for a wife." (Williams, 1983, p. 202)

In the United States kinship relations have never been so formal
and standardized, and children are rarely expected to learn very many
relatives' names and kinship titles. Nevertheless, family and kinship
relations are still important, and different subcultures have their own
special ways of describing kinship and family. Teachers can best talk
with children about kinship ideas if they learn about family relations in
different cultural groups.

For example, in Afro-American communities it is customary to
label close friendships with kinship terms (Liebow, 1967; Stack, 1974).
People who have established an important relationship may say that
they are "going for brothers" or "going for cousins." A person may
become part of another's family through this fictive kinship and be
called "aunt" or "uncle" by the children. Some of these bonds become

permanent. In Hispanic communities, the range of kinship is extended beyond genetic links by the institution known as *compadrazgo* or coparenthood (Madsen, 1973). The most important *compadres* are the baptismal godparents of children, and *compadre* relationships involve carefully defined roles and responsibilities.

Ethnic variability is an important reason why teachers should be careful not to impose one set of definitions of family and kinship terms on children. Another reason is that people define and understand these terms in more than one way and intend different meanings on different occasions.

The word "family" is a good example. American adults use this word in at least three distinct (though related) ways.[2] First, "family" can mean all one's relatives, as when one says, "We had a family reunion." Second, "family" can refer to two or more people who live together, share tasks and resources, and are responsible for each other's welfare. Third, "family" can mean a father, mother, and children (a nuclear family), as when someone says, "He's grown up and has his own family now."

Some teachers believe that the third meaning, "nuclear family," is too restrictive because it excludes too many household units in contemporary American society. The third definition seems outdated as a definition of what a group of people *must be* in order to call itself a family. However, the nuclear family remains important in American society as a cultural symbol and as a type of household in which many children live for at least part of their growing up. Of course, many children also have experiences living in other types of "families," in the sense of a group of two or more people with a long-term commitment.

How do children use and define kinship and family terms? As we shall see, mastering kinship and family concepts is a complex and multistep cognitive task. Children in all cultural groups develop through similar stages, from a first and simplest "concrete categorical" level to a fully systematic "abstract" level. Experience may speed up or slow down the course of development, but the steps involved have been found to be similar in a variety of cultural settings.[3]

Step 1: Concrete categorical concepts. At about age three, young American children often first begin to use kinship terms as social labels.[4] Typically they use only the most common kinship terms—"mother," "father," "grandmother," "grandfather"—and they apply the terms to people both within and without their family. For example, they may label any elderly people that they see with grandparent terms.

These very young children use kinship terms to assign people to concrete *categories* (sex and age groups), but they cannot understand kinship *relations*. Children under about age four cannot coordinate two social categories. They think of a "mother" as a woman, and a "son" as a boy, but they cannot relate the two categories to each other and realize that in order to *be* a mother, a woman must *have* a son or daughter. Therefore, they use the kinship terms "categorically" (to fit people into sex/age categories), not "relationally" (to describe kinship relations).

TEACHER: What is a brother?
CHRIS (age 5): Big and tall.
TEACHER: What do you have to have to be a brother?
CHRIS: Toys.

TEACHER: What is a brother?
JENNIFER (age 5): He's big and takes care of stuff.
TEACHER: What do you have to have to be a brother?
JENNIFER: Homework.

Further evidence of categorical thinking is seen when young children are asked "conservation" questions that address whether a certain kinship relationship is retained, or "conserved," even though a certain (irrelevant) change has taken place. An example of such a question is, "Will two girls who are sisters still be sisters when they grow up?" Children at the categorical stage tend to answer, "No, they will be mothers." Their focus is on the static gender and age attributes of the "sister" category, and they cannot conserve the relationship over the transformation of time. Similarly, they deny that an old man can be a father or brother, and say that he must be a grandfather.

Step 2: Early relational concepts. Elements of relational thinking enter young children's kinship concepts as soon as they can coordinate two social categories, usually at age four or five. Children now understand intuitively that a kinship term involves a relationship between two people. Yet they struggle with the problem of the exact nature of the relationship.

Because their thinking is still so concrete and present-oriented, they cannot take in all of the information that adults give them about kinship. To adults it is simple that a woman becomes a mother by having or adopting a baby and becomes a grandmother through gaining a grandchild. These facts are not at all obvious to young children.

An activity on kinship categories invites children to pick out the grandfather doll's "brother" from a set of family dolls.

TEACHER: What is a brother?
JEN (age 5): Someone you love.
TEACHER: What do you have to have to be a brother?
JEN: You have to share.

MOTHER: Are you a son, Sam?
SAM (age 3:2): The real sun is up in the sky, but the boy you love is another kind of son.

TOM (age 6:1) [to friend]: David, do you have a big sister named Jean and a big brother named Michael? I know them.
DAVID (age 5:4): I have a brother named Michael, but I don't have a sister named Jean because she went to college.

Four- and five-year-olds define kinship relationships in terms of close connections, and they think of the concrete kinds of closeness that they can directly experience—close feelings and living close together. People are relatives when "they live in the same house," "like each other so much," or "want to be." Similarly, they can become nonrelatives just as easily, through becoming "unclose" in some way. For example, when children are told an interview story about puppet sisters who fight over a book until one runs away, most preschoolers say the fighting dolls are no longer sisters.

TEACHER: When these dolls are fighting, are they sisters?
CRISTEN (age 3:10): No, because one of them ran away.
TEACHER: If she came back, would they be sisters again?
CRISTEN: Yes.

Children's ideas about family during the early relational period are also based on closeness rather than kinship. In the children's book *Families*, by Meredith Tax (listed in the bibliography at the end of this chapter), six-year-old Angie expresses this well: "Families are who you live with and who you love." Thus, when young children are asked to name everyone in their family, they usually name the members of their household, including their pets.

Step 3: Later relational concepts. During the middle childhood years, starting at about age six or seven, children begin to coordinate multiple kinship roles into a larger, objective system, or "web of relations." One signal of this is that they realize how a person can occupy many kinship roles at once and be, for example, one person's wife, another's mother, and a third's daughter. Another signal is that when explaining the relationship between two people, children are apt to mention some other, third person. Even when they make errors in explaining a relationship, they approach the problem in the right way.

MOTHER: What's a great-aunt?
ANNA (age 8:0): It's your great-grandmother's child. And your great-uncle is someone who is a child of your other set of great-grandparents.

At this stage children begin to move away from the "closeness" definition of the family toward a kinship-based definition. They now spontaneously include relatives such as grandparents and cousins on their family list. They may invent a term such as "my *big* family" or "my *whole* family" to refer to their extended family beyond their household. They construct for themselves the idea that when a family member moves out of the home, that person still remains part of the "big family" because he or she is still related to the child.

Certainly, even during the later relational period, some kinship concepts remain intrinsically more difficult than others for children to grasp or explain. Terms such as "mother" and "sister" are relatively easy because they can be defined from the child's point of view. In contrast, terms such as "daughter" and "granddaughter" are more difficult because they require the child to look at the self from an adult's perspective. Furthermore, kinship terms that are logically more complex are mastered relatively late. For example, terms such as "aunt," "niece," and "cousin" involve more logical steps to define than do such terms as "mother" and "son." Children show development in their ability to define kinship terms throughout middle childhood.

Step 4: Fully abstract concepts. With the onset of abstract thinking abilities in adolescence, teenagers become capable of fully objective concepts of kinship. At this point they can understand the framework of their culture's kinship system in an abstract or general way.

For example, American adolescents can appreciate a fundamental principle of our cultural kinship system—that there are two kinds of relatives. One kind (parents, children, siblings, and other "blood" relatives) are understood as permanent and given "by nature." Another kind (spouses and in-laws) are understood as "divorceable" and gained "by law."

This American kinship theory works to explain reality except for the special case of legal adoption. Under American law, adoption severs biological kinship and establishes new kinship relations based on law. This sets up a puzzling situation for adopted children, in the sense that the American cultural meanings surrounding kinship do not apply well to the facts of their lives.[5] Their adoptive parents, the people they love and live with, are not "natural kin" but "contractual kin," and their biological parents, "natural kin" at birth, are legally not their relatives at all.

One can also appreciate why adolescence, with its burgeoning logical powers, can present a time of special crisis to some adopted adolescents. Grappling with complex issues that have enormous personal and emotional significance to them, they may develop the desire to know more about their "birth parents."

By late adolescence, most young people develop the logical powers to understand that a kinship system *is* a system, that in fact, it is a cultural invention, like government. They can consider kinship abstractly and comprehend that kinship systems might be organized in many ways. For example, they are not surprised when they learn that in some cultural groups, people are taught to address each of their female relatives of the parental generation (those we might call aunts or first cousins once removed) as "Mother" and each of the corresponding males as "Father." Adolescents everywhere, if exposed to cultural diversity, have the capacity to step back mentally from their own kinship system and for the first time think of it as a cultural system.

Kinship Concepts and Parental Divorce

While kinship concepts as we have been describing them may seem overly intellectual and far-removed from the natural concerns of children, in fact they are closely implicated in young children's emotional life. Children's conceptions of kinship and family bear close connections to their emotions.

Parental separation and divorce present a difficult challenge to young children—cognitively and emotionally. Children experience acute distress when their parents divorce, and they may respond to the crisis with rage, sadness, fear, and feelings of deprivation. Teachers can be helpful because they are often the adults outside the immediate family who spend the most time with, and are closest to, the children.

Children's age is a very strong predictor of how children initially react to their parents' divorces.[6] Preschoolers, younger elementary-school children, older elementary-school children, and adolescents have been found to present characteristically different patterns of reaction. The differences result from the age groups' differing levels of cognitive development, as well as from their differing emotional needs. Young children, it is now widely agreed, often show the greatest disturbance and disorganization right after the divorce and the most confusion and difficulty in understanding the meaning of the events.

Because young children are considered to be particularly vulnerable to disturbance and confusion related to the immediate events of divorce, a large number of picture books have recently become available that explain divorce to young children. These books are intended to reassure children, in simple and concrete language, that they did not "cause" their parents' divorce, that their needs for care and love will continue to be met (though perhaps in new ways), and that they will eventually feel better about their new living arrangements.

Sometimes parents or other adults use these picture books hoping that children's confusions can be quickly cleared away through clear, accurate, concrete information. Such a hope may be unrealistic. Young children's confusions can be caused not only by a lack of information but also by age-appropriate cognitions. Children construct their own ideas, and adult instruction may not be able to quickly change them.

During the early relational period (before the age of about six or seven) young children conceive of a parent as someone who lives in the household; therefore, they tend to think that if the parent moves out, he or she is not the parent any more. Because they cannot understand how a person can have multiple kinship relations, they tend to think that when a father divorces his wife, he also divorces his children. When thinking about the cause of the divorce, they egocentrically focus on their own actions ("I did something bad") rather than thinking about the relationship between the parents.

Mary Ellin Logue obtained fascinating results when she used dolls to present a hypothetical story about divorce to elementary school children.[7] Most children under age six or seven gave similar answers, regardless of whether their parents were divorced. They said that a live-in housecleaner was a family member. They were certain that the father stopped being the father when he moved out of the house but became the father again by moving back home. They believed that the father moved out because of something bad that the children had done. Here is a typical interview with a kindergarten child.

TEACHER: Is Peter [housecleaner] part of the family now?
DONNY (age 5, parents divorced): Yes.
TEACHER: He is? Who is he?
DONNY: A man.
TEACHER: A man. Does he have another name? Is he a mom?
DONNY: No. [Laughs] Dad. Girls have long hair.
TEACHER: Is this man [pointing to father doll] the father now?
DONNY: No.
TEACHER: How do you know?
DONNY: He lives in the orange house.
TEACHER: Does the woman have a husband now?
DONNY: Peter.
TEACHER: Are you sure?
DONNY: Yes. But this guy [father] might move back in.
TEACHER: What would happen if he moved back in?
DONNY: He'd [Peter] clean the house again.
TEACHER: Is there anything he [father] can do to be the father again?
DONNY: Make her [mother] say him can come in the house again.
TEACHER: Why do you think he [father] moved to the orange house?
DONNY: Because of Peter.

TEACHER: But he [father] said it was okay.
DONNY: Or because the kids were too loud.

Contrast those answers with the following interview of Tasha
(age 6). Tasha denies that Peter is a "real" relative, and she can "conserve" fatherhood over parental divorce. She suggests that the divorce
was caused by a fight between the parents, not something done by the
children or Peter.

TEACHER: Is Peter part of the family now?
TASHA (age 6, parents divorced): Well, he isn't related but he is in a
way.
TEACHER: Can you tell me more?
TASHA: Well, he isn't a real part of the family, but he is in a way
because he lives with them—he's a roommate.
TEACHER: Is that different from being related?
TASHA: Yes.
TEACHER: Is this man [father] the father now?
TASHA: Well, he's still their father, but I don't think he's the mother's
husband anymore. He'll always be their father.
TEACHER: Why do you think the father moved to the orange house?
TASHA: They might have had a fight before the story—that you
didn't tell.
TEACHER: Who had the fight?
TASHA: The mother and the father.

How then can adults best talk to young children about divorce?
They must be prepared to hold many brief discussions over an extended period of time, to give children time to slowly build up understanding of their situation. Following divorce, young children must
have concrete experiences that allow them to construct new understanding. Even if they cannot comprehend the abstract logic of the
sentence, "She is not *your father's wife* anymore, but she will always
be *your mother*," they can construct through personal experience the
knowledge that their own noncustodial mother still remains "Mommy"
to them. Repeated low-key discussions can help children to gradually
evaluate and take stock of new experiences.

Adults should view these conversations as opportunities to learn
what children think, as well as to correct misconceptions. For instance,
in the conversations quoted at the start of this chapter, the teachers did
not immediately correct the errors of Megan, Freddie, Anne, and
Greg. The children seemed to want to share their feelings with a

trusted adult and were not primarily seeking adult instruction. On occasions when adults do need to correct young children's misconceptions, they can be most effective if they come down to the children's cognitive level. This requires careful listening as a basis for communication. For example, a teacher might help a young child understand his or her relationship to a noncustodial parent by suggesting a definition of "parent" that would make sense to someone at the early relational level but not require the parent to live with the child. Such a definition involves closeness of another sort than physical proximity—giving of a gift, calling on the phone, a physical similarity, or liking the same activity.

Classroom Activities on Kinship and Family

In addition to holding spontaneous discussions with children, teachers can plan structured learning encounters on kinship and family.

Such activities can meet either of two objectives. First, they can extend children's basic knowledge by widening their foundation of vocabulary and concrete experience. For example, some children may never have met a man called an uncle or realized that their friends also have people called grandmothers. They may not know that the size of families may vary from small to large.

When talking about families, teachers should avoid setting forth any one definition because such narrowness can create unintended problems. For instance, suppose a teacher asserts, "A family is the people with whom you live." If a child in the group is moving toward a kinship-based (later relational) definition, he or she may have a different idea—perhaps not consciously realized. If his or her parents are separated or divorced, and the child is struggling to retain an image of the noncustodial parent as "still in the family," the teacher's definition may be troubling.

Second, activities can be planned to stimulate children's reasoning and curiosity about the meaning of kinship and family words. These activities can support the general development of logical thinking abilities. They can also expand the range of children's intellectual concern, making them realize, for instance, that it is interesting to ask themselves, "What's a family?" That way, should children's personal situations ever require it, they may be cognitively more ready to deal with emotional challenges such as parental divorce or remarriage. They may be more able to bring their "highest level," their "best thinking," to bear on understanding changes in the real family situations of themselves or their friends.

1. *Children aged two and above can engage in activities that extend their vocabulary and concrete base of experience.*
  - Photographs of family members can be displayed on a bulletin board or made into a laminated book entitled *Our Families* for the reading area.
  - Children can first as a group discuss personal experiences involving a specific class of relatives—such as siblings, grandparents, uncles, aunts, or cousins—and then they can draw pictures or make picture books about them.
  - Children can act out the ways that the people in their own household help each other, and then they can discuss how families work together.
  - Children can talk about the roles of family members and act out experiences children have in their own families: "What do mothers do?" "What do grandmothers do?" "What do cousins do?"
  - Children can tape-record interviews with people in their school, asking the question, "Who is in your family?"
  - Parents can be invited to bring in family photo albums and show pictures of children's relatives and ancestors.
  - Teachers can bring their own relatives to visit the class (children, siblings, parents, etc.) to stimulate thinking about how adults occupy multiple roles (kinship and occupational).
  - Teachers can read a book to children that focuses on extended family relatives (e.g., *Darlene, Cousins Are Special, The Visit*) and then discuss with children their experiences with that type of relative.

2. *Children aged four and above can engage in a thinking-game interview on kinship concepts.* This problem-situation encourages children to consider the essential or defining characteristics of a kinship relationship.

A Thinking Game on Kinship Concepts: "Two Sisters"

MATERIALS: A family doll set containing two daughters; a friend doll; and a small "toy" for the dolls.

ACTION: The teacher introduces the dolls by saying, "Here is a family. There are parents, and two girls named Joanne and Sue" (other names may be substituted, of course).

DISCUSSION QUESTIONS
  - How are Joanne and Sue related to each other?
  - How many sisters are there in this family? Are Joanne and Sue sisters? Why (or why not)?

- Is the mother Joanne's sister, too? Why (or why not)?
- Here is another girl named Mary. She has a different mother, and they live in a different house over here [pointing]. Is Mary [pointing] a sister to Joanne and Sue? Why (or why not)?
- Someday, when Joanne and Sue grow up to be big women, will they still be sisters? Why (or why not)?
- One day Joanne and Sue are playing with toys. [Bring out toys and dramatize.] Then Joanne begins to take away Sue's toys and won't give them back. They get very angry and have a big fight. Sue runs away from Joanne. Are they still sisters when they are fighting? Why (or why not)? What are they when they are fighting? Are they still girls?

SUGGESTED VARIATIONS: This activity can be modified to focus on any kinship relationships.

3. *Children aged five or six and above can engage in a thinking-game interview on kinship concepts.* This small-group activity, adapted from Deutsch (1979), encourages children to think about kinship from a systemic point of view and is excellent for older children who have begun to appreciate later relational concepts.

A Thinking Game on Kinship Concepts: "The Four John Walkers"

MATERIALS: This learning encounter requires four cardboard figures, magazine cutouts, or felt-board people to represent four male characters: an elder, two middle-aged men, and a boy.

ACTION: The teacher relates, "Here are the four John Walkers. They all have the same name, John Walker! Isn't that funny? It is also confusing. This one [pointing to the elder] is the oldest. He has two children [pointing to middle-aged men]. They are both grown-up men now. This one [pointing to one of them] is married. He has one son of his own now [pointing to boy]."

DISCUSSION QUESTIONS

- This John Walker [boy] wants to call this John Walker [elder] on the telephone. Here goes! Ring! Ring! Now this man [elder] answers and says, "Hello." What does this John [boy] say? The boy needs a name to call the man besides "John," because there are four Johns in the family. So the boy says to the man, "Hi, ———." [If no answer] Does he say, "Hi, Mom"? No? Then what?
- Now this John Walker [boy] calls this John [his father figure] on the telephone. Ring! Ring! Now this man answers and says, "Hello." What does this John [boy] say? He says, "Hi, ———." Why?
- Now this John Walker [boy] calls this last John Walker [other middle-aged man] on the telephone. Ring! Ring! Now the man answers and says, "Hello." What does this John [boy] say? He says, "Hi, ———." Why?

The action is repeated using each of the John figures as the caller in turn. The teacher may also vary the action for interest, for example, substituting picture taking for telephoning. The point is to find out what the children think each figure calls the others—the kinship terms of address—and also to explain their reasons why, if possible.

THE DEVELOPMENT OF FRIENDSHIP CONCEPTS

Friendship, like family, is a source of close connections and companionship for young children. Friendship is especially necessary in a society such as ours where children meet many other children in their neighborhoods and schools who are not related to them in any way. Friendship is a means of providing close bonds based on affection.

Step 1: Concrete categorical concepts.   Children first use the term "friend" around the age of two or three as a simple social label.[8] They apply the word "friend" to any "special person" who has been so labeled for them. Toddlers and the youngest preschoolers do not talk about friendship much but do have favorite peers and strong attachments.

NATHAN (age 3:4) [seeing his best friend for the first time since vacation]: Sam! I didn't see you for a long time.
SAM (age 3:3): I was at my Granny's house.
NATHAN: Someone told me you were at your grandmother's.
SAM: Did you want me?
NATHAN: I wanted you a lot of times. I missed you.

Step 2: Early relational concepts.   Children first begin to spontaneously talk about friendship with one another at about age three, and they do so a great deal at ages four and five. During this time, friendship talk mostly serves the purposes of *bonding*, or facilitating access to play. When one young child says to another, "Are you my friend?" he or she usually means something like, "Will you play?" "Am I still part of this activity?" or "May I join you?" Similarly, when the child declares, "You're not my friend," he or she usually means something like, "I'm angry," "I want to be alone," or "I'd rather play with someone else right now."

BOBBY (age 4) [to Chico in sandbox]: Are you my friend?
CHICO (age 5): No.
BOBBY: Oh. Are you Matthew's friend? [Matthew is nearby.]

CHICO: No. . . . Maybe later I'll be your friend.
BOBBY: Don't you want to be my friend now?
CHICO: Yes. [Chico and Bobby go off to play.]

These young boys think of a friend as someone with whom one is playing (nicely and happily) in the immediate moment. Their concepts of friendship are self-centered, present-bound, and focused on the concrete and external. A friend is someone whom the self likes "right now." Friends play together and share food, toys, and other valued resources. They are close in terms of physical proximity or even looking alike.

Thus when teachers use the word "friend" in talking with preschool children, they should remember how focused children are on the externals of situations and on the immediate present. Most likely when they hear one child tell another, "You're not my friend!" or even, "I hate you!" they need to comfort the second child, but not in terms of his or her likability. The second child may indeed be angry or disappointed at the departure of the first child, but his or her feelings are not hurt. For example, the child is too young to worry that there is something about his or her personality that the first child does not like and is not concerned about whether the other child will ever play with him or her again. Those are the concerns of older children.

Further, when teachers wish to stop aggression or encourage positive behavior, they should avoid expressions like, "Be nice, he's your good friend!" based on an assumption that it will help to remind children of their enduring relationship. Before age six or seven, children have little awareness of the long-term nature of any of their relationships. Therefore, adults intervene most effectively with comments that describe the concrete situation: "Pushing hurts," "Simon would like to use that, too."

Similarly, when teachers wish to create a sense of community in a group of children, they should try to talk at children's own level. A kindly kindergarten teacher was once observed trying to convey a sense of community based on notions of mutual helping. "This is a friendly classroom," she said. "We are all friends here. We help each other, we are kind to each other, so we are all friends." What did the children make of these remarks? Not much, one fears, because moments later, the observer had the following conversation with a boy named George:

INTERVIEWER: I guess you have a lot of friends, George.
GEORGE (age 5): No, I don't. Jane is my friend. We go home from

school together. Graham is my friend. He plays with me at my house.

INTERVIEWER: Are these your only friends, George?

GEORGE: Well, Tim—but Tim is in Paris now. So I'm not sure if he is my friend or not.

George was independently constructing his own thoughtful conception of friendship focused on present association and playing together. Indeed, young children seldom seem reassured when teachers tell them, "We are all friends in this classroom." After all, from the children's point of view, it is evident that not everyone is playing together or wants to play together "right now," so how can they all be friends?

A better way for teachers to build community is through fostering bonds based on common activity and experience. For example, they can provide equipment that requires children to make eye contact and/or coordinate their activity. They can structure joyful moments of unity—marching, singing, dancing. They can use mealtimes and festive occasions to foster the affectionate feelings that are the basis of genuine community.

Steps 3 and 4: Later relational and abstract concepts. Eventually, at age seven or eight, or even later, children move on to more sophisticated concepts of friendship. Then friends are understood to be people who are kind and helpful to each other—either spontaneously or when one of them expresses a need. At first the focus is on concrete goods and services exchanged by friends, then gradually with time the focus shifts to more intangible kinds of resources—good feelings, secrets, promises. Friendship comes to be considered to be a long-term relationship, not limited to one exchange or situation. Furthermore, friendship becomes based on mutual trust and can be terminated by a refusal to help or by ignoring the needs or desires of the other. Friendship concepts come to fit those put forward by the kindly kindergarten teacher in the earlier example.

Finally, during adolescence and adulthood, friendship concepts may progress even further, based on highly complex concepts of social sharing and causality. Friendship comes to be seen as based on the *intimacy* of sharing common interests and personal secrets, and/or on a respectful *interdependence* that allows growth through a balance of dependence and independence. Friendship is understood as slowly built up or eroded over time; it can be preserved through acts (including symbolic ones) by which each person indicates to the other how much he or she values the friendship. Friendship concepts have at last come to be fully abstract, reciprocal, and future-oriented.

Classroom Activities on Friendship Concepts

Teachers can use an accurate knowledge of children's friendship concepts to guide their informal conversations with them. They can also use this knowledge to plan structured classroom activities.

1. *Children aged four and above can make books entitled* My Friends. This activity stimulates children to think about the kinds of things one does with a friend. The children can draw pictures of themselves having fun with different friends, and the teacher can write the children's comments under each drawing. The teacher can structure the drawing with such suggestions as, "Draw a picture of yourself with a *home* friend," or "Draw yourself having fun with your best *grown-up* friend," or "Draw yourself playing with someone who was your friend when you were *little*."

2. *Children aged five to six can make a "remembering book" for a child moving away and leaving the class.* This activity stimulates children to reflect on the basis of friendship and, when all of the contributions are viewed together, to take the perspective of others and consider how all have had different friendly relationships with the same person. The teacher should structure this activity at a time when the child who is soon to depart is absent, so the book can be given as a surprise goodbye gift. Each child draws a picture of something he or she remembers liking or doing with the departing child. The teacher writes each of the children's comments under the picture and puts all the pictures together into a book or album.

3. *Children aged three and above can engage in a small-group discussion about "what friends do together,"* with the teacher writing down the answers to display. Here is an example of the ideas of children in one day care group:

Play together
Walk around together
Don't push each other down
Take care of each other

An activity on friendship presents a choice about what makes a friend—giving a toy or (as shown here) giving a hug.

Hug each other
Sit next to each other
Hold hands

　　by Zachary, Wesley, Silvana, George (age 3)

4. *Children aged three to five can engage in a thinking-game skit on friendship.* This activity stimulates children to think about what friendship is for, that is, what valued resources (material and emotional) are exchanged by friends.

A Thinking Game on Friendship: "Best Friends"

CHARACTERS: Amy, her mother, and two friends, all acted by teachers.
MATERIALS: Two stuffed animals and a book.
ACTION: Amy sits on the floor reading a book. Along comes friend Valery, carrying the two stuffed animals.

AMY: Hi, Valery.

VALERY: Hi, Amy. I like you! Would you like one of my stuffed animals? You would? Okay, here's one. [Valery gives Amy an animal, then goes to stand to the side, still holding one animal. Friend Diane approaches Amy.]

AMY: Hi, Diane.

DIANE: Hi, Amy. I like you! Can I give you a big hug? I can? Oh, good! Here's one. [Diane hugs Amy warmly, then goes to stand by Valery at the side. The mother enters.]

MOTHER: There you are, Amy. It is time to go to the park. Here comes our bus! I have one extra ticket, so you can bring one of your friends with us. Which friend would you like best to bring along too? There are your two choices, Valery and Diane. Why don't you tell one of them to come with us.

DISCUSSION QUESTIONS
 * Whom should Amy tell to come, Valery or Diane? Why?
 * Who is Amy's best friend today—Valery, who gave her the stuffed animal, or Diane, who gave her the big hug? Why?
 * Are you a better friend if you give a stuffed animal or a hug? Why?
 * What do you like more, a toy or a hug? Why?

SUGGESTED VARIATIONS: This skit pits a concrete resource (toy) against an emotional resource (hug) as a basis for choosing to play with a friend. This conflict, not very compelling to adults, can seem quite interesting to pre-school children. Other variations of the same conflict can be created substituting food (such as a pretzel) or other tangible goods for the toy. Or the story can begin with Amy quarreling with her two friends, then with Valery offering to make up by giving Amy a turn with a toy, while Diane offers to make up by telling Amy, "I'm so sorry."

5. *Children aged four and above can engage in a thinking-game skit on friendship.* This activity stimulates children to think about how and why friendships are maintained and/or terminated.

A Thinking Game on Friendship: "Moving Away"

CHARACTERS: Barry, his mother, and his friend, Joanne.
MATERIALS: Suitcase, blocks.
ACTION: Barry and Joanne sit playing with blocks.

BARRY: Boy, this is fun. I am glad that we live right next door to each other so we can play together so much.

JOANNE: We can play together every day. We're friends.

BARRY: Yes, we are. I love playing blocks and everything with you. . . . But do you know what is going to happen soon? I have to move with my family.

We have to go live far, far away, and I won't get to see you anymore.
MOTHER [enters with suitcase]: Barry, did you tell Joanne about moving
away? It's time to go now. I packed our suitcase.
JOANNE [sadly]: What am I going to do?
MOTHER: Maybe we will come back and visit you sometime.
JOANNE [to audience]: Who will I play with?
BARRY [sadly, waving, going off]: Goodbye, Joanne.

DISCUSSION QUESTIONS

- Do you think Barry and Joanne are still friends? Why (or why not)?
- Can Barry have Joanne as a friend even if he lives far, far away?
- Do you think Barry will like Joanne if he doesn't see her everyday and live next door? Why (or why not)?
- Who will Joanne play with now?
- Does Joanne still like Barry? Why (or why not)?
- Will Joanne forget Barry if he moves away? Why (or why not)?

SUGGESTED BOOKS FOR CHILDREN

Books on Kinship and Family

This list includes books that discuss what families are in a general way or present images of specific families. Because so many children's books present the image of the nuclear household, some of the books were selected to provide children with images of other household types (one-parent, aunt/child, communal, "blended") or to portray children relating to extended kin (cousins, great-aunt and great-uncle, grandparents, etc.). They can provide a good background for a discussion based on the question, "Who is in your family?" and for talking about different kinds of relatives. The list also includes a number of "crisis-oriented" books that deal with parental separation or divorce. These are intended for use in helping a child and his or her classmates focus on what it means for a household to change due to separation or divorce.

Eber, Christine Engla. *Just Momma and Me.* Chapel Hill, N.C.: Lollipop Power, 1975.   A young child is adopted by a single woman, who soon marries and has a new baby. Provides a good basis for a discussion of what a family is.

Eichler, Margrit. *Martin's Father.* Chapel Hill, N.C.: Lollipop Power, 1971.   Martin and his father are a family, and the father cares tenderly for Martin.

Esley, Joan. *The Visit.* New York: Rand McNally, 1980.   Abigail is introduced to the world of her great-grandmother through a visit to her great-aunt and great-uncle. This book provides a good lead-in to discussing kinship concepts.

Goff, Beth. *Where Is Daddy? The Story of a Divorce*. Boston: Beacon, 1969.   This book mirrors the confused understanding and overwhelmed feelings of a preschooler whose parents divorce. Contains a good note for parents.

Goldman, Susan. *Cousins Are Special*. Chicago: Albert Whitman, 1978. What is a cousin? Carol Ann goes to visit hers and first thinks a cousin is a sort of special friend, then eventually discovers they are cousins because they share a grandmother!

Greenfield, Eloise. *Darlene*. New York: Methuen, 1980.   Darlene is left for the day with her uncle and girl cousin. The special warmth of kinship ties is concretely revealed.

———. *Grandmama's Joy*. New York: Collins, 1980.   The story of how Rhondy and her grandmother came to be a family unit accents an especially loving relationship.

Hazen, Barbara Shook. *Two Homes to Live In: A Child's Eye View of Divorce*. New York: Human Sciences, 1978.   The explanations of divorce, home, and family presented in this book seem well suited to the early relational thinker.

Kraus, Robert. *Whose Mouse Are You?* New York: Macmillan, 1970.   This book reassures the toddler that one's parents and sibling are not lost but always recoverable, even when one feels angry at them.

Lasker, Joe. *Merry Ever After*. New York: Penguin, 1976.   For older children, this masterfully illustrated book portrays two medieval-era weddings, focusing on the joining of extended families and the joyful community rituals.

Milgram, Mary. *Brothers Are All the Same*. New York: Dutton, 1978.   For the child with the later relational understanding of brothers, this book shows why an adopted brother is still a "real" brother.

Raynor, Dorka. *This Is My Father and Me*. Chicago: Albert Whitman, 1973.   A striking set of photographs provides images of fathers and children from around the world.

———. *Grandparents Around the World*. Chicago: Albert Whitman, 1977.   Another album of family photographs.

Schuchman, Joan. *Two Places to Sleep*. Minneapolis: Carolrhoda Books, 1979.   David, seven, describes living with his mother on weekends and father on weekdays. He begins to understand and accept his parents' divorce.

Severance, Jane. *Lots of Mommies*. Chapel Hill, N.C.: Lollipop Power, 1983.   Emily lives communally with a group of four "mothers" who love and care for her. Her friends at school at first doubt that someone can have four mothers, but then gain a sense of how all care for Emily. Good as a basis for discussing what a mother is.

Simon, Norma. *All Kinds of Families*. Chicago: Albert Whitman, 1975.   Best for young school-aged children, this book describes families. It first shows

families (households, really) from an early relational perspective, then
moves to a broader, more mature, kinship-based definition.

Sitea, Linda. "Zachary's Divorce," in *Free to Be Young and Me*. New York:
McGraw-Hill, 1974.   This book provides good insight into the thought
processes of the young child constructing an individual understanding of
divorce.

Surowiecki, Sandra Lucas. *Joshua's Day*. Chapel Hill, N.C.: Lollipop Power,
1972.   Joshua lives with his mother and attends day care. They pass
happily through their day. Good lead-in for discussing who is in a family.

Tax, Meredith. *Families*. Boston: Little, Brown, 1981.   Angie, six, defines
families from the early relational perspective and describes different ones
she knows in a warm, funny way.

Thomas, Ianthe. *Lordy, Aunt Hattie*. New York: Harper & Row, 1973.
Hattie lives with her aunt in the rural South. Written in black dialect, the
book captures the feelings and rhythms of that region in summertime.

Wensell, Ulises. *Come to Our House: Meet Our Family*. New York: Rand
McNally, 1978.   This book provides a portrait of an extended family
from a young child's point of view. We hear about a whole set of relatives
and their activities.

Books on Friendship

These selections portray friendship as young children understand
it. Some of the books portray the most concrete concept of friendship
(typical of two-to-four-year-olds), while others portray the early relational concept of friendship (characteristic of five-to-seven-year-olds).
Several of the books qualify as crisis-oriented books, that is, ones
useful for helping children to understand and talk about a specific
friendship problem.

Aliki. *We Are Best Friends*. New York: Greenwillow, 1982.   Robert's best
friend moves away, leaving him sad and lonely until he gradually makes a
new friend. The vision of friendship is appropriate to the later relational
thinker.

Cohen, Miriam. *Will I Have a Friend?* New York: Young Readers Press,
1972.   Jim worriedly enters preschool for the first time. But he easily
makes friends through his play.

Eastman, Philip D. *Big Dog . . . Little Dog: A Bedtime Story*. New York:
Random House, 1973.   Big Fred and little Ted have a friendship based
on differences that complement each other.

Hoff, Syd. *Who Will Be My Friends?* New York: Harper, 1960.   Freddy,
new to town, goes searching for "friends," that is, playmates. He makes
them, too, just by playing! Portrays children's early relational concepts of
how friends are formed.

Lobel, Arnold. *Frog and Toad Are Friends*. New York: Harper & Row, 1970.   This book and its sequels portray a memorable friendship. They share many experiences and solve many problems together, with Frog modeling middle-childhood maturity and Toad preschool immaturity.

Steig, William. *Amos and Boris*. Cedar Grove, N.J.: Rae, 1977.   A mouse and a whale, unlikely companions, become committed friends and save each other's lives in turn. Illustrates the later relational concept of friendship as long-term reciprocity and caring.

Stevenson, James. *Fast Friends*. New York: Greenwillow, 1979.   The process of making friends—establishing common interests and values—is portrayed in concepts typical of the later relational thinker.

Urdy, Janice May. *Let's Be Enemies*. New York: Harper & Row, 1961. Realistically portrays the casual way in which friendships end and resume again throughout early childhood.

Zolotow, Charlotte. *New Friend*. New York: Abelard-Schuman, 1968.   A child plays closely and often with a certain friend, and then feels the hurt of loss when that friend finds a "new friend" and won't play anymore.

———. *The Hating Book*. New York: Harper & Row, 1969.   The word "hate" has a different and temporary meaning when used by young children. This book concretely illustrates something young children have difficulty understanding—the role of both parties in the start of a conflict.

———. *Hold My Hand*. New York: Harper & Row, 1972.   For the toddler, this book provides concrete images of friendship: hand-holding, playing, sharing pleasure.

CHAPTER 7

Understanding Society

TEACHER: Here are some pictures of people working—an astronaut, cowboy, teacher, doctor, ice cream seller, policeman, and the President. Who should get the most money for their work?
KERI (age 5): I think the ice cream lady, because she sells things. If she sells things, she has to have some money there, so she can give it [change] to you.

Society is organized by institutions that coordinate the actions of people and groups. Governmental, legal, and commercial systems regulate the workings of adult society. Young children participate only indirectly in institutions, but they are curious about the mysterious activities of "buying things" and "going to work" that so engross adults. Children too wish to be in the know.

Yet adult society is a complicated reality for young children to understand. They cannot go far in understanding its workings on the basis of their own interaction or experimentations. They must construct their knowledge through observing adult behavior, reading books or watching television, listening to adult conversations, and asking questions. From age four onward, children ask many questions about adult society.

SAM (age 4): Mom, how do robbers get the job of robbering?
LYNN (age 5): Why do bus drivers always wear blue shirts?
DON (age 6): When do policemen put people in jail?

Early childhood educators need to know how they can best support children's construction of knowledge about social, political, and economic institutions. What should their basic goals be? What can children actually understand? Will too much information overwhelm children? Will telling them about realities such as inequality, crime, and unemployment discourage or frighten them? Will correcting their childlike errors disorient or confuse them? How can teachers best encourage children's curiosity, optimism, and excitement about their own futures?

Before answering these questions, we need to study how society is understood by young children, in particular what ideas they have about the institutions most visible to them: money and commerce (the *economic system*), and work and jobs (the *occupational system*).[1] Other institutions, such as politics and government, are more remote and abstract and become interesting only during later childhood or adolescence (Connell, 1971; Jahoda, 1964; Weinstein, 1957).

THE DEVELOPMENT OF ECONOMIC CONCEPTS

Economic relations are basic to social life, and most children have observed commercial transactions. Whether they dwell in the city or country, they see people buy things. American children may see adults use cash, checks, food stamps, coupons, and credit cards. They may also go with parents to the bank to withdraw or deposit money. They may observe their parents at home paying the monthly bills. Yet how much do young children actually understand about money and its use?

The Use and Value of Money

Watching young children play store or bank can be a fascinating experience for the teacher. The children handle the play materials in ways that they obviously believe are exact replicas of adult behavior, and indeed they are often humorously apt in their renditions of mothers snapping open their handbags and clerks slamming their cash registers. Yet a close inspection of young children's behavior reveals how different their ideas of money are from adults'. Moreover, gradual and systematic changes can be clearly seen to take place during childhood. Such changes are tied both to accumulated real-life experiences with buying and selling and to cognitive development. Over the early and middle childhood years, children construct notions of how money corresponds to goods and serves as a medium of exchange.

Research has shown that the understanding of money develops in definite steps.[2] Children aged three to four only vaguely recognize that money is necessary for buying. In playing store, their clerk and customer roles can merge, overlap, and disappear. A child acting as customer may or may not give money to the person at the cash register, and a child acting as salesperson may or may not ask for money and give change back to the buyer. The money is evidently not seen as part of an exchange of any kind. Rather, the child supposes that when people want or need something, they just go to the store and find it.

Older preschool children (age four to five) understand that money has to do with buying, but they lack the mathematical concepts to make sense of its value. Either they think any coin can buy any object, or they use a rough qualitative rule, such as "More coins can buy bigger things," or, a bit later, "A big money can buy a special thing." Buying becomes a kind of magical ritual to them. They often think that buyer and seller are "paying each other" as money goes back and forth between storekeeper and customer.

This magical thinking is illustrated by a young Italian child, observed as he and an interviewer "played coffee bar." The interviewer acted as customer and gave the child a 100-lire coin (about 12 cents U.S.) to buy chocolate. The child returned a 500-lire coin.

> INTERVIEWER: Why are you giving me that?
> CHILD: Eh, because in this [coffee] bar we give money.
> INTERVIEWER: Every time somebody comes to buy something?
> CHILD: Yes.
> INTERVIEWER: You are very kind!
> CHILD: Eh, all the bars do that!
> INTERVIEWER: How come?
> CHILD: I don't know. (Berti & Bombi, 1981b, p. 1180)

With increasing experience (or instruction by adults), young children gradually come to realize that not all types of money can buy all things and that sometimes the money is not enough, but they do not understand why. Not until age six or seven do they establish a correspondence between money and goods that has to do with money having value and goods having prices. By this time they have an understanding of the number system and of one-to-one correspondence. At first (about age six), they apply a rigid correspondence. In the storekeeper role, they reject bills or coins that they think are too much or too little for the price, or they insist that the customer take away more goods than wanted. Eventually, they realize the compensating value of change. This is seen in another example from the Italian study. The interviewer pays a child 500 lire for a chocolate.

> CHILD: But I have to give you some change.
> INTERVIEWER: How much do you have to give me?

CHILD: [It costs] 50 lire for a chocolate?
INTERVIEWER: Yes.
CHILD: 450 lire.
INTERVIEWER: Why are you giving me change?
CHILD: Because you gave me too much. (Berti & Bombi, 1981b, p. 1181)

The Chain of Transactions from Production to Consumption

The goods sold in the store and even the money itself are usually thought of by young children as being made or grown on the spot by the storekeeper.[3] Young children do not think of the retail store as just one step in a long chain of transactions that begins with production and culminates at consumption. They think about only one aspect at a time.

MOTHER: Where does our little store next door get the bread we buy?
SAM (age 4:5): They must make it in the back of the store.
MOTHER: Don't you remember when your school went to the bakery factory and saw them make bread?
SAM: Yes. They must have a little machine like that in the back of the store.
MOTHER: How about the vegetables that they sell?
SAM: They must grow them right out back of the store.
MOTHER: Sometimes we go on drives in the countryside and see farms where vegetables are growing.
SAM: That food is sold in stores in the country. But not in our store here.

It is not until age six or seven that children understand that shopkeepers usually obtain their goods from elsewhere. At first children assume that producers make new goods out of fragments of old, broken ones. Later they become more realistic in their ideas about production. They also come to understand that retailers and producers are connected through a string of intermediaries—wholesalers and transporters. Children assemble into a whole all of their heretofore disconnected images about production, packaging, transportation, and selling.

Young children also have no notion of the profit mechanism. They benevolently assume that storekeepers just like to give things to people. They also assume that clerks have free access to the money in their cash registers. They believe that policemen can have the money they find on robbers, that bus drivers can use the money they collect, and so forth. Only in later childhood can children make the distinction between "personal" and "societal" money and realize that employees get paid in what adults call wages and salaries, while employers get money from their profits.

The Ownership and Management of Economic Resources

The ownership and management of economic resources is also understood by young children in their own way.[4] Younger preschoolers think of owning in terms of using or being closest to something (Piaget, 1924). By age four or five, most children think of owning as being in charge of something. Thus, children's early notions of property do not involve any notion of economic control.

TEACHER [showing a picture]: Who owns the school here?
PHILIP (age 3:8): The teachers, because they live in it. They sleep there.
DAE-SUN (age 4:4): Well, the person who made it.
WILL (age 6:0): I know, the director owns it!
TEACHER: Who owns this little baby brother?
MATTHEW (age 4:10): The mother because she got it. How would a boy get it? [Laughs.] My mom owns me, and your mom owns you.
TEACHER: Who owns the school bus?
PHILIP: The kids riding in it.
DAE-SUN: The bus driver, because he's driving it.
TEACHER: Who owns this sun up in the sky?
DAE-SUN: God, because it is up in the sky.
MATTHEW: Mother Nature.

Similarly, young children lack concepts of economic hierarchy: owner at the top, manager or boss in the middle, and workers at the bottom. Younger preschoolers generally have no idea of what a boss is; they do not realize that a request can change in significance according to the status of the person who makes it. Older preschoolers think of a boss as someone in charge. Thus, children's first definition of "boss" merges with their definition of "owner," as illustrated in the following Italian interview.

INTERVIEWER: Is there a boss in this school?
ANDREA (age 6:8, child of a factory worker): Yes, it's Gino [the janitor] and the teachers.

INTERVIEWER: How did Gino become a boss?

ANDREA: He got big.

INTERVIEWER: And getting big he also became the boss?

ANDREA: Yes, because he made the school. . . .

INTERVIEWER: How did your dad's boss become the boss?

ANDREA: Because he made a house then some people wanted to go there to work, and so they helped him. (Berti, 1981, p. 115)

Gradually the concept of boss as manager develops during the middle childhood years as children differentiate property ownership from managerial authority.

Social Inequality and the Difference Between Rich and Poor

Society is subdivided. There are ethnic, religious, and regional differences—but surely socioeconomic class is the most salient source of division. In the United States, the distribution of wealth is unequal; some people have luxurious quantities of things and privileges, while others lack the barest necessities. All normal adults know that this is true and have definite opinions about what differentiates rich and poor people, how people become rich or poor, and whether it is okay for some people to be rich while others are poor.

But how is this knowledge acquired and organized? Young children cannot understand the social-class system in the abstract, but does this mean that they are unaware of inequality? The answer is important, because children's beliefs, like adults', are probably connected to their attitudes and behavior toward others, as well as to their self-esteem and sense of well-being.

Much recent research has been conducted on the development of concepts of wealth and poverty.[5] We do not yet know how children's understanding of these concepts affects their feelings, aspirations, and behavior, but we do know that the ability to make distinctions between rich and poor emerges early in American children of both middle- and lower-class backgrounds and in both black and white racial groups.

Only young preschoolers (aged three to four) have little or no understanding of the words "rich" and "poor." In one classroom a teacher showed children a set of magazine pictures depicting people obviously rich or poor (by adult standards). Most of the children did not know how to divide them into "rich people" versus "poor people." One child separated the pictures of children from the pictures of adults. "Children are poor because they don't have money," she said. "Grown-ups are rich because they have all the money."

At age five or six, children first begin to be able to categorize people into "rich" and "poor" on the basis of obvious differences in clothes and other concrete possessions. Their understanding of how people get rich or poor focuses on immediate events and circumstances.

TEACHER: What does "rich" mean?
EDWARD (age 6:4): Somebody that has lots of money, diamonds, and gemstones.
TEACHER: What does "poor" mean?
EDWARD: Somebody that has, like, only three cents, sometimes not even enough to buy a house or food. They have to dig in the trash like cats do.
TEACHER: How do people get rich?
EDWARD: By working at their job.
TEACHER: How do people get poor?
EDWARD: They don't have the right job. Or robbers take away all of their money.

Over time, children's perception of what differentiates rich and poor people develops from an exclusive focus on concrete possessions to a consideration of more abstract attributes. Lower-class children tend to empathize with the poor and talk about how the ideas or feelings of the poor differ from those of the rich. Well-off children tend to empathize with the rich and describe the rich as having superior personal qualities (intelligence, diligence, etc.). Children also move toward more abstract understanding of the structural bases of the socioeconomic system. They begin to point out structural factors (unemployment, educational opportunity, inheritance of wealth) as sources of inequality. They develop beliefs about whether the system is fair or unfair, necessary or unnecessary.

Older children's ideas are more complex and realistic, yet younger children's ideas can be appreciated for their optimism. Because they consider differences between the rich and the poor to be a matter of concrete possessions rather than abstract values, life-styles, or character traits, they see no reason why rich and poor people cannot be friends. Older children are much more likely to talk about barriers to friendship between the rich and poor. Furthermore, because young children do not realize that money and resources are limited and controlled, they optimistically believe in easy social mobility. White and black children, of middle- and lower-class backgrounds, assume that any poor person can become rich by getting a good job or asking a rich person for money.

TEACHER: Where does the bank get its money?
JENNY (age 5:3): From the rich people.
TEACHER: Where do the rich people get it?
JENNY: From the money-making factory. Then they give the bank some money to give to the poor people.

Classroom Activities on Economic Concepts

What are the implications of the developmental findings for educators? We agree with Berti and Bombi (1981a) that educators cannot—and should not—try to supply young children with an abstract and complete understanding of the economic system. Young children are well served by their egocentric and often friendly view of society, which answers *their* questions (about where money comes from, why stores contain the things they want, etc.) and reassures them that society is a comprehensible place where their needs are central. Adult interventions aimed at supplying children with adult concepts will only leave them with an equally incomplete—and less satisfying—picture of society. When teachers deal with children whom the adult world has let down, for example, with poor children, their goal should be to build the children's self-confidence and to communicate their regard for the children's families and cultures, but they should not try to discuss with children the social structural bases of inequality. That issue is most appropriately discussed with older children and adolescents.

Instead, educational efforts with young children should be mostly indirect and experiential, aimed at stimulating their constructive curiosity and providing them with a rich and varied storehouse of concrete images and experiences concerning different aspects of the economic world. At a later age they will integrate these images into a systematic understanding of the economy as a functioning whole.

In addition, classroom activities that provoke children to formulate economic concepts can stimulate children to reflect upon related issues in terms of their own highest level of understanding. Over time, children will spontaneously and slowly transform their concepts and construct a more abstract understanding of the economic system as a functioning whole.

1. *Children's concrete information about the economic system can be expanded through direct, personal experience.* Field trips are the best way to expose young children (aged three and above) to the processes of production and consumption of goods and services. Such trips can be integrated into curriculum units on such themes as trans-

portation, community helpers, public services, industry, agriculture, building and road construction, and buying and selling (Walsh, 1980). Suggested places to take children include the local shoe store, laundromat, hairdresser's, post office, health clinic, town collector's office, television repair shop, computer dealership, auto dealership, car rental business, bakery factory, rug factory, and fire department.

Field trips require adequate preparation of the children beforehand. This can include use of films and books, class visitors who speak on a related topic, photograph displays, and group discussions about what the trip will involve and what might be seen.

Field trips promote learning most when followed up by activities that allow children to rehearse and reflect on what they have seen. Group discussions, picture drawing, model construction, and dramatic reenactments are effective.

2. *Children's understanding of economic concepts can be consolidated and elaborated through sociodramatic role playing.* Play allows young children (aged about three and above) to rehearse and examine their knowledge in a nonthreatening, active context. The teacher can promote sociodramatic play involving economic concepts by preparing the role-play area of the classroom as a "grocery store," "bank," "bakery factory," "laundromat," "fast food restaurant," and so forth. Moreover, if the classroom is large enough, the teacher may wish to provide for a "home area" (which never varies in its basic elements) next to the "factory" or "business" (which may vary from week to week). This will allow the children to play out the experiences and feelings involved in going from home out into the world and back again.

The teacher's role will mainly be to observe and support the children's play without active intervention. On occasion, however, the teacher may wish to learn about the children's ideas and at the same time challenge children cognitively. Then the teacher may actively enter the play, for example, by taking on the role of storekeeper or customer in the "grocery store." A subtle way of entering the play involves taking on a role and then manipulating the materials present so as to pose a cognitive problem to the children, for example, taking all of the money out of the cash register so that children need to find more. A more direct way of entering the play is through asking questions. This must be done sensitively so that the children's interest and stream of activity are not disrupted. Here are questions suitable for children aged four and above:

• Why do you pay for things?

Before they understand how money works as a medium of exchange, children eagerly watch and play at buying and selling.

- Do you have the right money to buy that item?
- Where does the money in the cash register come from?
- Why is the money put in a cash register? Would a shoebox work just as well?
- Why do you get money (change) back?
- What happens if you don't pay for something?
- What happens if all of the money in the cash register gets used up? Where can you get more?
- What is the difference between coins and bills? Between different kinds of coins?
- Where do all of the goods in the store come from?
- What happens when something runs out? Where do we get more?
- Can the storekeeper keep some money from the cash register? Is it his/her money?

3. *Children aged five to six can classify products as necessities or luxuries.* This activity stimulates children to think about why objects are bought. The teacher supplies magazines or catalogs containing pictures of products and discusses with children the difference between things we "must have" (necessities) and things we "just want to have" (luxuries). The children should then cut out examples of each and paste them on a large sheet of paper divided into two clearly labeled halves.

4. *Children aged five to six can use play money to practice making choices of objects to buy.* The teacher can cut out pictures of a variety of products from catalogs and mount them on heavy paper, marking the price of each (in even dollars) underneath. Areas of the classroom can be designated as "clothing store," "hardware store," "grocery store," "shoe store," "toy store," and so forth. The children can each be given a small pile of pictures of products and asked to place them in the appropriate store. One child can then act as the banker and give each child $100 to spend. Several other children can act as storekeepers in each store. The remaining children can spend their money in some designated way, for example, to get gifts for each member of their family or to buy the necessities their family most requires. Before spending their money, the buyers should spend time planning their choices.

5. *Children aged four and above can engage in a thinking-game interview about ownership.* This activity (suggested by the discussion in Berti, Bombi, & Lis, 1982) encourages children to consider the meaning of the term "own." Some of the items in the questions are not really "ownable" (in the adult sense), and the questions usually elicit a variety of answers. The teacher should not correct children's answers but can encourage children to comment on one another's ideas.

A Thinking Game on Ownership: "Who Owns This?"

MATERIALS: Felt board and felt figures representing a mother, father, boy, baby brother, teacher, two school friends, various toys of any kind, bed, automobile, moon, and stars.

ACTION: The teacher acts out the following story. "One morning a boy named Chris woke up and ate breakfast with his mother, father, and baby brother. Then he and his brother played with their toys for a little while. His father told Chris it was time for school, so Chris drove with his father to his school. Chris got out of the car and went inside. At school he saw his teacher and played with his friends with the toys at school. After school, his father came again and drove him home. That night while Chris was sleeping in his bed, the moon and stars came out and shone in the sky over his house."

DISCUSSION QUESTIONS: For each of the items (things and people), the children should be asked, "Who owns ——? Why do you think so? Does anyone have another idea?" The questions should be asked for all of the items in turn—Chris's shirt, Chris's shoes, toys at home, baby brother, Chris, mother and father, car, house, school, toys at school, friends at school, teacher, moon, and stars.

SUGGESTED VARIATIONS: The same activity can be conducted varying the story, perhaps replacing it with one involving a factory or business store. For older children (aged about six and above) who may have begun to differentiate ownership and authority concepts, the discussion questions can be made more advanced by asking, for each item, "Who is *in charge* of this? Who *owns* this? Is the *boss* of the —— the same person as the *owner* of the ——? Why (or why not)?"

6. *Children aged four and above can engage in a thinking-game skit on money and prices.* The goal of this activity is to encourage children to consider money as a medium of exchange for goods in buying and selling.

A Thinking Game on the Use and Value of Money: "Birthday Purchase"

CHARACTERS: Grandfather, girl, and storekeeper.

MATERIALS: A one-dollar bill (real or play money) and six items bearing conspicuous price tags. (Of course, comparable items can be substituted for the ones suggested here.)
- Necklace—$10.00 (small but valuable item)
- Deck of cards—$1.00 (small, common item)
- Tricycle—$10.00 (large, valuable item)
- Hoola hoop—$1.00 (large, common item)
- Plastic bag of cardboard puzzle pieces—$10.00 (overpriced item)
- Attractive baby doll—$1.00 (underpriced item)

ACTION: The grandfather knocks on the door of the girl's house and greets his granddaughter. He tells her that because it is her birthday, he is going to give her one dollar to pick out a present. He hands her the dollar bill and they walk to the store. They tell the storekeeper that they want to pick out a present for the girl with her one-dollar bill. The girl then walks around the store, examining each item and naming and describing it to the audience but *not* saying anything about prices or pointing out the price tags.

DISCUSSION QUESTIONS
- How much do you think the necklace costs? Why? Can she buy it? [After answers are given] Now let's check what this price tag says. Ten dollars! [This questioning procedure is then repeated for each of the other items in turn]

- How can you tell whether something will cost a lot or a little money? Does it matter how *big* it is? Why (or why not)? Does it matter how *special* it is? Why (or why not)? Does it matter how many *parts* it has? Why (or why not)?
- If the girl needs more money to buy the present she wants, where can she get it? [If someone suggests from her parents] Where do her parents get money? Where do your parents get their money? [If someone suggests the cash register in the store] Can she get money out of the cash register? Can her grandfather? Why (or why not)? [If someone suggests the girl should get a job] What kind of job can she do? Why do you get money when you do a job?

THE DEVELOPMENT OF OCCUPATIONAL CONCEPTS

Young children's interest in adult work begins even in infancy. All parents know how closely their infants watch when they are performing any kind of active work. By toddler age, children trail their parents around the house and yard and seek to participate in household tasks as if they realized that work is important, interesting, and worthwhile. Their attraction to adult work motivates them to learn about all of the hundreds of procedural details necessary for living in their society: how to handle sharp knives, hammer nails, weed crops, paint walls, feed babies, drive trucks, ride horses, and so forth. Early childhood is a period of intense growth in which children are open to influence from many people in many walks of life, because they are interested in almost everything that adults do.

Younger preschoolers' imitations of adults reveal their earliest ideas of roles. At age two to three, most children use dolls or dress-up materials to act out a few familiar roles (e.g., father, mother, doctor), and they can perform some appropriate actions for each. They think of each role in isolation from others; for example, when acting out the "doctor," they do not also think about what the "patient" should do. Thus, young preschoolers cannot usually coordinate their fantasy play to act out roles in a complementary way.

Children's understanding of roles takes a big step forward at about age four or five, however, when they begin to understand that roles involve *complementary relationships*.[6] For instance, doctors need patients, teachers need students, sellers need buyers, and actors need an audience. At this age, when children engage in sociodramatic play, they assign one another complementary roles and they become concerned that their partners act in appropriate ways, that is, live up to their internalized images of proper role behavior.

Nevertheless, their occupational role concepts are still immature in several ways. First, they are limited in their ability to understand multiple roles—that a person can simultaneously occupy several roles. Before about age six or seven, they cannot take the multiple perspectives involved in seeing, for example, that a man can be at the same time a father to his child, a husband to his wife, and a carpenter to his clients. Second, they cannot separate the idea of the role from the concrete activities involved in it. Therefore, they think that a person stops being, for example, a nurse, carpenter, or secretary when he or she is off the job. Third, in a similar way, young children cannot separate the role from the person who occupies it. Especially when thinking about other people (as opposed to themselves), they have difficulty imagining how a person can change his or her occupational role: a person who is a doctor cannot be an artist, for example. At about age six, however, children overcome all of these ways of thinking and move to a new level of understanding.

TEACHER: Can a carpenter also be a teacher?
ELLEN (age 6:4): Well, no, because a carpenter spends all of his time building. He doesn't usually have time to do other stuff, like be a teacher. But if he has time, then he can do two jobs.
TEACHER: When the carpenter goes home, is he still a carpenter?
ELLEN: Yeah. He works during the day, then he comes home and has supper. He is still a carpenter all the time.
TEACHER: While he is eating supper, he is still a carpenter?
ELLEN: Yes, no matter where he is, he is always a carpenter, unless he quits work.
TEACHER: Can he quit?
ELLEN: Yes, once he is . . . 65, I think. Yeah, 65.
TEACHER: What if he wants to quit before that?
ELLEN: He can, as long as the mother works and they have enough money. Instead of quitting, he should change his job.

The Selection of a Job

How do young children understand the world of adult work? They think of it as a kind of conflict-free fantasy zone, in which people simply choose the job they want or have it chosen for them by a benevolent authority figure. They think that people select a job purely on the basis of its emotional qualities, such as how much action, fun, and power it provides. Young children do not understand that in most societies, people must compete for jobs. Job entry is dependent on education or training, and there is a limited supply of jobs open to people. The desirability of jobs varies according to their status, pay, and work conditions, and some jobs are more sought-after.

> MOTHER: How do you think your teacher, Franca, decided to be a teacher?
> SAM (age 4:4): I think she just chose it.
> MOTHER: What makes you choose one job instead of another?
> SAM: You just pick the job that you want to do. One job that you think is very fun.
> MOTHER: What if Franca wanted to be a teacher, but there wasn't room for a new teacher at any school anywhere?
> SAM: She would get someone else to do a different job, and then she could be the teacher.

In later childhood, children begin to construct a more realistic vision of the job market. For example, now knowing that behavior may be determined by multiple reasons, not just by one (Erwin & Kuhn, 1979), they construct the idea that people work to get money for living, as well as for individual, personal reasons.

> PAUL (age 10:10): I don't think you can do a job without getting money . . . but I think you should enjoy a job. If you don't like that job, it's not really worth doing it—unless you can't find any other job which you would like to do. (Furth, 1980, p. 207)

When older children put this more sophisticated understanding of job selection together with an understanding of profit, they become capable of a whole new level of thinking about societal phenomena. They begin to think that salary and educational scales may be related to job choice. Their initial formulations of these relationships are naive, however, and remain so until adolescence or adulthood.

> ELLEN (age 8:2): If you work hard at school, you'll get to be what you really want, like a doctor. (Furth, 1980, p. 188)

> SAM (age 9:6): Factory workers get paid the most. (Furth, 1980, p. 189)

The Social Division of Labor

Another way in which young children show their egocentric understanding of adult work is in their answers to the question of why there are so many different kinds of jobs in the world. Rather than taking the adult perspective and thinking about all the different needs in society that must be met, young children again take a personalistic view of the matter. They say that there are many kinds of jobs so that they can choose the particular job that they want.

ALEXIS (age 5): There are so many jobs because there are so many fun things to do. I would like to do three jobs.

ANN (age 4): If you don't like one job you have, you can just get a different one!

Alternatively, thinking about all of the many services that are provided by different kinds of workers, young children say that there are so many jobs because they themselves need so many different things. They do not understand that the needs of everyone are met by a social division of labor and exchange of goods and services. Just as young children think that the moon and sun follow them as they travel, so they innocently place themselves at the center of society. Constructing an objective view of society requires coordinating all the perspectives of the different members of society into one generalized perspective— an achievement of adolescence or adulthood.

Classroom Activities on Occupational Concepts

What are the implications of these findings for teachers? Young children are generally reassured and satisfied by their benevolent and providential view of adult society, and only in certain cases will teachers need to worry that children's unrealistic ideas will cause them distress. Parental unemployment is one cruel fact of life that does not fit well into young children's conceptual schemes. Because they assume that every act is motivated by a person's likes or dislikes, they tend to think that workers are laid off because their bosses don't like them. In the case of a boy with an unemployed father, for example, a teacher might intervene to find out why the child thinks his parent lost his job, and if necessary, to try to correct any idea that his parent lost his job because his boss didn't like him. Perhaps the child's parents have already explained to him that his parent lost his job through no fault of his own, but he needs to have it told him more than once, in the context of repeated brief talks.

More commonly, however, teachers' role with respect to the occupational system will be to feed children's tremendous curiosity about the world of work and answer their many questions. Their goal should be to support children's interest; increase their range of knowledge of different occupational roles; provide them concrete evidence that jobs are not necessarily limited to people of a certain gender, race, or age group; and stimulate them to think about the occupational system at their own highest level.

1. *The occupational interest of children aged two and above can be expanded through exposure to a variety of roles portrayed in books and photographs.* Young children are often unaware of the variety of jobs that exist. Pictures of people at work in different occupational roles can be displayed around the room, and the reading area can be stacked with books containing information or stories about different occupations. Gender, age, and racial stereotypes should be counteracted through use of materials portraying both genders, young and old adults, and different races of people. Frequent change will sustain a high level of interest in the materials. As teachers discuss the materials with children (either individually or in groups), the work involved in each role can be described. The materials can also be used as a springboard for discussion of other topics related to occupational roles, for example, what is good about each job.

2. *Children's understanding of occupational concepts can be elaborated and expanded through sociodramatic play.* Sociodramatic play allows children aged two and above to try out the activities associated with different occupations and to vicariously experience the power and instrumental effectiveness of adult work. Teachers can prepare the role-play area of the classroom with the clothing and equipment required for children to act out one role (e.g., firefighter) or a set of complementary roles (e.g., the building trades). A "home" area provided next to the "work" area will allow many more possibilities for play and encourage the children to coordinate roles (e.g., parent and worker). The equipment provided to the children should consider their skill and judgment level, but more equipment will encourage richer play:

- Construction worker—hard hat, nail apron, hammer holster, play tools, sawhorses
- Sales clerk—cash register, money, merchandise, price tags, telephone, sales slips
- Baker—apron, rolling pins, cookie cutters, trays, spatula, mixing bowls, spice jars, wooden spoons
- Plumber—plastic piping, play tools, faucet and sink
- Office worker—typewriter, pads, carbon paper, pens, erasers, telephone, mailing stickers, envelopes, briefcase

Books provide a most important way to broaden children's knowledge of adult occupations.

3. *Children's concrete information about the occupational system can be enriched through contact with working adults.* Field trips and visits to class by speakers can expose children aged three and above to different occupational roles. Young children have a great appetite for concrete information about adult work—the tools, uniforms, and procedures involved and the ways in which teams work together or complementary jobs intermesh. Children will want to see demonstrations, handle equipment, try things out themselves, and ask many questions. During the question period, teachers can introduce new issues into the children's thinking by asking a selected few of the following questions that may not have been brought up by the children:

- How did you learn to do your job?
- What made you choose this job?
- Did you ever do any other type of job before this one?
- What kind of person likes this job and does it well?

- Why is this a good job? Anything bad about it?
- Why do you work?
- [For young preschool children] Where do you sleep at night?
- Are you a parent, in addition to your other job?

Good preparation and follow-up activities for field trips and class visits related to occupational topics are the same as those described earlier for economic topics. Some specific ways to organize class visits or field trips include the following:

- To enhance children's family pride, their parents can be visited at work, by small groups of four to five children.
- To give children concrete experience with the social division of labor, a factory, department store, or supermarket can be visited; children can observe the diversity of jobs (e.g., at a grocery store there are clerks, baggers, shelf stockers, managers, etc.).
- To help children realize that men and women can hold the same jobs, male/female *pairs* of doctors, nurses, carpenters, and so forth can be invited to visit the class.
- To give children another view of the women they already know as one another's mothers, several mothers can be invited to come at one time as "experts" to teach and demonstrate a skill; another day, fathers or other relatives might be the focus.

4. *Children aged four and above can make up plays about particular occupations.* This activity allows children to consolidate their knowledge and develop representational skills. The teacher can ask children to describe what people in some selected occupations do, what they are like, and how they act. Then the children in small groups can be given props and asked to make up and act out scenes to demonstrate the role. (The teacher should make sure that children of both sexes are part of each small group.)

5. *Children aged three and above can make a concrete representation of a community in terms of the network of vital services provided.* This activity allows children to gain a concrete sense of the social division of labor. The teacher can read children the book *Katy and the Big Snow* and then ask the children to create Geoppolis. They can do this in the sandbox using miniature transportation toys as props, or draw a map on a large piece of butcher paper, or create the city with felt buildings and vehicles on a large felt board.

6. *Older children's informational base about the occupational system can be enriched through interviews conducted by children*

themselves. Children aged five to six and above can conduct their own interviews with people about their work. The class as a group can decide upon the questions, and children can go individually or in pairs to conduct interviews. For example, they can interview the director or principal, custodian, cook, and secretary of their school. The interviews can be tape-recorded, or an accompanying teacher can act as recorder. The results of the interviews can be played or read back, and discussed, at class meeting.

SUGGESTED BOOKS FOR CHILDREN

Some of the following selections focus on money as a medium of exchange. Others focus on work—its satisfactions, its importance, how and where it takes place. The more recent books on adult careers present nontraditional images of men's and women's job possibilities. Because much children's literature presents traditional images, these selections give teachers a way to offer children a more balanced perspective.

Baker, Jeannie. *Grandfather*. London: Andre Deutsch, 1977.   The interesting goings-on at a junk shop are portrayed through the eyes of a young granddaughter.

Barton, Byron. *Building a House*. New York: Puffin, 1981.   Attractive illustrations and simple text lay out all of the steps and occupational roles involved in building a house.

Burton, Virginia L. *Katy and the Big Snow*. Boston: Houghton Mifflin, 1971.   Katy, the strongest crawler tractor in Geoppolis, saves the day when a blizzard blankets the city. The book shows how a community is a network of interconnected parts.

Delton, Judy. *My Mother Lost Her Job Today*. Chicago: Albert Whitman, 1980.   A young girl grapples with the meaning of her mother's loss of her job.

Gibbons, Gail. *Department Store*. New York: Crowell, 1984.   In rich and detailed pictures, this book describes the inner workings of a big department store.

Greenberg, Polly. *O Lord, I Wish I Was a Buzzard*. New York: Macmillan, 1968.   Two rural children show the spirit and maturity their lives require as they spend a long and hot day helping their father pick cotton.

Hazen, Barbara Shook. *Step on It, Andrew*. New York: Atheneum, 1980.   Andrew's mother says "step on it" and the astounding splash of the mud puddle lands on everyone in town. This funny story for older children serves as a good springboard for discussion: "What is a mayor's job? What does the greengrocer do? The robber? The city councilors?"

Homan, Dianne. *In Christina's Toolbox*. Chapel Hill, N.C.: Lollipop Power, 1981.   A young girl knows how to use her set of adult tools. Many details of carpentry and repair work are simply portrayed.

Isadora, Rachel. *Ben's Trumpet*. New York: Greenwillow, 1979.   Ben, an inner-city boy of the 1920s, listens to the musicians at the Zig Zag Jazz Club and yearns to play. This book labels the musicians—pianist, saxaphonist, trombonist, drummer, and trumpeter—and the striking artwork conveys the sound and feeling of their work.

Jenness, Aylette. *The Bakery Factory: Who Puts the Bread on Your Table*. New York: Crowell, 1978.   This book is for older children but can be used with young ones by talking about the excellent and interesting photographs of the work and workers at a Massachusetts bakery.

Kaufman, Joe. *Busy People and How They Do Their Work*. New York: Golden, 1973.   This picture book portrays the work of men and women in several common occupations.

Lasker, Joe. *Mothers Can Do Anything*. Chicago: Albert Whitman, 1972. Striking illustrations accompany a simple, rhythmic text describing the variety of occupations held by women.

———. *The Do-Something Day*. New York: Viking, 1982.   Bernie wants to participate in work. No one in his family will let him help, but while "running away" through his New York neighborhood, he is invited to work with many of the familiar adults.

Leiner, Katherine. *Ask Me What My Mother Does*. New York: Franklin Watts, 1978.   This book is unusual in that it not only describes a variety of jobs for women but also uses photographs and diagrams to explain many interesting facts about the work.

Lenski, Lois. *Lois Lenski's Big Big Book of Mr. Small*. New York: Derrydale, 1985.   The six Mr. Small stories were originally published in the 1930's. They present traditional images of male occupations in a captivating way that has made this a classic for young children.

Maury, Inez. *My Mother the Mail Carrier: Mi Mama la Cartera*. Old Westbury, N.Y.: Feminist Press, 1976.   In English and Spanish, Lupita describes the daily work and happy day of her mother, a mail carrier.

Merriam, Eve. *Mommies at Work*. New York: Scholastic, 1973.   This book pictures the diversity of women's work, from bridge building to air-traffic control.

Nolan, Madeena S. *My Daddy Don't Go to Work*. Minneapolis: Carolrhoda, 1978.   The father in this family cannot find another job. His wife is employed, and he takes over cooking and cleaning. The family (black) is anxious but sticking firmly together. Good basis for discussion: "Why did the father lose his old job? Why can't he get a new one?"

Rockwell, Harry. *My Doctor*. New York: Macmillan, 1973.   The stethoscope and other tools in a physician's kit are explained for toddlers through a visit to a pediatrician.

Simon, Norma. *I'm Busy, Too*. Chicago: Albert Whitman, 1980.   This book portrays busy children and adults "at work" all over town and suggests the parallels and interconnectedness of child and adult activity.

Viorst, Judith. *Alexander, Who Used to Be Rich Last Sunday*. Hartford, Conn.: Atheneum, 1978. The humorous trials of Alexander illustrate, for older children, the way in which a dollar consists of many small portions to spend or lose.

Wandro, Mark, R.N., and Blank, Joanie. *My Daddy Is a Nurse*. Reading, Mass.: Addison-Wesley, 1981. This book tells about 10 fathers who work in traditionally "feminine" occupations (as nurse, weaver, flight attendant, dental hygienist, etc.).

Williams, Vera B. *A Chair for My Mother*. New York: Greenwillow, 1982. A little girl and her hardworking mother save up coins in great jar until they can buy a beautiful armchair.

Wilson, Julia. *Becky*. New York: Crowell, 1966. The event of shopping for, selecting, and paying for a doll is portrayed through the eyes of Becky, a young inner-city girl. ("Magic" is involved too.)

CHAPTER 8

Becoming Moral

In a college classroom, an instructor led a discussion on moral education with a group of students majoring in early education. "What do you look for in a 'moral' young child?" she asked the group.

One student said, "I look for a child who cares about other people's needs and feelings—who helps others."

"To me," suggested one student, "a moral child is one who seems to have a conscience. I know a four-year-old who always feels bad when she's done something wrong or mean, and she tries to make up for it afterwards."

"That's okay," commented another, "but I'm more impressed by deeds than feelings. I look for a child who can remember and follow the rules, even when no adult is there watching."

"Actually, I disagree with this whole question," a fourth student told the instructor. "Young children can't really be called 'moral.' They don't have enough sense yet, enough judgment, to take responsibility for their actions."

At this point an adult visitor spoke up. This man was a kindergarten teacher in a nearby school, and he said, "You know, talking about what makes a 'moral child' makes me also think about what makes an adult moral. As a teacher, I continually reexamine myself and my values. What really is right and wrong and how do I know it? What rules should I have in my classroom and how should they be decided upon? What values should I try to live by in my personal life and as a teacher?"

Each participant in this discussion made a valuable point. The diversity of ideas reflects the difficulty of describing in a simple way what the task of becoming moral entails. Yet, simple or not, morality is the business of teachers, and moral education is an essential part of teachers' work. Teachers must manage a classroom group and help children to learn, live together, and control themselves. In a larger sense, they share with parents and the rest of society the responsibility for preparing the young to appreciate basic values, respect the rights of others, and recognize their responsibilities as members of society.

DEFINING MORALITY AND THE TEACHER'S ROLE

What is morality? Philosophers say that it is a system of standards for good or right conduct (Gewirth, 1968, 1978). Morality is a necessary and universal part of human life because people everywhere face common problems such as dividing resources, controlling aggression, and organizing the tasks of production and childrearing. In all societies people have rules and a language for communicating about what people ought to or must do, about what is worthy and valuable to strive for, and about what people's duties and responsibilities are.

Yet, though people everywhere use moral language to talk about what people should strive for, they disagree about the content of their moralities. Throughout history, many ethical systems—coherent and defensible—have been built on different visions of the good life,[1] and even within the same society, people disagree on how to rank moral values. Philosophers have searched since the dawn of civilization for the most valid way to describe moral experience and justify moral standards. What guiding assumptions, then, can teachers bring to the task of moral education?

Three assumptions can guide teachers as they work to support children's development:

1. Overarching the diversity of cultural traditions in America are certain general moral values—compatible with all groups' specific values—that teachers must recognize in their classrooms and help children to understand. These values are binding on everyone because reason tells us that some set of guiding principles is necessary for life in our kind of society. There must be some building blocks for a general or shared morality. The guiding principles go back to the ideals of justice and love—two values ethically defensible as ultimate "goods." They are defined specifically and concretely for Americans by the founding documents of the country. Thus, Americans may disagree about what is right or wrong to do in specific concrete situations, but they usually do agree that the social contract is founded on *justice* (the principle of treating each person equally), *liberty* (the principle that individual freedom of action should be lim-

ited only where necessary to protect individual rights or the group welfare), and *avoidance of harm* (the principle that unnecessary harm or suffering to living beings should be avoided). The ethics of the early childhood profession reflect these guiding principles; teachers must respect the rights of each child equally and work to promote each child's present and future well-being (Katz & Ward, 1978).

2. Beneath the sheltering umbrella of the overarching morality, a diversity of cultural traditions can coexist side by side even though they offer divergent views of moral virtue and the good life. Different cultural groups have evolved their own views of human excellence—the qualities of mind or character thought to be essential to the realization of the common good. For example, spirituality, harmony with nature, physical courage, honesty, moderation, respect for elders, humility, self-assertion, devotion to family, and love of the arts have been differentially prized by cultural groups throughout history. Teachers cannot promote all these moral virtues at the same time; there is no one right way to choose among them. However, teachers can try to find out which values are prized by children's parents, the surrounding community, and other staff at their school. Teachers can work to create a moral atmosphere in the school based on tolerance, respect, a celebration of cultural diversity, and ultimately a particular prizing of some key virtues—those common to all the groups involved and/or those about which people care most deeply. Over time, teachers can contribute toward building a school community based on an evolving, shared vision of the good life.

3. The task of becoming moral—of developing moral sense and understanding—belongs ultimately to the child. Adults must support and guide children, because children attend closely to the words and actions of loved, admired adults. But in the end, children themselves are responsible for what they know, feel, believe, and value. Hence, the crux of the teacher's role in the moral realm (as in others) is to facilitate children's natural development toward a state of mature autonomy in which they can think for themselves and adopt an inquiring stance. Young children cannot understand abstract moral principles or reason impartially and consistently. They do, however, have a dawning appreciation of the values of justice and concern for others that—if supported—will evolve into a mature morality. In order to best support and guide children's moral growth, teachers

need to be as aware as possible of the developmental steps by which children acquire moral sense and understanding.

This chapter reviews some of the findings on the development of moral sense and understanding and considers implications for the teaching of young children.

MORAL-DECISION TASK ONE: INTERPRETING A SOCIAL SITUATION

Psychologist James Rest (1983) has suggested that morality involves two steps of decision making. First is the cognitive task of *interpreting* a social situation in terms of how people's welfare has been, or may be, affected by one's actions. Second is the task of *moral judging*, that is, deciding or reasoning about what is "the right thing to do." Moral behavior or action then follows a moral decision when someone *chooses* to do what he or she thinks to be right and *executes* that intention.

Research has elucidated a great deal about the cognitive tasks of both interpreting and moral judging. Interpretation, it seems, involves at least two skills that even young children can begin to accomplish and that teachers can facilitate—perspective taking and causal reasoning.

The Development of Perspective Taking

JESSICA (age 4): Mommy, let's close our ears and see what it's like for a deaf person to see fireworks. And let's close our eyes and see what it's like for a blind person to just listen.[2]

Perspective taking involves sensing or comprehending the thoughts and feelings of others. Whenever people are in the company of others, they naturally engage in almost continual perspective taking as they monitor other people's expressions, gestures, words, and actions to get a sense of what the other is thinking, feeling, wanting, intending.

Perspective taking can be seen as a multifaceted capacity that develops continuously and gradually with age and experience.[3] Rather than being self-contained, it is embedded inextricably in many social-cognitive skills. *Spatial* perspective taking is revealed when children try to understand others' visual experience. How does something look to a person who is situated in a place in space that is different from one's own location? *Social* perspective taking is revealed when children try to infer the motivations of others. What do others want? What do they intend? *Affective* perspective taking is revealed when children try to understand how others feel about a situation. Are they happy? Are they sad? Are they angry? *Moral* perspective taking is revealed when children seek to resolve moral conflicts by balancing competing claims. Who deserves what? Who needs what? What is fair?

Thus, there are many types of perspective taking, and they all develop through specific experience and practice. Children typically show uneven levels of skill across aspects. Even within one aspect, their level of performance seems tied to particular demands of the situation.

Although perspective taking is not one unified capacity, the various skills that constitute it show parallel changes with age. Underlying all perspective-taking skills are information-processing strategies. Young children, as has been discussed throughout this book, are limited in how many representations they can control and manipulate mentally at one time. Before the age of about seven, children cannot simultaneously coordinate the perspectives of several people. Instead, they focus on the perspective of one person at a time—often but not always their own perspective. As their information-processing capacities increase, they become more able to "calculate" the perspectives of others, keeping in mind their own perspective, too.

Furthermore, underlying all perspective-taking skills is a cognitive sense of the other as an independent self. A good example of how this sense changes over time can be seen in the evolving nature of empathy. Infants experience a primitive kind of empathy because they cognitively fuse self and others. They may cry when they see or hear another infant in distress but not really know whether what bothers them is inside or outside the self. By about 18 months, however, children understand self and others to be distinct objects in the physical world. Then, at about two or three years of age, they construct the idea that others have their own inner lives, and that everyone's thoughts and feelings are different. Yet they still may not be able to consistently apply this insight. Young children often project their feelings and thoughts onto others, because when concentrating on their own feelings, they cannot simultaneously calculate how the other person feels. During adolescence, finally, children develop "true sympathy," a compassion for the suffering of others based on knowledge of the individuality of every human being (Hoffman, 1975, 1978a, 1978b, 1983).

Teachers can promote the develoment of perspective-taking skills in young children by providing a range of opportunities for social sharing and cooperation. For example, teachers can help children to identify and differentiate the feelings of self and others. A light touch is required, in which teachers echo children's remarks and invite them to talk about how they feel, how others may feel, and how they are affected by the feelings of others (Axline, 1947; Moustakas, 1953; Ginott, 1972). It is important to avoid pushing children into talking about feelings—especially those of which they have no conscious awareness. A comment such as, "Do you happen to feel sad today because your cat is lost? Your face looks sad to me," is more effective than, "I know that you are angry because you have a new sister." As children then gain increasing cognitive control of their empathic feelings, they will become more and more able to incorporate prosocial feelings into moral decision making.

The mandated inclusion of special-needs children in early education settings presents today's teachers with another kind of opportunity to promote perspective taking in young children. Integration and positive social relations do not occur automatically when handicapped children are brought into contact with nonhandicapped children. Experts believe that interventions are required in order to directly confront the issue of differences between handicapped and nonhandicapped peers (Hanline, 1985; Thurman & Lewis, 1979). "Mainstreaming should not be viewed as an effort to teach children to minimize or ignore differences, but as an effort to teach them *positive, appropriate* responses to these differences" (Sapon-Shevin, 1983, p. 24). A key to this teaching is fostering both empathy and role taking. Three strategies can be helpful.

1. Children should be given concrete information about the nature of the specific handicaps of their classmates. If possible, this information should be provided before a handicapped child joins the classroom. Enjoyable activities can be planned that allow children to experience the world as a specific handicapped person might. Teachers should at first focus on the one aspect of the handicapped person's situation that other children most notice; teachers will need to find out about that aspect by listening to the children. The purpose of giving children information is to reduce any fears of the strangeness of the handicapped child's appearance or behavior.

2. The talents and strengths of handicapped children should be pointed out to help others see them more holistically. For example, a child who uses a wheelchair may have impressively strong

arms. The kinds of capabilities that most interest young children are what people can *do*; small skills are valued by them. This strategy is important for counteracting some children's tendencies to treat handicapped children as pitiful.

3. The feelings of handicapped children should be highlighted to increase others' awareness of them as selves. This is especially important when handicapped children cannot speak well for themselves. Teachers can comment, "Jackie is enjoying your company. Look at her smile at you!" or "Kim misses her mom. Have you noticed how she always gets her doll when she misses her mom?" Empathic feelings are easily formed when children become aware that others share wants and needs for food, affection, comfort, fun, rest.

These strategies—and others—establish a concrete basis for all young children in a classroom to appreciate and enjoy each other.

Understanding Causality in Social Interaction

Cause-and-effect reasoning is another important way in which children seek to interpret social situations. Cause-and-effect reasoning allows children to accomplish their goals and be socially effective. For example, it occurs when a child notices that his behavior is not getting the desired result and switches tactics—for instance, ceases whining for attention and asks in a more pleasant way. It also occurs when a child tries to determine which social event was the cause of some other event. What was it about spilling the milk bottle that made her parent angry? Was it the magnitude of the mess all over the floor or the fact that she was holding the bottle in a silly way?

Many investigators have described ways in which young children only slowly, gradually, and with much practice build up skills for causal reasoning and planning.

Three-year-olds cannot yet be expected to consciously plan their social strategies because they cannot focus on more than one cognitive representation at a time (Fischer et al., 1984). In classroom situations, these children often persist in repeating actions that lead to undesired results and only gradually, through trial and error, build up more successful alternatives. They generally cannot be expected to take account of how their behavior caused a certain effect—for instance, their hitting caused another child to push them away.

In contrast, by age four or five most children are able to coordinate two cognitive representations and reflect on simple cause-and-effect sequences. They can talk in a group about the different possible actions that one might take to get a certain desired result; they can also consider the likely effect of each type of action.[4] They become more aware of other people's intentions and motivations and, when other, more concrete aspects of the situation do not compete to steal their attention, they evaluate other people's actions as good or bad depending on their motivations.[5] For example, when their friend knocks down the block structure on which they are working, they may be forgiving rather than angry if it is obvious that their friend did it "by accident" and "is sorry."

By age six or seven, most children go on and take another major step in understanding social causality. They can coordinate many cognitive representations at once. They can consider several aspects of their own behavior while also considering several of their partner's. They can plan in terms of multiple goals—finding a way to accomplish their own desires while at the same time satisfying the desires of the other person. They can realize that people's actions may have multiple motivations rather than just one motivation (Erwin & Kuhn, 1979; Selman, 1980). When assessing moral responsibility—whether someone should be praised or blamed for a certain action—they can begin to develop more complex frameworks. For example, they begin to realize that the motivational context surrounding an action contains many factors, such as whether the action was done intentionally or accidentally, carelessly or carefully, while acting of one's own free will or under pressure, in a normal or impaired mental condition, and so forth. As Piaget (1932/1948) first pointed out long ago, school-aged children begin to consistently evaluate the motivations behind an act as critical for evaluating an offender's guilt.

By becoming aware of these developmental changes, teachers can become both more realistic in their expectations for children and more creative in helping children to develop causal reasoning skills appropriate for their age. Of course, the natural practice that children get through play with other children remains the single most important experience needed for developing skill in interpreting social situations.

Classroom Activities to Promote Skills of Social Interpretation

The following activities can be used to foster skills of social interpretation. They are also beneficial because they promote thinking skills of general use, for instance, drawing inferences from available information, considering not just one aspect of a situation but multiple aspects, and increasing representational competence.[6]

1. *Children aged two and above can engage in activities that enhance social perspective taking (role taking) by requiring children to cooperate or to coordinate their actions.*[7]

- *Sociodramatic play* fosters complementary role playing.
- *Cross-age caring* allows older children to take the lead and respond to the inferred needs of younger ones in a context that is nonthreatening, particularly for socially withdrawn children.
- *Multichild gross-motor equipment* requires children to coordinate and time their movements (two-child rocking horse, rocking boat, "moon buggy," and see saw are good examples).
- *Circle and group games* (London Bridge, Duck-Duck-Goose, Farmer in the Dell, etc.) promote role taking and coordination in an exciting context.

2. *Children aged three and above can engage in activities that help them become aware of how feelings are communicated by the face* (from Smith, 1982):

- Children can use paper plates, collage materials, paste, and paints to make "face plates." The teacher prepares the activity by cutting a wide variety of eyes, noses, and mouths out of construction paper (reflecting different feelings). The children can practice identifying the facial parts, then construct their face plates. These can be displayed on the wall, with the group discussing why particular faces look happy, sad, scared (or scary), angry, or surprised.
- Children can make "feeling face masks" out of paper bags and paint, yarn, construction paper, and so forth. The teacher should suggest that children make masks that are either happy, angry, sad, or frightened. (Completed models should be available to show if children need help in understanding the task.) When children are finished, they can try to guess what feelings each mask displays and act out the feelings of their masks.
- The teacher can take "emotion photographs" of children acting out particular feelings. These can be displayed on the wall or made into a deck of cards that children can classify and discuss.
- Children can work on "emotion puzzles" made out of photographs or magazine pictures glued to cardboard and cut in half. The pictures should clearly represent the simple emotional states. As the children work on the puzzles, the teacher can discuss with them why the top and bottom halves of the face show the same feeling.

This rocking horse encourages children to take each other's perspective and coordinate their movements together.

3. *Children aged four and above can engage in a sensory-awareness activity to promote perspective taking and problem solving on behalf of people with handicaps* (from Smith, 1982). The teacher leads a group discussion on how the children would feel if they *could not hear at all* because they had something wrong with the inside of their ears. The teacher asks, "If you could not hear, how could other people tell you that it's time for dinner? Or, that it's time to go to bed? Or, that they like you? Or, goodbye?" (After each question, the children act out their ideas.) Then the teacher can tell the children that he or she would like to find out what it would be like to be in the classroom and be someone who cannot hear. The children should first discuss the sounds they hear and then try on ear covers. The children should remove their ear covers, but the teacher should continue to wear his or

hers for a while to force the children to find nonverbal ways of communicating with him or her. The same activity can be conducted to focus on other handicaps, such as inabilities to talk or see.

4. *Children aged three to five can engage in a thinking-game skit on perspective taking.* This activity (adapted from Flavell et al., 1968) helps children to differentiate the wants and needs of self and others.

A Thinking Game on Different Perspectives: "The Birthday Store"

CHARACTERS: A teacher acts as "storekeeper" and leads the discussion.
MATERIALS: A "gift shop" equipped with a choice of items to buy: pipe, necktie, women's shoes and blouse, fire hat, baby doll.
ACTION: The storekeeper says, "This is a gift shop. There are things here to buy." Children are invited to name each item.
DISCUSSION QUESTIONS: Let's pretend that it is your ———'s birthday. Which present would you buy: the necktie, pipe, shoes, blouse, fire hat, or baby doll? Why? [These questions are repeated for a set of relatives, such as father, grandfather, mother, baby sister.]

5. *Children aged three and above can engage in a thinking-game interview that encourages young children to generate multiple alternatives and consider their causal consequences* (adapted from Spivack and Shure, 1974).

A Thinking Game on Social Problems: "What Happens Next?"

MATERIALS: Dolls or puppets representing two friends and a teacher; miniature sand toys—shovel and watering can.
ACTION: The teacher narrates, "Here are Gloria and Gertie, and here is their teacher. Gloria and Gertie are playing in the sand box building a big castle together. Their teacher is standing nearby watching them. Gloria is using the shovel to dig a deep hole around the castle. Gertie is using the watering can to sprinkle water on the castle. Gertie says, 'I am so *tired* of the watering can. I need to use the shovel now, to build a tower.' Gloria says, 'No, I am not finished yet.'"
DISCUSSION QUESTIONS
   • What can Gertie do so that she can have a chance to use the shovel? [Solicit as many alternatives as possible, using such probes as, "What can Gertie *do*?" "What can Gertie *say*?" As each suggestion is made, it should be restated for the group: "Joey says that Gertie can *grab* the shovel. That is one idea. Can someone think of another idea?" When a number of suggestions have been offered, ask for each one.]
   • What will happen next if Gertie ———? [To child who made that suggestion] Can you use these dolls to show me what might happen next if

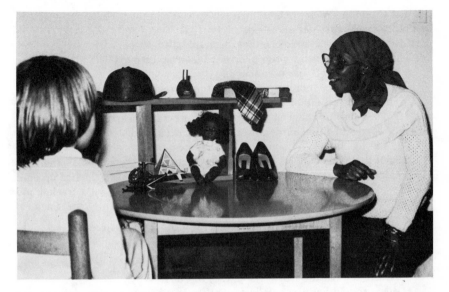

The Birthday Store activity promotes perspective taking by asking children to select gifts for their different family members.

Gertie ——— ? [Let children handle materials and act out their own consequences.]
SUGGESTED VARIATIONS: This activity can be expanded by adding additional problems, for example, a child who wants to play with Gloria and Gertie, one of the children wandering off and getting lost, or whatever seems appropriate given the age and real-life problems of the children in the classroom group.

6. *Children aged four and above can engage in a thinking-game skit on moral intentionality.* This activity[8] allows children to consider whether an evaluation of "naughtiness" should be based more on *subjective purposes* or *objective outcomes.* In the story, Billy has two kinds of good purposes (the motive of trying to help and the absence of any intention of breaking glasses), while Jack has two bad ones (the motive of disobeying and a purposeful intention of breaking a glass).

A Thinking Game on Moral Responsibility: "Billy and Jack Break Cups"

This activity involves two stories acted out back-to-back, followed by a discussion. Before the stories, it is a good idea to provide reassurance: "These stories are just pretend. We are acting them out so you can think about the problem, but no one will really get punished."

CHARACTERS: Billy and his father; Jack and his father.

MATERIALS: Tray, set of prebroken cups (styrofoam cups with chunks taken out, then replaced), jar of crackers.

ACTION: The teacher first narrates the story about Billy: "This is Billy. He was trying to help his father wash dishes. The father asked Billy to carry a trayful of clean cups into the dining room. Billy was carefully carrying the tray when he slipped and dropped the whole tray. Billy *accidentally* broke *fifteen* cups."

The teacher then continues: "The second story is about Jack. He was playing in the kitchen. He wanted to have another cracker but his father said no. Jack got angry, and when his father left the room, Jack climbed up onto the sink to get a cracker for himself. Jack climbed up and got a cracker and then he was still so mad that he knocked a cup onto the floor. Jack *on purpose* broke *one* cup."

DISCUSSION QUESTIONS
- Tell me what Billy, the first boy, did.
- Tell me what Jack, the second boy, did.
- Which boy did the worse thing, Billy or Jack? Why?
- What should happen to Billy next? Why?
- What should happen to Jack next? Why?

MORAL-DECISION TASK TWO:
DECIDING WHAT IS RIGHT AND WRONG

Many parents and teachers think that a child can know what is right and wrong simply by learning the rules of society. According to this point of view, adults know what is right and wrong, children do not. Adults must tell the rules to children, and then, once children have been instructed sufficiently clearly and often, they too will know the rules.

The problem with this point of view is that it is factually incorrect and pragmatically ineffective as a guide to teaching. Adults do "tell" children the rules and children do "listen," but children have their own ways of understanding and deciding what is right and wrong that are different from adults'.

Adults' most important role is to orient children to the moral aspects of social situations. Children constantly monitor the words and actions of the adults with whom they have a close relationship. Children attend closely to the vocabulary of these adults and to their emotions, and they incorporate the adults' meanings as best they can into their emerging frameworks of the world. The content of adults' moral language critically shapes children's moral sensitivities. Yet children cannot just drink in the adults' message; they must make sense of it themselves in their own ways. Teachers can best facilitate children's moral development if they understand the nature of children's moral knowledge and decision-making strategies. Teachers can use such understanding to work with children toward establishing a moral classroom—one in which the principles of truth and justice are respected and upheld by children at the highest level of which they are capable.

The difference between the adult and preschool approaches to moral decision making is illustrated by the following conversation. At first, Nathan's remarks impress us with their mature, almost adult consideration of the purpose of different rules. Only at the end of the conversation, as the child wearies of the task, does his own unique viewpoint emerge.

TEACHER: What is wrong with hitting at school?
NATHAN (age 4:4): It hurts the kids.
TEACHER: What is wrong with a boy wearing a dress to school?
NATHAN: Usually we see girls wearing dresses.
TEACHER: What is wrong with yelling at school?
NATHAN: It hurts people's ears.
TEACHER: What is wrong with not sharing the toys?
NATHAN: Other children get bored.
TEACHER: What is wrong with running around the cafeteria during lunchtime?
NATHAN: You're supposed to eat, not run around.
TEACHER: What is wrong with chewing with your mouth open?
NATHAN: Babies usually do that.
TEACHER: What is wrong with stealing people's things?
NATHAN: They don't belong to you, and the other people don't like it.
TEACHER: What is wrong with a big boy who only likes to play with babies?
NATHAN: There's nothing wrong, only if there's nobody that he likes.
TEACHER: What is wrong with messing up all of the laundry that your mother just folded?
NATHAN: The mother will have to fold them all again. Why don't you see if you can figure some of these out yourself?
TEACHER: Okay. But I have another kind of question. Do you think there are any mothers who let their children steal and hit other people?

NATHAN: Yes, there are.

TEACHER: What kind of mother would do that?

NATHAN: A nice one who wanted her child to do what he likes.

Children's strategies for moral decision making show characteristic features at each level of development. Lawrence Kohlberg's work lays the foundation for understanding this sequence.[9] Inspired by Piaget, Kohlberg and his colleagues have studied how people of all ages resolve moral dilemmas. They have pioneered an approach to moral education that has been widely used in many types of educational settings. Their focus is not on *what* choices people make but on *why* they make them. They have found that with age and experience, people's moral-judging strategies tend to become more *universalized* (applied to every relevant case, not just the one) and *reversible* (impartial, involving a perspective that is fair to every party in the situation). Moreover, they have established that people generally prefer, or rate as better, reasoning that is above rather than below their own general stage.

Kohlberg's six stages can be briefly summarized as follows:

- *Stage 1. Heteronomous Morality*: "Right" action consists of obedience to authority for its own sake, avoiding physical damage of people and property, and not breaking rules backed by punishment.
- *Stage 2. Concrete Exchange and Individualism*: "Right" action consists of acting fairly—but for concrete, pragmatic reasons. The goal is to serve one's own needs and interests in a world where one has to recognize that other people have their own needs and interests, too.
- *Stage 3. Mutual Interpersonal Expectations*: "Right" action involves good motives, maintaining long-term relationships, and living up to socially defined roles.
- *Stage 4. Social System and Conscience*: "Right" action involves fulfilling one's defined duties and contractual obligations and contributing to the good of the whole (institution, society, world) understood as a complex system.
- *Stages 5 and 6. Principled, Postconventional Understanding*: These stages involve a metaethical or philosophical perspective on virtue or justice, in which basic principles are consciously explored as a rational system. (Adapted from Kohlberg, 1984, pp. 174–76.)

Most adults in all societies use Stages 2, 3, and/or 4 predominantly; some adults who have had certain types of cultural and/or educational experiences employ "principled" judging strategies.

Building on Kohlberg's work, other psychologists have studied, elaborated upon, and used stage theory. William Damon (1975, 1977, 1980, 1983a, 1983b) has described in greater detail the reasoning processes of younger children, especially with respect to their concepts of authority and justice. Elliot Turiel has explained how American children divide rules into domains of justice/welfare "morality" versus other social regulations and "conventions." The work of both of these theorists has direct implications for early childhood educators. Their findings can help teachers understand children's actual thinking so they can talk at a level not too far removed from children's own.

Children's Understanding of Authority

Respect for authority is central to children's relationship to adults. At every age, children consider their moral relationship to elders to require respect and obedience. Piaget and Kohlberg have described how avoidance of negative consequences and unquestioning deference to adult authority form the basis for children's first understanding of right and wrong.

But why, then, does "behavior management" occupy so much time of parents and teachers? If young children are really so submissive to authority, why are they not more obedient and cooperative? Most parents and teachers find that young children often ignore or "forget" rules and are more anxious to do what *they* want rather than what adults want.

Damon has discovered the curious fact that preschool children cannot differentiate their own perspective on rules and commands from the adult perspective. He has outlined six authority levels for children aged four to twelve years. Damon's first two levels (characteristic of ages four and five) actually precede Kohlberg's and Piaget's first stages. These first two levels are helpful for explaining why preschool children's awe of adults does not translate into consistent obedience.

At Level 0-A, children think that the authority's desires are the same as their own. Because they feel that adults exist to fulfill their needs, they see adults as an extension of themselves. They tend either to mold their own wishes to fit with the authority's, or to transform the authority's commands into their own wishes. At level 0-B, children still see authority from their own perspective but now perceive it as being an obstacle obstructing the self's desire. (Level 0-A is illustrated by the answers of Nicholas, Danny, Daniella, Gregory, Sean, and Seth in the sample discussion on authority at the end of this chapter; Level 0-B is illustrated by the answers of Alexis, Jenna, and Kurt.)

The descriptions of preschool reasoning can be helpful to teachers in their daily work in the classroom. For instance, on one occasion a teacher was standing near a climber when she noticed Justin (age 4) starting to come down the ladder backwards—a dangerous action prohibited by a classroom rule. She moved closer to him. Justin looked at her, said, "Oh, yeah," and turned himself around to come down correctly. Later the teacher commented, "I used to think that children break rules mainly to be defiant. Now I realize how hard it is for them to think about rules when they are doing something else, like playing. When they are thinking about what *they* want to do, they sort of forget what *you* told them to do."

During the early school years, children usually move on to more mature authority concepts. They now differentiate their own perspective from the authority's and see authority as "out there." At Level 1-A, children consider that authorities have an inherent right to be obeyed because of their general power, superiority, and position. At Level 1-B, they think that they obey in return for the concrete help, care, and material goods that adults give them. Brian and Gregory, in the sample discussion, are closest to Level 1-A.

In later childhood, most children advance to Level 2-A and understand authority as a relationship in which one person (with greater training, knowledge, or experience) offers guidance or leadership to the other. Obedience is seen as voluntary. Ultimately, at Level 2-B, authority is seen as a social contract. Authorities govern "with the consent of the governed" and are legitimate only when they act within designated bounds.

Damon's research has shown that developmental progress in authority concepts is slow but steady throughout childhood. Most children show upward change of one level or less per year. Development is gradual, and children usually show a mixture of levels at any one time.

Children's Understanding of Justice

Authority and respect are at the moral heart of the adult/child relationship, but a different situation prevails in the world of peers.

Authority does not regulate relationships between children close in age. It does not encompass all that children know about right and wrong.

Rather, justice is a central issue in children's relationships. Children in the classroom, playground, and neighborhood encounter constant problems that require them to construct moral ideas about the fair use of resources so that they can coordinate and arbitrate disputes in play.

Both sharing and rightful possession are pivotal values involving justice in American society. In our capitalist economy, most productive resources, such as farms and factories, are privately owned, as are personal consumption goods such as clothes, homes, and cars. Yet at the same time, laws, customs, and institutional processes allow for some redistribution and sharing of resources. How are children in this society to learn when to "hold on" and when to "let go"? These are emotional and complex issues, and adults do not always transmit clear messages to children about possession rights versus obligations to share.

The following observation illustrates the difficulty for both adults and children in deciding who should "hold on" and who should "let go" when two people want the same object. Teachers must sometimes mediate and help children to solve problems involving issues of sharing versus rightful possession. But does this teacher intervene *justly*? He strongly enforces the value of sharing, yet is his solution fair from the point of view of the children involved? There is no simple answer, but the sadness of one child, Phil, suggests that perhaps his claims and feelings were not adequately considered. The main question for a teacher must always be, What can I do to help the children involved in this situation *learn and deepen their moral understanding*?

Five three-year-olds in a community day care center were seated at a round table with five toys placed on it. Ed saw Phil reaching for the train and tried to get it first. Ed said, "I want train. I want train." Phil said, "No—mine." Both boys tugged at it, each trying to wrench it from the other's grasp.

The teacher said, "Phil, you need to share. Ed asked for it nicely." The teacher took the train and handed it to Ed. Phil screamed, "Mine," and hit Ed. The teacher repeated his statement about sharing and removed Phil to a seat in the corner of the room. Phil began to cry and whimper, saying, "I want my mommy."

After a few minutes, the teacher allowed Phil to return. Ed, still playing with the train, looked up at Phil and said, clearly in a

pleased way, "My train!" Phil sat quietly at the table looking with a
sad expression at the train. He then picked up the cash register. Ed
repeated, "My train."

Teachers' goals in handling conflicts should not be simply to end
them as quickly as possible (Katz, 1984). Conflicts are both an inevita-
ble and a valuable part of children's experience. Children need practice in solving conflicts in order to develop concrete knowledge of
what fairness means to them.

In intervening, teachers should try to provide children with an
opportunity to express and work through their conflicting emotions
within a climate of support and encouragement. The following guidelines are important:

1. Support both children's initiative and self-determination.
2. Encourage the children to negotiate at the highest interpersonal
   level they are capable of. Try to expand upon their existing
   repertoire of strategies.
3. Help the children become aware of each other's feelings.
4. Point out the results of the children's actions upon each other.
5. Respect the children's own standards of what constitutes a fair
   or acceptable solution to the problem.

The last guideline is particularly important. Teachers should not
impose adult standards of morality on the children. They cannot
permit children to hurt one another, but they can accept outcomes that
are not strictly fair from the adult point of view.

Children's concepts of justice are different from adults' and develop dramatically with age and social experience. Damon has established that there are six levels of understanding "fairness in the distribution of resources." These levels parallel the levels of authority
concepts.

At the first two levels, characteristic of the preschool years, children focus on the perspective of only one person in the conflict. They
justify giving the resources to someone by saying, "He *wants* it," or
"He needs it," or "He's my friend." At the second two levels, characteristic of young school-aged children, strict equality enters children's
reasoning about justice. Because they now can simultaneously see
more than one person's perspective, they painfully experience the
problem of justice. At Level 1-A, they insist so rigidly on everyone's
getting equal shares that they may force someone to accept something
that he or she does not even want. Finally, at the third level, character-

istic of later childhood, children try to discern the true claims and needs of people in a conflict. In a concrete way, they try to balance "equality," "merit," and "need."

This theory can be useful to teachers. As one teacher put it, "I used to think that children should *always* share immediately with each other—that it should just be a *rule*—and if they didn't, they should be disciplined quickly. Now I allow all of the children involved to express how they think about the situation, and I encourage solutions to be developed by *them*."

Children's Understanding of Rule Domains

In order to master the knowledge of their culture and take their place in society, children must learn the rules. This is not an easy task, because there is a complicated and bewildering variety of rules (Much & Shweder, 1978). *Interpersonal* moral rules prohibit people from harming themselves and others or violating their rights: "Do not murder," "Do not steal," "Do not abandon the members of your family," "Do not have sex with your own child." These moral rules are considered to be sacred or universally right. *Conventional rules*, or *customs*, prescribe important behavioral uniformities: "Chew with your mouth closed," "Wear clothes in public," "Comb your hair and dress nicely when going to a party." These rules are considered to be based on group consensus and important to the quality of group life. *Regulations* ensure smooth, orderly, safe, and/or fair procedures by people as a collectivity: "Drive on the right side of the road," "Pay your taxes by April 16," "Be at school by 8:30 A.M. and place your jacket on the hook with your name on it." Regulations derive from governing figures or bodies who have authority to set them.

How can teachers best help children to develop knowledge of rules? Should they try to reduce the confusion by de-emphasizing the distinctions between types of rules? Or should they help clarify the distinctions for children?

Turiel, Nucci, and Smetana[10] have put forth the theory that children intuitively appreciate distinctions between rule domains from an early age. This theory, if true, is important because it suggests that young children do *not* see all rules as true and important simply because they come from authorities (as Piaget and Kohlberg had claimed). The evidence collected to test the theory suggests that from a young age, children are aware of some of the main ways in which rules vary.

First, adults and children agree that some rules in our culture are more important than others. For example, in many societies, people see violations such as stealing, physically harming others, and violating their rights as worse than violations of propriety. The hierarchy of moral values varies from society to society (Edwards, 1985b), but in every society adults communicate to children a sense of what rules are most important. Adults explain their justifications better, but both age groups share intuitive knowledge of the hierarchy of values.

A practical implication of this finding is that teachers should explain clearly to children why they do not treat all rule violations as equally serious. Obviously, throwing a rock at someone is a worse offence than throwing food on the floor. Teachers should support young children's developing understanding of the differential importance of rules.

Second, adults and children agree that some rules are more universally right than others, that is, right regardless of time, place, and circumstances. In general, Americans see rules concerning aggression and individual rights as universal and other conventions and regulations as relative. Young children cannot explain this distinction very clearly or rationally, but they display their intuitive knowledge in the different ways that they respond to transgressions.

> Paulo (age 6) got into a physical scuffle with several other boys at a public park. Paulo pushed one boy down, causing him to scrape his elbow. Paulo's mother came running and angrily scolded and spanked him as she took him away. Sam (age 4:6) observed this incident intently. His mother asked him, "Sam, do you think that there is a rule in this park about pushing?"
> Sam replied, "Yes, I do."
> His mother then asked, "If there wasn't a rule, then would it be all right to push?"
> "No," Sam said, "because you could still get hurt."

Nucci (1982) summarizes a series of studies in which children were asked to comment on transgressions that they witnessed in classrooms or playgrounds. When questioned about *harm* and *justice* transgressions, over 85 percent of preschool and school-aged children said that the act would *not* be right even if there were no school rule about it. In contrast, when questioned about other transgressions such as *school regulations*, over 80 percent of children in each grade said the act *would* be right.

Because children see some rules as more universal than others, they also see them as more unconditional. Children see rules prohibiting

harm to people as most unconditional. When accused, their best de-
fense is to try denial ("I did not do it") or extenuating circumstances
("He hit me first"). In contrast, children see many conventional rules as
conditional. They often try to negotiate exceptions to the rules: "If I
wear my boots outside, my feet will get hot," "It's not my bedtime
because I took a long nap," "I can't go out on the playground because I
have a sore throat" (Much & Shweder, 1978).

A practical implication of this finding is that teachers should expect
and welcome children's excuses and arguments about rules. They are
part of children's learning to think about the logic of rules and the
conditions associated with them.

Finally, adults and children agree about the social function of
different kinds of rules. Americans, who typically have a "rights-
centered" perspective on morality, believe that interpersonal rules are
needed to ensure justice, avoidance of harm, and liberty. In contrast,
they generally assume that other social conventions are needed to
maintain social order, harmony, and the quality of life.

The practical implication of this finding is that teachers should not
treat all rules as being the same. Instead of instructing children to
follow a rule simply because "at this school, the rule is x," teachers
should offer different reasons for following different rules. As Stengel
(1982) puts it, "Ground rules must be based on good reasons that are
aimed at optimal learning and development for all children and that
take into account the interests of teachers and parents" (pp. 26–27).
Here are some examples of "good reasons" that distinguish between
the purposes behind different rules.

- "You must wear a smock to paint, to keep your clothes clean."
- "You need to put away materials after using them so that the play
  area doesn't get all jumbled."
- "Hitting hurts. I can't allow you to hurt someone else."
- "Calling people bad names is wrong because it makes them feel
  sad."

Teachers' goals in moral development must go beyond teaching
children to respect rules. Teachers should also enhance children's
intellectual and moral autonomy by letting them participate as far as
possible in the process of establishing classroom rules and procedures.
They should encourage children to both take responsibility for their
own actions and help their peers do so also. They should allow children the freedom to make mistakes and learn for themselves why it is
important to follow specific rules. They should support children in

resolving conflicts and expressing their ideas and feelings within a classroom atmosphere of acceptance and respect for all.

Classroom Activities to Promote Moral Judging

Moral discussions are an important way in which teachers can help children to develop an awareness of moral issues. Spontaneous discussions give the best opportunity to heighten children's awareness of the values pervading interpersonal interaction and social life. When teachers make comments such as, "John thinks it is unfair that he can't play, too," they label a situation as one with a moral dimension without getting into a long lecture that only annoys children. They also thereby model ways for children to state their own moral concerns and listen to other people's.

Structured classroom discussions of moral dilemmas provide another way to heighten children's awareness and stimulate their reasoning. The content of the discussions may be about either actual or hypothetical cases. Whether real or hypothetical, the problems presented to children should be *genuine* moral conflicts—ones in which the issues seem significant and in which there is no one right or wrong answer. A genuine moral conflict has "right" on both sides, and that is why it makes people sit up and think. Where the conflict is genuine, the teacher's goal can honestly be to encourage each child to express a position and explain why he or she has taken it. Young children cannot express complex positions, but they can begin to feel they have ideas and that moral positions require thought and justification.

As teachers become more practiced in leading moral discussions, they will feel more comfortable in encouraging children without trying to draw out certain ideas or evaluating some ideas as better or right. During the discussion, children will get the chance to hear answers that vary in their level of maturity. Because children themselves naturally prefer more adequate reasons to less adequate ones, teachers actually promote development most effectively by *not* evaluating children's answers and by instead reinforcing the critical stance that is the beginning of moral autonomy.

Moral discussions can be fascinating learning experiences for teachers, too. They provide an exciting way to learn about children's thinking and develop good questioning strategies. Moral discussions can spark personal as well as professional growth in teachers because they provoke everyone involved to think about the fundamental values involved.

Most teachers will want to develop their own moral problem-situations appropriate to the developmental level and daily experiences of their group. The following five thinking games provide models of problems that have been found to interest young children. Following this section, the transcript of a tape-recorded moral discussion is provided to illustrate the method in practice.

1. *Children aged four and above can engage in a thinking-game skit on fair distribution in sharing* (adapted from Damon, 1977). The problem encourages children to consider and balance the claims of different parties to a justice dispute. The underlying issues are equality, merit, and need.

A Thinking Game on Justice: "Dividing the Cookies"

CHARACTERS: Mother and two children.
MATERIALS: About 20 round objects (such as poker chips) to represent cookies.
ACTION: The narrator explains that a mother and her children are busy decorating cookies for a party that night. The mother says, "Children, the party is tonight. We have to get all these cookies ready. Please decorate as many as you can, because we will need a lot for our friends." After working for a while, the first child says, "Look mother, I decorated 10. Count them— one, two, three, four, five, six, seven, eight, nine, ten." The second child says, "I only decorated one, but it broke." Then, the mother stands up to leave, saying, "Well, thank you, children, for your help. As a reward you may have these five cookies—one, two, three, four, five. I will take the rest to the party. Now you children split up these five cookies and decide who should get them."

The first child says, "I should get the most because I decorated most cookies. I worked hardest."

The second child says, "I should get the most because I want them. I'm little and I need them."
DISCUSSION QUESTIONS
• Who should get the cookies? How should they be divided up?
• What is the fairest way to divide the cookies? Why?
• What should happen to the extra cookies?

2. *Children aged five and above can engage in a thinking-game skit on possession rights.* The problem encourages children to consider the weight of different claims to use a valued object.

A Thinking Game on Possession Rights: "Nina and Her Skipper Doll"

CHARACTERS: Three girls at a birthday party.
MATERIALS: Two dolls (we use a Skipper and a Snoopy).
ACTION: The narrator explains, "This is a birthday party. The children are

watching as Nina opens her presents." Nina opens one box and exclaims, "Oh, a Skipper doll! I love it." A second girl reaches for it, saying, "Nina, please let me hold it. You should let me use it first because you are going to have this Skipper all the time, and I'll be going home." A third girl says, "You should let me take a turn because I let you use my new Snoopy last week." Nina looks dejected and says, "Oh, maybe you all are right. But it's my new Skipper doll, so I should be able to do whatever I want with it."

DISCUSSION QUESTIONS
- Who should get the Skipper doll, and why?
- What is the fairest thing to do with it?
- Nina *owns* the doll. Does that mean she can always have it? Why (or why not)?
- To be a good friend, should Nina share her new Skipper doll? Why (or why not)? What about her other toys? Is there any difference?
- Why should kids take turns, anyway? What will happen to them if they don't?
- One of Nina's friends wanted to use the Skipper doll because she would be going home soon. Another friend wanted to use it because Nina had used her new Snoopy last week. Which friend should Nina share her Skipper with first? Why?

3. *Children aged three and above can engage in a thinking-game skit concerning valid exceptions to conventional rules.* This problem encourages children to reason about conditions under which a rule might not apply.

A Thinking Game on Conventional Rules: "No Running"

CHARACTERS: Mother, daughter, and daughter's friend.
MATERIALS: None.
ACTION: The daughter is running inside the house and falls down. Her mother tells her, "Kelly, I want you to remember. The rule in this house is, No running. Do you promise you won't run?" Kelly agrees, and her mother leaves. Soon Kelly's friend arrives, and they begin to play. A few moments later, the friend seems to cut her hand. She cries out, "Ouch, ouch, I'm bleeding! I cut my hand! Kelly, run. Hurry, run and get your mother."

DISCUSSION QUESTIONS
- What should Kelly do? Her mother told her not to run in the house, but her friend says to run and get help.
- Is it ever all right to disobey your mother? Why (or why not)?

4. *Children aged four and above can engage in a thinking-game skit on rule domains.* This problem focuses on the universality (versus situation-dependency) of different rules.

Children watch attentively as teachers act out a problem situation about "the Yellow Blanket School, where there are no rules and children can do anything they want."

A Thinking Game on the Universality of Rules:
"The Yellow Blanket School"

CHARACTERS: Two children and a teacher.

MATERIALS: A large yellow blanket and some toys.

ACTION: The narrator says, "This is the Yellow Blanket School. It is different from other schools. In the Yellow Blanket School, there are no rules. Children can do anything they want." After a pause to let that idea sink in, the two children begin to play with the toys. They play, then the teacher comes over and begins to pick up the toys and put them away. One child says, "I'll help you." The teacher says, "Okay, thanks." The teacher immediately leaves, and the first child continues to pick up toys. He says to the second one (who just plays), "You come help pick up, too." The second child says, "No, I can go on playing. In this school there are no rules."

DISCUSSION QUESTION: What do you think? Can he go on playing, or does he have to pick up? Why?

ACTION (continued): The two children resume playing together. Soon they get into a scuffle over a toy. One hits the other hard. The victim cries and says, "You are bad. It's wrong to hit." The aggressor says, "I'm not bad. In this school there are no rules, so I can do anything I want."

DISCUSSION QUESTION: What do you think? Is he wrong (or bad) to hit in this school? Why (or why not)?

5. *Children aged four and above can engage in a thinking-game skit on authority* (adapted from Damon, 1977). The objective is to encourage children to consider why one should obey (what is the rationale for obedience) and what gives an authority figure the right to command (what is the legitimate basis of authority).

A Thinking Game on Obedience to Authority: "The Circus Parade"

CHARACTERS: Mother, daughter, and daughter's friend.
MATERIALS: Miscellaneous toys, clothes (scattered about the floor).
ACTION: A mother tells her daughter, Anna, that she must clean up her messy room before she can go outside to play. The toys must be put away, the dirty clothes put in the laundry hamper, and so on. Anna agrees and sets to work. Just then, however, her friend comes rushing in, shouting, "Anna, Anna, come outside! There is a parade near your house, with an elephant, a woman dressed up and riding a horse, and clowns doing tricks. You have to come right now! The parade will be gone in just a minute." Anna asks her mother if she can go, but her mother says firmly, "No, Anna, you must clean up your room before you can go anywhere, even if you miss the parade."
DISCUSSION QUESTIONS
- What should Anna do? Why?
- Is it fair of the mother to make Anna clean up first?
- Would it be all right for Anna to sneak out? Why (or why not)?
- What should the mother do to Anna if she catches her sneaking out? Why?
- What is it about mothers that gives them the right to tell children to clean up?

A SAMPLE MORAL DISCUSSION: "THE CIRCUS PARADE"

This observation illustrates how to conduct moral dilemma discussions with young children. The discussion was recorded in a preschool classroom in Amherst, Massachusetts, and took place toward the end of the school year, when children were well accustomed to thinking games. The discussion leader, Mitchell Worth, was an undergraduate student teacher. His questioning strategies are labeled in brackets.

TEACHER: What do you think the girl should do? Should she put her toys away the way her mother said? Or should she run outside to see the circus parade? [*Lead-off question*]
GREGORY (age 3:10): Put her toys away.

TEACHER: Why, Greg? [*Why question*]

GREGORY: [No answer]

BECKY (age 4:9): Put her toys away.

JESSE (age 4:6): Yeah.

NICHOLAS (age 4:4): How about if she plays with them in her room because that's all right. That's still all right.

DANNY (age 4:8): I think she should clean up *fast*.

DANIELLA (age 4:10): Or look out the window.

TEACHER: She'll miss the parade if she cleans up her toys right now. Should she miss the parade, do you think? [*Refocuses on conflict*]

SEAN (age 4:5), BECKY, JESSE: No.

TEACHER: Do you think it was *fair* that her mother told her that she had to put her toys away? [*Issue probe*]

GREGORY: Yes.

TEACHER: Why, Greg? [*Why question*]

GREGORY: And they have to be quiet.

KURT (age 4:3): No.

TEACHER: How come, Kurt? [*Why question*]

KURT: She should go without cleaning up.

TEACHER: She should go outside without cleaning up? [*Encourages communication; seeks to understand his perspective*]

SEAN: That's what I do.

TEACHER: You go outside and don't clean up? [*Follows up on personal example*]

SEAN: I don't have any jobs in my house.

TEACHER: You don't have any jobs? [*Encourages communication*]

SEAN: I do, but I keep forgetting.

TEACHER: Oh, you always forget. [*Encourages communication*]

SEAN: I always push them in the corners.

TEACHER: You push toys in the corner? Do you think that it is *good* to do that? [*Issue probe*]

SEAN: Yeah, my father lets me go out and so does my mother.

TEACHER: But what if your father said that you have to pick up all your toys, Sean, and put them in the right places before you went? [*Refocuses on moral dilemma*]

SEAN: They would never say that.

TEACHER: Brian, do you think it was *fair* that the mother said the girl couldn't go outside until she picked up her toys? [*Refocuses on issue probe*]

BRIAN (age 5:4): Yes, I think that would be.

TEACHER: Why, Brian? [*Why question*]

BRIAN: Because if her mother finds out, she'll tell her to come back in.

SETH (age 4:4): Looking out the window is a pretty good thing.

ALEXIS (age 4:10): No, it's not fair.

TEACHER: Why, Alexis? [*Why question*]

ALEXIS: Because then her mother would be nasty.

TEACHER: Do you think that the girl should *sneak outside*? Would that be okay for her to do? [*Issue probe*]

GREGORY: I'd kick those blocks.

TEACHER: You would kick those blocks. Would you sneak outside and not put your toys away like your mother told you? [*Encourages communication; tries to understand his perspective*]

GREGORY: I will put my toys away. Mommy said I can put my toys away. Her doesn't do it. I do it myself.

JENNA (age 4:9): I think, sneak out.

TEACHER: Jenna, you think she should sneak out? Do you think she should get *punished* if she sneaks out? [*Issue probe*]

JENNA: Sneak out the back door.

TEACHER: You think she should sneak out the back door. Do you think her mother should get *angry*? [*Refocuses*]

SETH: No, because she wouldn't find her in the back. There's no window in the back.

TEACHER: Kurt, do you have an answer? [*Encourages communication*]

KURT: Jump out the window.

TEACHER: Jump out the window? What if her mother caught her? [*Refocuses on issue probe*]

KURT: Punch her.

TEACHER: Punch her? Who should punch? [*Seeks to understand his perspective*]

KURT: The girl should punch.

TEACHER: Do you think it would be *good* to do that? [*Issue probe*]

KURT: She can jump out the window again.

TEACHER: What is it about mothers that gives them *the right* to tell their children what to do? [*Issue probe*]

CHILDREN: [No answers]

TEACHER: Well, that's the end of the skit. Some of you thought that the girl should clean up her toys and miss the parade, because that's what her mother told her to do. Others of you thought that she should run outside, or sneak outside, even though her mother told her to clean up first. Thank you for sharing your ideas today! [*Summarizes*]

SUGGESTED BOOKS FOR CHILDREN

Books to Help Children Take the Perspective of Others "Different" from Themselves

Fassler, Joan. *Howie Helps Himself.* Chicago: Albert Whitman, 1975. Howie has cerebral palsy. This book presents information about Howie and portrays his unusual determination and his father's pride.

Kraus, Robert. *Leo the Late Bloomer.* New York: Windmill, 1971. Leo the Lion's delays in walking, talking, reading, and writing are positively reframed as "late blooming," that is, a matter of different timing of development.

Larsen, Hanne. *Don't Forget Tom.* New York: Crowell, 1978. The text and photographs present an exceptionally clear and tactful discussion of Tom's intellectual disability.

Simon, Norma. *Am I Different?* Chicago: Albert Whitman, 1976. This book is about differences of all kinds. Though handicaps are not mentioned, the book serves as an excellent basis for discussion.

Stefanik, Alfred T. *Copycat Sam: Developing Ties with a Special Child.* New York: Human Sciences, 1982. Freddie comes to understand and appreciate Sam, his new neighbor with Down's syndrome.

Wolf, Bernard. *Anna's Silent World.* Philadelphia: Lippincott, 1977. The protagonists of this book are young children and the photographs are superb. The text should be simplified for young listeners. (Also see Wolf's other books, *Don't Feel Sorry for Paul* and *Connie's New Eyes.*)

Books Promoting Perspective Taking and Causal Thinking

Alcona, George. *I Feel: A Picture Book of Emotions.* New York: Dutton, 1977. This book contains vivid photographs illustrating 14 simple emotions.

Berger, Terry. *I Have Feelings.* New York: Human Sciences, 1971. Photographs and text illustrate, for older children, complex emotions such as pride, disappointment, shyness, shame, jealousy, and others.

Brandenberg, Franz. *It's Not My Fault.* New York: Greenwillow, 1980. Typical sibling bickering and conflicts are worked through by the fieldmouse children. Skills of playing, working, and eating together in a large group are illustrated.

Crary, Elizabeth. *A Children's Problem Solving Book: I Want It.* Seattle: Parenting Press, 1982. This book and others in the series (*I'm Lost, I Can't Wait, I Want to Play, My Name Is Not Dummy*) are excellent for helping young children develop the cognitive skills of generating alternative solutions and considering likely consequences of actions.

Hefter, Richard. *Turtle Throws a Tantrum.* New York: Harper & Row, 1978. This book is part of a series in which animal characters get into difficulty because of troublesome habits or personality traits. In this book, Temper Tantrum Turtle finally experiences temper outbursts from the receiving end.

Kroll, Steven. *The Candy Witch*. New York: Scholastic, 1979.   Maggie is a small witch who switches to negative deeds in order to get attention, but they make people unhappy, a consequence Maggie does not want. A good book for focusing upon social cause-and-effect sequences.

Low, Joseph. *Don't Drag Your Feet. . . .* New York: Atheneum, 1983.   Peggy is domineering and inconsiderate to her dolls until, through a dream in which she and her dolls reverse roles, Peggy discovers how it feels to be treated that way.

Panek, Dennis. *Matilda Hippo Has a Big Mouth*. Scarsdale, N.Y.: Bradbury, 1980.   Matilda makes unkind remarks to others until she constructs the idea that her behavior has undesired consequences.

Preston, Edna Mitchell. *The Temper Tantrum Book*. New York: Penguin (Puffin), 1974.   This amusing book allows younger children to label and describe the emotions of others and to think about cause and effect (how parental actions cause anger or frustration).

Books Focused on Moral Issues

Books provide an important means of discussing moral issues with children. The following list contains only a few of the many books that address moral issues and/or the purpose of different rules for social living. In using these books, the reader may wish to consult several references that discuss how to use children's literature for moral education, including Krogh and Lamme (1985), Fassler and Janis (1983), and Rudman (1984).

Albert, Burton, Jr. *Mine, Yours, Ours*. Chicago: Albert Whitman, 1977. Pictures and brief text illustrate, for younger children, concepts of mine, yours, ours, ownership, sharing.

Chorao, Kay. *Molly's Lies*. New York: Seabury, 1979.   This book is intended to help young children understand why someone might invent false stories and what kinds of unintended consequences may follow lying.

Hogrogrian, Nonny. *One Fine Day*. New York: Collier, 1971.   A fox loses his tail and tries to get other animals to share materials and skills. Most want something in return. Good for asking, "Is sharing giving, or can it be trading?"

Keats, Ezra J. *Peter's Chair*. New York: Harper & Row, 1967.   A brother is reluctant to share his outgrown things with his baby sister but eventually changes his feelings.

Scarry, Richard. *Richard Scarry's Please and Thank You Book*. New York: Random House, 1973.   Moral and conventional rules are illustrated in a somewhat oversimplified way, but also with humor and explanations of the purposes of the rules.

Suess, Dr. *The Lorax.* New York: Random House, 1971.   Many of Suess's books address important moral themes (*The Grinch*, the control of greed; *The Lorax*, respect for the environment; *The Sneetches*, pointlessness of intergroup prejudice; *Horton Hatches the Egg*, keeping a promise; *Horton Hears a Who*, individual worth; *The Butter Battle Book*, how aggression escalates toward mutual destruction). Children of all ages enjoy the rhymes and stories and gradually over time develop deeper understandings of the moral content.

Supraner, Robyn. *It's Not Fair!* New York: Frederick Warne: 1976.   The young school-aged child typically conceptualizes justice in terms of exact, concrete equality. The girl in this story cannot understand why she and her baby brother are treated differently.

Wells, Rosemary. *Morris's Disappearing Bag.* New York: Dial, 1975.   This book illustrates sharing as concrete exchange: Morris's older siblings don't want to share what is theirs until they find that he has something of his own to share.

Appendix
Notes
References
About the Authors
Index

Appendix

SUMMARY OF DEVELOPMENTAL CHANGES IN SOCIAL KNOWLEDGE DURING THE EARLY CHILDHOOD YEARS

	Early Preschool Level[1] 2–3 Years Old[2]	Later Preschool Level[1] 4–5 Years Old[2]	Early School Level[1] 6–8 Years Old[2]
GAINING AGE, GENDER, AND RACIAL AWARENESS			
Child's Concerns	What am I? What are you? What do different categories of people do? [behavioral roles]	What will I (and you) become? What am I not? What do different categories of people want or like to do?	What defines one's identity? What changes, what stays the same? What should different categories of people do (as role members)?
New Skills	Identifying self & others. Associating concrete behaviors or features of appearance with each category.	Relating 2 categories as opposites. Attaching personal preference to some aspects of one's roles.	Understanding defining attributes. Understanding what attributes change. Understanding roles as systems that are objective and prescriptive.
Examples	"I am a girl." "Girls wear dresses."	"Girls grow up to be women." "Girls wear dresses—boys don't."	"I will always be a girl because of my girl's body." "I should play with girls because I'm a girl."

Child's Concerns	What are you called? (mother/father/brother/sister/etc.)	Are you my relative? (mother/father/brother/sister/etc.)	What defines why we are relatives; what is the connection?
New Skills	Using kinship terms as category labels, e.g., boys as brothers, women as mothers, etc.	Using kinship terms in an early relational way, to define bonds of closeness between people.	Using kinship terms in a later relational way, to describe people connected by descent & marriage.
Examples	"A daddy is a man." "A family is me and my mom."	"A daddy takes care of you." "A family is who lives together."	"A daddy is a man with children." "Your family is your relatives."

UNDERSTANDING FRIENDSHIP BONDS

Child's Concerns	Whom can I call 'friend'?	Are you my friend right now?	What should friends do for each other?
New Skills	Using friend term to label playmates or others liked right now.	Using friend term to facilitate bonding & access to play.	Understanding friendship as a relationship of concrete reciprocity.
Examples	"I don't like you! You're not my friend!"	"Will you be my friend and play with me?"	"I have to help you because you're my best friend."

1. The early preschool level corresponds to Kurt Fischer's Skill Level 4 (the child cognitively controls one symbolic representation at a time), for example, using the word 'boy' to label a peer. The later preschool level corresponds to Skill Level 5 (the child cognitively coordinates two representations), for example, thinking about how someone must be either a boy or girl. The early school level corresponds to Skill Level 6 (the child controls and coordinates many symbolic representations simultaneously), for example, constructing a system relating the male/female dimension of bodily differences to masculine/feminine differences in clothing, toys, adult jobs, and so forth. Fischer's Skill Level 6 is equivalent to the beginning of Piaget's concrete operational stage.

2. These ages are not exact and would not be expected to be the same for all children. Children vary in the rate at which they develop. Moreover, children are typically not even in their development; they progress more rapidly in some content areas than in others.

(Appendix continued next page)

	Early Preschool Level[1] 2–3 Years Old[2]	Later Preschool Level[1] 4–5 Years Old[2]	Early School Level[1] 6–8 Years Old[2]
Child's Concerns	What is that job called? What do they do in that job? What is each kind of money called? What happens in each store?	[With reciprocal roles such as buyer/seller and teacher/student] What does each person do in the relationship or transaction?	What are the skills for each job? How do you get a certain job? How much do different things cost? Where do the store's goods come from?
New Skills	Recognizing adult jobs & behaviors associated with each. Recognizing coins and bills as money.	Recognizing the complementary nature of societal roles. Realizing money is for exchange.	Understanding how jobs require skill & fulfill needed functions. Understanding price and value.
Examples	"Food comes from the store." "Clerks use cash registers." "That paper is called a dollar."	"We give money to the clerks, then they give us the things we need to take home."	"Storeowners buy things from farms & factories." "Goods have a price; if you pay too much, you get the right amount of change back."

	Early Preschool Level[1] 2–3 Years Old[2]	Later Preschool Level[1] 4–5 Years Old[2]	Early School Level[1] 6–8 Years Old[2]
Child's Concerns	What do the adults I care about say to do?	What do I want to do? What do adults want me to do? [These questions beginning to be distinguished.]	What should I do in order to be good & earn praise from people I respect and admire?

	Young preschool	Later preschool	Early school
New Skills	Developing regard for beloved authorities & their commands.	Attaching personal desire to act of obedience. Beginning to see authority's desires as different from self's.	Developing true respect for authority, knowing authority & self may have different desires. Knowing adults too are bound by moral rules.
Examples	"I do what my teacher says; I stay inside the fence."	"I stay inside the fence. My teacher wants me to, & I don't want to get hurt by a car."	"Children must stay inside the fence. Their teachers who know all about it say it's not safe in the street."

MAKING DECISIONS ABOUT RIGHT AND WRONG: VALUING JUSTICE AS FAIRNESS[3]

	Young preschool	Later preschool	Early school
Child's Concerns	Is it my turn? How much is my portion?	Whose turn is it? How much is everyone's portion?	Has everyone had equal turns? Does everyone have equal portions?
New Skills	Using justice words to talk about people doing or using things together.	Recognizing that fairness involves settling conflicts in a good way. Knowing that reasons should be given for a division of shares.	Conceptualizing justice as strict equality of turns or portions and insisting on a fair solution in a conflict.
Examples	"You share now and give me some of your toys."	"It's fair for me to get that now." [Why?] "Because I'm biggest."	"We have to get the same amount or it won't be fair!"

3. The material on understanding right and wrong is based on William Damon's levels, discussed in Chapter 8. The young preschool level corresponds to Damon's Level 0-A, the later preschool level to Level 0-B, and the early school level to Level 1-A.

Notes

CHAPTER 1

1. Brazelton (1981); Brazelton et al. (1979). For more information about young children's social networks, see Bronfenbrenner (1979), Lewis & Feiring (1979), and Whiting & Whiting (1975).

2. Throughout this book, we will use the term "teacher" to refer to any early childhood professional, whether that person works in a setting called a preschool, nursery school, day care center, or kindergarten.

3. This definition of social cognition derives from James Youniss (1975). Comprehensive research reviews may be found in Damon (1977, 1983a, 1983b) and Shantz (1975, 1983).

4. Many books presenting Piagetian approaches to early education are listed in the references section and include the following fine works: Copple, Sigel, & Saunders (1979); Forman & Hill (1980); Forman & Kuschner (1977); Hohmann, Banet, & Weikart (1979); Kamii (1985); Kamii & DeVries (1978); Saunders & Bingham-Newman (1984); Sigel & Cocking (1977).

5. See the helpful discussion in Gallagher & Reid (1981). We have based our discussion of empirical and reflexive abstraction on theirs but have elaborated and reinterpreted their distinctions to incorporate the special case of social knowledge, which they do not discuss. Piaget himself used the term "social knowledge" in a different way than does this book. We believe that our use is more in accord with current social-cognitive theory and research. Piaget (1983) considered "physical knowledge" to be a different source of knowledge than social knowledge. He defined physical knowledge as that which comes directly from observation and action on objects. He defined social knowledge as arbitrary cultural information, knowledge of labels, rules, and practices that must be taught. The difficulty with Piaget's usage is that it sets up what many psychologists would regard as a false dichotomy. The construction of all knowledge, no matter what its subject matter, involves "guided reinvention," that is, the mediation of culture. Thus, the construction of knowledge about both the physical and the social worlds involves identical, parallel cognitive processes. Cultural values and information influence both in the same way.

6. For full discussion of representational competence, see the works of Irving Sigel and colleagues (Sigel, 1970; Copple, Sigel, & Saunders, 1979; Sigel & Cocking, 1977a, 1977b; Sigel & Saunders, 1979). These works lay out a theory of the relationship of representational competence to the social envi-

ronment, including parental, familial, and cultural factors. Adult strategies that require the child to separate self from the ongoing present and to create representations of objects, events, and people are called distancing behaviors. Distancing behaviors are used as part of an educational strategy called guided inquiry.

CHAPTER 2

1. Reimer, Paolitto, and Hersh's (1983) book, *Promoting Moral Growth: From Piaget to Kohlberg*, presents a valuable model of moral education, including the art of leading moral discussions. Although the book is primarily focused on teaching elementary and secondary students, the basic principles are equally applicable to working with young children—with suitable adaptations. Our discussion of initial and follow-up questioning strategies draws heavily from this model, and their book is recommended to those who wish to study moral education in depth.

CHAPTER 3

1. Unless otherwise noted, the quotations presented throughout this book are drawn verbatim from a corpus of observational records collected by the authors and their student colleagues in preschools, day care centers, kindergarten classes, and homes in the western Massachusetts area. If the child's birthdate is known, his or her age is presented in years and months (e.g., "age 4:3"). Otherwise the age is presented in years only (e.g., "age 4"). Sometimes the names of children were changed. The quotations are intended to illustrate points in the theoretical description and to remind readers of their own personal experiences. In all cases, the quotes were selected because they were believed to be typical of children's thinking at that age, though of course future research may show otherwise. We hope that readers will let us know where we may have made serious or minor errors in our characterizations of children's thinking.

2. Research findings on children's ability to rank people as younger and older and to assess chronological age are presented in Britton & Britton (1969); Clark (1972); Kogan, Stephens, & Shelton (1961); Kratochwill & Goldman (1973); Kuczaj & Lederberg (1977); Looft (1971); Looft, Rayman, & Rayman (1972); Piaget (1924/1976); Stevenson, Miller, & Hale (1967).

3. Research findings on boys' and girls' nurturance toward infants are presented in Berman, Monda, & Myerscough (1977); Edwards & Whiting (1980); Weisner & Gallimore (1977); Whiting & Edwards (1973); Whiting & Whiting (1975).

4. Research on children's conceptions of age roles is found in Edwards &

Lewis (1979); Emmerich (1959, 1961); Fischer et al. (1984); French (1984); Phenice (1981); Tucker (1979); Watson & Amgott-Kwan (1983).

5. Descriptions of children's responsible work and sibling caretaking may be found in Edwards (1985b); Edwards & Whiting (1980); Munroe & Munroe (1975); Weisner & Gallimore (1977); Werner (1984); Whiting & Whiting (1975); Williams (1983).

6. *Beginnings*, a magazine for early childhood educators, devoted its Spring 1985 issue to "multiage caregiving." This issue (volume 2, number 1) suggests many ways of promoting caring relations between people of different ages and generations.

CHAPTER 4

1. Research validating the sequence of steps in the development of gender identity includes: Emmerich et al. (1977); Gouze & Nadelman (1980); Kohlberg (1966); Marcus & Overton (1978); McConaghy (1979); Thompson (1975); Wehren & DeLisi (1983). Cross-cultural research exploring the sequence in children from Belize, Kenya, Nepal, and American Somoa is described in Munroe, Shimmin, & Munroe (1984).

2. See Albert (1983); Ashton (1983); Best et al. (1977); Bradbard & Endsley (1983); Carlson (1984); Davidson, Yasuna, & Tower (1979); Flerx, Fidler, & Rogers (1976); Hyde (1984); Koblinsky & Sugawara (1979); Ruble, Balaban, & Cooper (1981); Ullian (1976); Weinraub et al. (1984).

3. Elliot Turiel (1983) has proposed a theory of the development of knowledge about conventional rules. Carter & Patterson (1982) and Damon (1977) have applied and tested the theory with respect to sex-role concepts.

4. Good practical discussions of strategies to use in the classroom include: Eaton (1983); Guttentag & Bray (1976); Sprung (1975); Ullian (1984).

CHAPTER 5

1. Numerous studies have been done in this area. Good descriptions of some of this work can be found in Goodman (1952), Katz (1976, 1982, 1983), and Porter (1971).

2. See Katz (1976, 1983). Derman-Sparks, Higa, and Sparks (1980) describe how children's ideas about race develop, as evidenced by the kinds of questions they ask parents and teachers and by the kinds of spontaneous remarks they make about racial differences.

3. One classic review is by Proshansky (1966). Many studies on this topic have also been done by Asher and his colleagues (Asher, Oden, & Gottman, 1977; Asher, Singleton, & Taylor, 1982; Singleton & Asher, 1979).

CHAPTER 6

1. Family life in cross-cultural perspective is surveyed and discussed in Munroe & Munroe (1975); Stephens (1963); Werner (1984); Williams (1983); Whiting & Whiting (1975).

2. David Schneider (1968), anthropologist, has written the classic description of American kinship. Schneider & Smith (1973) discuss social class and ethnic variations in family and kinship emphases.

3. Research findings on the development of kinship concepts by children living in Australian, German, Mexican, Hawaiian, and Nigerian communities are found in Danziger (1957); Deutsch (1979); Greenfield & Childs (1977); LeVine & Price-Williams (1974); Price-Williams et al. (1977).

4. The following discussion on the development of kinship definitions is based on Chambers & Tavuchis (1976); Danziger (1957); Edwards (1984); Elkind (1962); Haviland & Clark (1974); Jordan (1980); Piaget (1946/1971). The theory of cognitive development comes from Fischer et al. (1984). A good related discussion of developmental changes in children's concepts of how people get babies may be found in Bernstein & Cowan (1975).

5. Research findings on the development of an understanding of adoption (what it is, why someone might adopt a baby, why someone might give up a baby for adoption, etc.) are presented in Brodzinsky, Singer, & Braff (1984).

6. Young children's responses to parental separation and divorce are discussed in Kurdek (1983). Samuels (1977) and Skeen & McHenry (1980) discuss how teachers can help young children to cope with the crisis. Children's understanding of death, an issue related to separation by divorce, is discussed in White, Elsom, & Prawat (1978).

7. I wish to thank Mary Ellin Logue for permission to publish these interview excerpts and also for her help in developing an understanding of children's concepts of friendship and family, especially divorce. Logue's divorce interview was used as part of a formal research study. We would not recommend it for regular classroom use because it might stir up powerful emotions in children whose parents are separated or divorced.

8. The following discussion of the development of friendship concepts is based on Corsaro (1979); Damon (1977); Rubin (1980); Selman (1980); Youniss (1980, 1983).

CHAPTER 7

1. Furth (1980), Furth, Baur, & Smith (1976), and Pickert & Furth (1980) are basic sources for a theoretical and empirical description of societal understanding in children. Many other researchers, noted below, have contributed to the field. Research studies have been conducted in several countries besides the United States—England, Scotland, Italy, Australia, Switzerland.

2. Children's development of concepts of money has been studied by Berti & Bombi (1981b); Furth (1980); Strauss (1952).

3. Children's development of concepts of the chain of transactions has been studied by Berti & Bombi (1981a); Danziger (1957); Furth (1980); Furth, Baur, & Smith (1976); Jahoda (1979).

4. Children's development of concepts of ownership and management of economic resources has been studied by Berti (1981); Berti, Bombi, & Lis (1982); Danziger (1958); Piaget (1924/1976).

5. Children's development of concepts of rich and poor and of social inequality has been studied by Danziger (1958); Leahy (1981, 1983a, 1983b); Luce (1981); Naimark & Shaver (1982).

6. Children's development of occupational concepts (and role concepts) is explored in works by Fischer et al. (1984); Furth (1980); Furth, Baur, & Smith (1976); and Jordan (1980).

CHAPTER 8

1. See Kagan's (1984) and Whiting, Chasdi, Antonovsky, and Ayres's (1966) reflections on the acquisition of standards during childhood. Also relevant is Wong's (1984) philosophical analysis of cultural differences in ethical systems: "A virtue-centered morality gives a central place to the concept of a good common to all members of a community. . . . The virtues are identified as the qualities necessary for the performance of one's roles and thus for successful contribution to the common good. A rights-centered morality does not give a central place to the common good and a shared life. Rather, it emphasizes the notion of what each member of the community is entitled to claim from other members. . . . Ancient Greek morality is virtue-centered and constitutes a morality of that type. . . . The moralities of modern Western Europe and North America have become various interpretations of rights-centered morality" (pp. 3–4).

2. Quotation from A Notebook from Side by Side, describing a mainstreamed preschool in Greenfield, Massachusetts. The notebook was prepared by the Hampshire Educational Collaborative.

3. The description of perspective taking presented here is based on Damon (1983b) and Turiel (1983). Not all developmentalists view perspective taking in this way. Robert Selman (1980) is a leading proponent of the position that role taking is a unified cognitive capacity in its own right, developing in its own sequence of stages. Damon (1983b, Chapter 4) presents a valuable consideration of the pros and cons of each position, ultimately concluding that the research best supports the view of role taking as a multifaceted skill embedded in specific task domains.

4. Shure, Spivack, & Jaeger (1971), Shure & Spivack (1978), and Spivack & Shure (1974) discuss an interventional approach to helping young children acquire skills of social problem solving, including causal reasoning.

5. Piaget (1932/1948); also see the reviews of research on moral intentionality in Gruenich (1982), Karniol (1980), Keasey (1978).

6. Copple, Sigel, & Saunders (1979, Chapter 7) provide an in-depth discussion of social-affective development from a cognitive perspective. This chapter also contains many practical suggestions and activities.

7. Forman and Hill (1980) call all of these activities "encounters with perspective" and offer many additional ingenious ideas, such as the Co-op Board, Twin-Line Tennis, Co-op City, and Tilt-a-Hole Tray. Smith (1982) lists many other activities to promote cooperation among young children.

8. This skit is adapted from Piaget (1932/1948) in light of suggestions by Berndt & Berndt (1975) and Keasey (1978). Experimenters since Piaget have devised many variations on the activity to simplify it or highlight different variables. (See, for example, Berg-Cross, 1975; Berndt & Berndt, 1975; Lyons-Ruth, 1978; Rybash, Roodin, & Hallion, 1979; Suls & Kalle, 1978.) These procedures allow more experimental control but, in our opinion, make the activity more time-consuming and less exciting to children than an open-ended learning encounter.

9. The key pieces of Kohlberg's work have been collected in Kohlberg (1981, 1984). His work is summarized in two highly recommended books: one for parents by Lickona (1983) and one for teachers by Reimer, Paolitto, and Hersh (1983). The book by Reimer, Paolitto, and Hersh has been our main guide in conducting moral discussions with children. A good evaluation of Kohlberg's approach to moral education from a philosophical point of view can be found in Carter (1984). The cross-cultural validity of Kohlberg's theory is explored in Edwards (1975, 1982) and Snarey (1984).

10. Elliot Turiel and his colleagues have presented their theory and research findings in a large number of publications, including Nucci (1981, 1982); Nucci & Nucci (1982a, 1982b); Nucci & Turiel (1978); Smetana (1981, 1984); Turiel (1975, 1978, 1983); Turiel & Smetana (1984). A discussion of their theory that disputes certain aspects of its cultural universality can be found in Edwards (1985b).

References

Albert, Alexa A., & Porter, Judith R. 1983. Age patterns in the development of children's gender-role stereotypes. *Sex Roles, 9,* 59–67.

Asher, Steven R., Oden, Sherri, & Gottman, John M. 1977. Children's friendships in school settings. In L. G. Katz (Ed.), *Current Topics in Early Childhood Education, Volume 1.* Norwood, N.J.: Ablex.

Asher, S. R., Singleton, L. C., & Taylor, A. R. 1982. Acceptance versus friendship: A longitudinal study of racial integration. Paper presented at the annual meeting of the American Educational Research Association, New York.

Ashton, Eleanor. 1983. Measures of play behavior: The influence of sex-role stereotyped children's books. *Sex Roles, 9,* 43–47.

Axline, Virginia M. 1947. *Play Therapy.* Boston: Houghton Mifflin.

Baldwin, James Mark. 1973. *Social and Ethical Interpretations in Mental Development.* New York: Arno (originally published 1899).

Berg-Cross, Linda Gail. 1975. Intentionality, degree of damage, and moral judgments. *Child Development, 46,* 970–74.

Berman, P. W., Monda, L. C., & Myerscough, R. P. 1977. Sex differences in young children's responses to an infant. *Child Development, 48,* 711–15.

Berndt, Thomas J., & Berndt, Emily G. 1975. Children's use of motives and intentionality in person perception and moral judgment. *Child Development, 46,* 904–12.

Bernstein, Anne C., & Cowan, Philip A. 1975. Children's concepts of how people get babies. *Child Development, 46,* 77–91.

Berti, Anna E. 1981. The "boss": Its conceptual development in children. *Italian Journal of Psychology, 8,* 111–19.

Berti, Anna E., & Bombi, Anna S. 1981a. Children's conception of economics. Paper presented at the annual meeting of the LEPS, Aix-en-Provence, France.

———. 1981b. The development of the concept of money and its value: A longitudinal study. *Child Development, 52,* 1179–82.

Berti, Anna E., Bombi, Anna S., & Lis, Adriana. 1982. The child's conceptions about means of production and their owners. *European Journal of Social Psychology, 12,* 221–39.

Best, Deborah L., Williams, John E., Cloud, Jonathan M., Davis, Stephen W., Robertson, Linda S., Edwards, John R., Giles, Howard, & Fowles, Jacqueline. 1977. Development of sex-trait stereotypes among young children in the United States, England, and Ireland. *Child Development, 48,* 1375–84.

Beuf, Ann. 1974. Doctor, lawyer, household drudge. *Journal of Communications, 24,* 142–45.

Bradbard, Marilyn R., & Endsley, Richard C. 1983. The effects of sex-typed labeling on preschool children's information-seeking and retention. *Sex Roles, 9,* 247–60.

Brazelton, T. Berry. 1981. *On Becoming a Family: The Growth of Attachment.* New York: Delta.

Brazelton, T. Berry, Yogman, Michael W., Als, Heidelise, & Tronick, Edward. 1979. The infant as a focus for family reciprocity. In M. Lewis and L. A. Rosenblum (Eds.), *The Child and Its Family.* New York: Plenum.

Britton, Jean O., & Britton, Joseph H. 1969. Discrimination of age by preschool children. *Journal of Gerontology, 24,* 457–60.

Brodzinsky, D. M., Singer, L. M., and Braff, A. M. 1984. Children's understanding of adoption. *Child Development, 55,* 869–78.

Bronfenbrenner, Urie. 1979. *The Ecology of Human Development.* Cambridge, Mass.: Harvard University Press.

Brooks, Jeanne, & Lewis, Michael. 1976. Infants' responses to strangers: Midget, adult, and child. *Child Development, 47,* 323–32.

Brooks-Gunn, Jeanne, & Matthews, Wendy S. 1979. *He and She: How Children Develop Their Sex-Role Identity.* Englewood Cliffs, N.J.: Prentice-Hall.

Carlson, Bonnie E. 1984. The father's contribution to child care: Effects on children's perceptions of parental roles. *American Journal of Orthopsychiatry, 54,* 123–36.

Carter, D. Bruce, & Patterson, Charlotte J. 1982. Sex roles as social conventions: The development of children's conceptions of sex-role stereotypes. *Developmental Psychology, 18,* 812–24.

Carter, Robert E. 1984. *Dimensions of Moral Education.* Toronto: University of Toronto Press.

Chambers, James C., Jr., & Tavuchis, Nicholas. 1976. Kids and kin: Children's understanding of American kin terms. *Journal of Child Language, 3,* 63–80.

Clark, Eve V. 1972. On the child's acquisition of antonyms in two semantic fields. *Journal of Verbal Learning and Verbal Behavior, 11,* 750–58.

Connell, R. W. 1971. *The Child's Construction of Politics.* Calton, Australia: Melbourne University Press.

Copple, Carol, Sigel, Irving E., & Saunders, Ruth. 1979. *Educating the Young Thinker: Classroom Strategies for Cognitive Growth.* New York: Van Nostrand.

Cordua, Glenn D., McGraw, Kenneth O., & Drabman, Ronald S. 1979. Doctor or nurse: Children's perception of sex typed occupations. *Child Development, 50,* 590–93.

Corsaro, William A. 1979. "We're friends, right?": Children's use of access rituals in a nursery school. *Language in Society, 8,* 315–36.

Damon, William. 1975. Early conceptions of positive justice as related to the development of logical operations. *Child Development, 46*, 301–12.

———. 1977. *The Social World of the Child*. San Francisco: Jossey-Bass.

———. 1980. Patterns of change in children's social reasoning: A two-year longitudinal study. *Child Development, 51*, 1010–17.

———. 1983a. The nature of social-cognitive change in the developing child. In Willis F. Overton (Ed.), *The Relationship Between Social and Cognitive Development*. Hillsdale, N.J.: Lawrence Erlbaum Associates.

———. 1983b. *Social and Personality Development: Infancy Through Adolescence*. New York: Norton.

Danziger, K. 1957. The child's understanding of kinship terms: A study in the development of relational concepts. *Journal of Genetic Psychology, 91*, 213–32.

———. 1958. Children's earliest conceptions of economic relationships (Australia). *Journal of Social Psychology, 47*, 231–40.

Davidson, Emily S., Yasuna, Amy, & Tower, Alan. 1979. The effects of television cartoons on sex-role stereotyping in young girls. *Child Development, 50*, 597–600.

Derman-Sparks, L., Higa, C. T., & Sparks, B. 1980. Children, race and racism: How race awareness develops. *Interracial Books for Children Bulletin, 11*, 3–9.

Deutsch, Werner. 1979. The conceptual impact of linguistic input: A comparison of German family-children's and orphan's acquisition of kinship terms. *Journal of Child Language, 6*, 313–27.

Duckworth, Eleanor. 1972. The having of wonderful ideas. *Harvard Educational Review, 42*, 217–31.

Dyk, Walter. 1966. *Son of Old Man Hat: A Navaho Autobiography*. Lincoln: University of Nebraska Press (originally published 1938).

Eaton, Warren O. 1983. Gender understanding and sex-role stereotyping in preschoolers: Implications for caregivers. *Child Care Quarterly, 12*, 28–35.

Edelbrock, Craig, & Sugawara, Alan I. 1978. Acquisition of sex-typed preferences in preschool-aged children. *Developmental Psychology, 14*, 614–23.

Edwards, Carolyn P. 1975. Societal complexity and moral development: A Kenya study. *Ethos: The Journal of Psychological Anthropology, 3*, 505–27.

———. 1982. Moral development in comparative cultural perspective. In D. Wagner and H. W. Stevenson (Eds.), *Cultural Perspectives on Child Development*. New York: Freeman, 248–79.

———. 1984. The age group labels and categories of preschool children. *Child Development, 55*, 440–52.

———. 1985a. Multi-age caretaking: Insights from other cultures. *Beginnings, 2*(1), 41–43.

———. 1985b. Another style of competence: The caregiving child. In A. Fogel & G. Melson (Eds.), *Origins of Nurturance*. Hillsdale, N.J.: Lawrence Erlbaum Associates.

Edwards, Carolyn P., & Lewis, Michael L. 1979. Young children's concepts of social relations: Social functions and social objects. In M. Lewis and L. Rosenblum (Eds.), *The Child and Its Family*. New York: Plenum.

Edwards, Carolyn P., Logue, Mary Ellin, & Russell, Anna S. 1983. Talking with young children about social ideas. *Young Children, 39*(6), 12–20.

Edwards, Carolyn P., & Whiting, Beatrice B. 1980. Differential socialization of girls and boys in the light of cross-cultural research. In C. Super and S. Harkness (Eds.), *Anthropological Perspectives on Child Development*. San Francisco: Jossey-Bass.

Eisenberg, Nancy, Murray, Edward, & Hite, Tina. 1982. Children's reasoning regarding sex-typed toy choices. *Child Development, 53*, 81–86.

Elkind, David. 1962. Children's conceptions of brother and sister: Piaget replication study V. *Journal of Genetic Psychology, 100*, 129–36.

Emmerich, Walter. 1959. Young children's discriminations of parent and child roles. *Child Development, 30*, 403–19.

———. 1961. Family role concepts of children ages six to ten. *Child Development, 32*, 609–24.

Emmerich, Walter, Goldman, Karla, Kirsh, Barbara, & Sharabany, Ruth. 1977. Evidence for a transitional phase in the development of gender constancy. *Child Development, 48*, 930–36.

Erwin, Joan, & Kuhn, Deanna. 1979. Development of children's understanding of the multiple determination underlying human behavior. *Developmental Psychology, 15*, 352–53.

Fassler, Joan, & Janis, Marjorie G. 1983. Books, children, and peace. *Young Children, 38*(6), 21–30.

Field, Tiffany F. 1979. Infant behaviors directed toward peers and adults in the presence and absence of mother. *Infant Behavior and Development, 2*, 47–54.

Fischer, Kurt W. 1980. A theory of cognitive development: The control and construction of hierarchies of skills. *Psychological Review, 87*, 477–531.

Fischer, Kurt W., & Bullock, Daniel. 1984. Cognitive development in school-age children: Conclusions and new directions. In W. A. Collins (Ed.), *Development During Middle Childhood: The Years from Six to Twelve*. Washington, D.C.: National Academy Press.

Fischer, Kurt W., Hand, Helen H., Watson, Malcolm W., Van Parys, Martha M., & Tucker, James L. 1984. Putting the child into socialization: The development of social categories in preschool children. In L. Katz (Ed.), *Current Topics in Early Childhood Education, Volume 5*. Norwood, N.J.: Ablex.

Flavell, J. H., Botkin, P. T., Fry, C. L., Wright, J. W., & Jarvis, P. E. 1968. *The Development of Role-Taking and Communication Skills in Children*. New York: John Wiley.

Flerx, Vicki C., Fidler, Dorothy S., & Rogers, Ronald W. 1976. Sex role stereotypes: Developmental aspects and early intervention. *Child Development, 67*, 998–1007.

Fogel, Alan. 1979. Peer versus mother directed behavior in 1–3-month-olds. *Infant Behavior and Development, 2,* 215–26.

Forman, George E., & Hill, Fleet. 1980. *Constructive Play: Applying Piaget in the Preschool.* Monterey, Calif.: Brooks/Cole.

Forman, George E., & Kuschner, David S. 1983. *The Child's Construction of Reality: Piaget for Teaching Children.* Washington, D.C.: National Association for the Education of Young Children (originally published 1977).

French, Doras C. 1984. Children's knowledge of the social functions of younger, older, and same-age peers. *Child Development, 55,* 1429–33.

Furth, Hans G. 1980. *The World of Grown-ups.* New York: Elsevier.

Furth, Hans G., Baur, Mary, & Smith, Janet E. 1976. Children's conception of social institutions: A Piagetian framework. *Human Development, 19,* 351–74.

Gallagher, Jeanette M., & Reid, D. Kim. 1981. *The Learning Theory of Piaget and Inhelder.* Monterey, Calif.: Brooks/Cole.

Garrett, C. S., Ein, P. L., & Tremaine, L. 1977. The development of gender stereotyping of adult occupations in elementary school children. *Child Development, 48,* 507–12.

Gewirth, Alan. 1968. Ethics. *The New Encyclopedia Britannica, Macropaedia, Volume 6 (Knowledge In Depth),* pp. 976–98. Chicago: Encyclopedia Britannica.

———. 1978. *Reason and Morality.* Chicago: University of Chicago Press.

Ginott, Haim. 1972. *Teacher and Child.* New York: Avon Books.

Goodman, M. 1952. *Race Awareness in Young Children.* Cambridge, Mass.: Addison-Wesley.

Gouze, Karen R., & Nadelman, Lorraine. 1980. Constancy of gender identity for self and others in children between the ages of three and ten. *Child Development, 51,* 275–78.

Greenfield, Patricia Marks, & Childs, Carla P. 1977. Understanding sibling concepts: A developmental study of kin terms in Zinacantan. In Pierre R. Dasen (Ed.), *Piagetian Psychology: Cross-Cultural Contributions.* New York: Gardner.

Grueneich, Royal. 1982. Issues in the developmental study of how children use intention and consequence information to make moral evaluations. *Child Development, 53,* 29–43.

Guttentag, Marcia, & Bray, Helen. 1976. *Undoing Sex Stereotypes: Research and Resources for Educators.* New York: McGraw-Hill.

Hanline, Mary Francis. 1985. Integrating disabled children. *Young Chlidren, 40*(2), 45–48.

Haviland, Susan E., & Clark, Eve V. 1974. "This man's father is my father's son": A study of the acquisition of English kin terms. *Journal of Child Language, 1,* 23–47.

Hoffman, Martin L. 1975. Developmental synthesis of affect and cognition and its implications for altruistic motivation. *Developmental Psychology, 11,* 607–22.

────. 1978a. Empathy, its developmental and prosocial implications. In C. B. Keasey (Ed.), *Nebraska Symposium on Motivation, Volume 25.* Lincoln: University of Nebraska Press.

────. 1978b. Toward a theory of empathic arousal and development. In M. Lewis and L. A. Rosenblum (Eds.), *The Development of Affect.* New York: Plenum.

────. 1983. Empathy, guilt, and social cognition. In Willis F. Overton (Ed.), *The Relationship Between Social and Cognitive Development.* Hillsdale, N.J.: Lawrence Erlbaum Associates.

Hohman, Mary, Banet, Bernard, & Weikart, David. 1979. *Young Children in Action: A Manual for Preschool Educators.* Ypsilanti, Mich.: High Scope Press.

Hooper, Frank H., & DeFrain, John D. 1980. On delineating distinctly Piagetian contributions to education. *Genetic Psychology Monographs, 101,* 151–81.

Hyde, Janet S. 1984. Children's understanding of sexist language. *Developmental Psychology, 20,* 697–706.

Jahoda, Gustav. 1964. Children's concepts of nationality: A critical study of Piaget's stages. *Child Development, 35,* 1081–92.

────. 1979. The construction of economic reality by some Glaswegian children. *European Journal of Social Psychology, 9,* 115–27.

Jalongo, Mary R. 1983. Using crisis-oriented books with young children. *Young Children, 38*(5), 29–36.

Jordan, Valerie Barnes. 1980. Conserving kinship concepts: A developmental study in social cognition. *Child Development, 51,* 146–55.

Kagan, Jerome. 1984. *The Nature of the Child.* New York: Basic Books.

Kamii, Constance. 1985. *Young Children Reinvent Arithmetic: Implications of Piaget's Theory.* New York: Teachers College Press.

Kamii, Constance, & DeVries, Rheta. 1978. *Physical Knowledge in Preschool Education: Implications of Piaget's Theory.* Englewood Cliffs, N.J.: Prentice-Hall.

Karniol, Rachel. 1980. A conceptual analysis of immanent justice responses in children. *Child Development, 51,* 118–30.

Katz, Lillian. 1984. The professional early childhood teacher. *Young Children, 39*(5), 3–9.

Katz, Lillian G., & Ward, Evangeline H. 1978. *Ethical Behavior in Early Childhood Education.* Washington, D.C.: National Association for the Education of Young Children.

Katz, Phillis A. 1976. The acquisition of racial attitudes in children. In P. A. Katz (Ed.), *Towards the Elimination of Racism.* New York: Pergamon.

────. 1982. Development of children's racial awareness and intergroup attitudes. In L. G. Katz (Ed.), *Current Topics in Early Childhood Education, Volume 4.* Norwood, N.J.: Ablex.

────. 1983. Developmental foundations of gender and racial attitudes. In R. L. Leahy (Ed.), *The Child's Construction of Social Inequality.* New York: Academic.

Keasey, Charles Blake. 1978. Children's developing awareness and usage of intentionality and motives. In C. B. Keasey (Ed.), *Nebraska Symposium on Motivation, Volume 25.* Lincoln: University of Nebraska Press.

Koblinsky, Sally A., & Sugawara, Alan I. 1979. Effects of nonsexist curriculum intervention on children's sex role learning. *Home Economics Research Journal, 7,* 399–406.

Kogan, Nathan, Stephens, Judith W., & Shelton, Florence C. 1961. Age differences: A developmental study of discriminability and affective response. *Journal of Abnormal and Social Psychology, 62,* 221–30.

Kohlberg, Lawrence. 1966. A cognitive-developmental analysis of children's sex-role concepts and attitudes. In E. E. Maccoby (Ed.), *The Development of Sex Differences.* Stanford, Calif.: Stanford University Press.

———. 1968. Early education: A cognitive-developmental view. *Child Development, 39,* 1013–62.

———. 1981. *Essays on Moral Development, Volume 1. The Philosophy of Moral Development.* New York: Harper & Row.

———. 1984. *Essays on Moral Development, Volume 2. The Psychology of Moral Development.* New York: Harper & Row.

Kohlberg, Lawrence, & Meyer, Rochelle. 1972. Development as the aim of education. *Harvard Educational Review, 42,* 449–96.

Kratochwill, Thomas R., & Goldman, Jane A. 1973. Developmental changes in children's judgments of age. *Developmental Psychology, 9,* 358–62.

Krogh, Suzanne L., & Lamme, Linda L. 1985. "But what about sharing?": Children's literature and moral development. *Young Children, 40*(4), 48–51.

Kropp, Jerri Jaudon, & Halverson, Charles F. 1983. Preschool children's preferences and recall for stereotyped versus nonstereotyped stories. *Sex Roles, 9,* 261–72.

Kuczaj, Stan A., II, & Lederberg, Amy R. 1977. Height, age, and function: Differing influences on children's comprehension of "younger" and "older." *Journal of Child Language, 4,* 395–416.

Kuhn, Deanna, Nash, Sharon Churnin, & Brucken, Laura. 1978. Sex role concepts of two- and three-year-olds. *Child Development, 49,* 445–51.

Kurdek, Lawrence A. 1983. *Children and Divorce.* San Francisco: Jossey-Bass.

Lamb, Michael E., & Roopnarine, Jaipaul L. 1979. Peer influences on sex-role development in preschoolers. *Child Development, 50,* 1219–22.

Lambert, W. E., & Klineberg, O. 1967. *Children's Views of Foreign People.* New York: Appleton-Century-Crofts.

Leahy, Robert L. 1981. The development of the conception of economic inequality. I. Descriptions and comparisons of rich and poor people. *Child Development, 52,* 523–32.

———. 1983a. Development of the conception of economic inequality. II. Explanations, justifications, and concepts of social mobility and change. *Developmental Psychology, 19,* 111–25.

———. 1983b. *The Child's Construction of Social Inequality.* New York: Academic.

LeVine, Robert A., & Price-Williams, Douglass R. 1974. Children's kinship concepts: Cognitive development and early experience among the Hausa. *Ethnology, 13*, 25-44.

Lewis, Michael. 1980. Newton, Einstein, Piaget and the concept of self. Invited address, the Jean Piaget Society, Philadelphia, May-June 1980.

Lewis, Michael, & Brooks-Gunn, Jeanne. 1979a. *Social Cognition and the Acquisition of Self*. New York: Plenum.

———. 1979b. Toward a theory of social cognition: The development of self. In I. C. Uzgiris (Ed.), *Social Interaction and Communication During Infancy*. New Directions in Child Development, no. 4. San Francisco: Jossey-Bass.

Lewis, Michael, & Feiring, Candice. 1979. The child's social network: Social objects, social functions, and their relationship. In M. Lewis and L. A. Rosenblum (Eds.), *The Child and Its Family*. New York: Plenum.

Lickona, Thomas. 1983. *Raising Good Children: From Birth Through the Teenage Years*. New York: Bantam Books.

Liebow, Elliot. 1967. *Tally's Corner: A Study of Negro Streetcorner Men*. Boston: Little, Brown.

Logue, Mary Ellin. 1985. Kindergarten children's concepts of parental divorce. Unpublished manuscript, Westbrook College, Portland, Maine.

Looft, William R. 1971. Children's judgments of age. *Child Development, 42*, 1282-84.

Looft, William R., Rayman, Jack R., & Rayman, Barbara B. 1972. Children's judgments of age in Sarawak. *Journal of Social Psychology, 86*, 181-85.

Luce, Terrence S. 1981. Political development and attribution of poverty by youth. Paper presented at the annual convention of the American Psychological Association, Los Angeles.

Lyons-Ruth, Karlen. 1978. Moral and personal value judgments of preschool children. *Child Development, 49*, 1197-1207.

Maccoby, Eleanor. 1985. The nature and implications of gender segregation in childhood. Paper presented at the annual meeting of the American Educational Research Association, Chicago.

Madsen, William. 1973. *The Mexican-Americans of South Texas*. New York: Holt, Rinehart & Winston.

Marcus, Dale E., & Overton, Willis F. 1978. The development of cognitive gender constancy and sex role preferences. *Child Development, 49*, 434-44.

McConaghy, Maureen J. 1979. Gender permanence and the genital basis of gender: Stages in the development of constancy of gender identity. *Child Development, 50*, 1223-26.

Moore, Shirley. 1979. Research in review: Social cognition: Learning about others. *Young Children, 34*(3), 54-61.

Moustakas, Clark. 1953. *Children in Play Therapy*. New York: Ballantine Books.

Much, Nancy C., & Shweder, Richard A. 1978. Speaking of rules: The analysis of culture in breach. In W. Damon (Ed.), *Moral Development*. New Directions for Child Development, no. 2. San Francisco: Jossey-Bass.

Munroe, Robert L., & Munroe, Ruth H. 1975. *Cross-Cultural Human Development*. Monterey, Calif.: Brooks/Cole.

Munroe, Ruth H., Shimmin, Harold S., & Munroe, Robert L. 1984. Gender understanding and sex role preference in four cultures. *Developmental Psychology, 20,* 673–82.

Naimark, Hedwin, & Shaver, Phillip. 1982. Development of the understanding of social class. Paper presented at the annual convention of the American Psychological Association, Washington, D.C.

Nucci, Larry. 1981. Conceptions of personal issues: A domain distinct from moral or societal concepts. *Child Development, 52,* 114–21.

———. 1982. Conceptual development in the moral and conventional domains: Implications for values education. *Review of Educational Research, 52,* 93–122.

Nucci, Larry P., & Nucci, Maria Santiago. 1982a. Children's responses to moral and social conventional transgressions in free-play settings. *Child Development, 53,* 1337–42.

———. 1982b. Children's social interactions in the context of moral and conventional transgressions. *Child Development, 53,* 403–12.

Nucci, Larry P., & Turiel, Elliot. 1978. Social interactions and the development of social concepts in preschool children. *Child Development, 49,* 400–407.

Paley, Virginia G. 1984. *Boys and Girls: Superheroes in the Doll Corner*. Chicago: University of Chicago Press.

Phenice, Lillian A. 1981. *Children's Perceptions of Elderly Persons*. Saratoga, Calif.: Century Twenty-One Publishing.

Piaget, Jean. 1960. *The Language and Thought of the Child*. London: Routledge & Kegan Paul (originally published 1923).

———. 1976. *Judgment and Reasoning in the Child*. Totowa, N.J.: Littlefield, Adams (originally published 1924).

———. 1948. *The Moral Judgment of the Child*. Glencoe, Ill.: Free Press (originally published 1932).

———. 1971. *The Child's Conception of Time*. New York: Ballantine Books (originally published 1946).

———. 1970. *The Science of Education and the Psychology of the Child*. New York: Viking.

———. 1983. Piaget's theory. In P. H. Mussen (Ed.), *Handbook of Child Psychology*. 4th ed. *Volume 1, History, Theory, and Methods*. New York: John Wiley.

Pickert, Sarah M., & Furth, Hans G. 1980. How children maintain a conversation with adults. *Human Development, 23,* 162–76.

Porter, J. D. 1971. *Black Child, White Child: The Development of Racial Attitudes*. Cambridge, Mass.: Harvard University Press.

Price-Williams, Douglass, Hammond, Ormond W., Edgerton, Ceel, & Walker, Michael. 1977. Kinship concepts among rural Hawaiian children. In

Pierre R. Dasen (Ed.), *Piagetian Psychology: Cross-Cultural Contributions.* New York: Gardner.

Proshansky, H. M. 1966. The development of intergroup attitudes. In I. W. Hoffman & M. L. Hoffman (Eds.), *Review of Child Development Research, Volume 2.* New York: Russell Sage Foundation.

Reimer, Joseph, Paolitto, Diana P., & Hersh, Richard H. 1983. *Promoting Moral Growth: From Piaget to Kohlberg.* 2nd ed. New York: Longman.

Rest, James R. 1983. Morality. In P. H. Mussen (Ed.), *Handbook of Child Psychology,* 4th ed. *Volume 3, Cognitive Development,* pp. 556–629. New York: John Wiley.

Rubin, Zick. 1980. *Children's Friendships.* Cambridge, Mass.: Harvard University Press.

Ruble, Diane N., Balaban, Terry, & Cooper, Joel. 1981. Gender constancy and the effects of sex-typed televised toy commercials. *Child Development, 52,* 667–73.

Rudman, Masha K. 1984. *Children's Literature: An Issues Approach.* New York: Longman.

Rybash, John M., Roodin, Paul A., & Hallion, Kenneth. 1979. The role of affect in children's attribution of intentionality and dispensation of punishment. *Child Development, 50,* 1227–30.

Samuels, Shirley, C. 1977. *Enhancing Self-Concept in Early Childhood.* New York: Human Sciences.

Sapon-Shevin, Mara. 1983. Teaching children about differences: Resources for teaching. *Young Children, 38*(2), 24–32.

Saunders, Ruth, & Bingham-Newman, Ann M. 1984. *Piagetian Perspective for Preschools: A Thinking Book for Teachers.* Englewood Cliffs, N.J.: Prentice-Hall.

Schneider, David M. 1968. *American Kinship: A Cultural Account.* Englewood Cliffs, N.J.: Prentice-Hall.

Schneider, David M., & Smith, Raymond T. 1973. *Class Differences and Sex Roles in American Kinship and Family Structure.* Englewood Cliffs, N.J.: Prentice-Hall.

Selman, Robert L. 1980. *The Growth of Interpersonal Understanding.* New York: Academic.

Shantz, Carolyn U. 1975. The development of social cognition. In E. M. Hetherington (Ed.), *Review of Child Development Research, Volume 5.* Chicago: University of Chicago Press.

———. 1983. Social cognition. In P. H. Mussen (Ed.), *Handbook of Child Psychology, Volume 3.* New York: John Wiley.

Shure, Myrna B., & Spivack, George. 1978. *Problem-Solving Techniques in Childrearing.* San Francisco: Jossey-Bass.

Shure, Myrna B., Spivack, George, & Jaeger, M. A. 1971. Problem-solving thinking and adjustment among disadvantaged preschool children. *Child Development, 42,* 1791–1803.

Sigel, Irving. 1970. The distancing hypothesis: A causal hypothesis for the acquisition of representational thought. In M. R. Jones (Ed.), *The Effects of Early Experience*. Miami, Fla.: University of Miami Press.

Sigel, Irving E., & Cocking, Rodney R. 1977a. *Cognitive Development from Childhood to Adolescence: A Constructivist Perspective*. New York: Holt, Rinehart & Winston.

———. 1977b. Cognition and communication: A dialectic paradigm for development. In M. Lewis & L. A. Rosenblum (Eds.), *Interaction, Communication, and the Development of Language*. New York: John Wiley.

Sigel, Irving E., & Saunders, Ruth. 1979. An inquiry into inquiry: Question asking as an instructional model. In L. G. Katz (Ed.), *Current Topics in Early Childhood Education, Volume 2*. Norwood, N.J.: Ablex.

Singleton, L. C., & Asher, S. R. 1979. Racial integration and children's peer preferences: An investigation of developmental and cohort differences. *Child Development, 50*, 936–41.

Skeen, Patsy, & McHenry, Patrick C. 1980. The teacher's role in facilitating a child's adjustment to divorce. *Young Children, 35*, 3–12.

Smetana, Judith G. 1981. Preschool children's conceptions of moral and social rules. *Child Development, 52*, 1333–36.

———. 1984. Toddlers' social interactions regarding moral and conventional transgressions. *Child Development, 55*, 1767–76.

Smith, Charles A. 1982. *Promoting the Social Development of Young Children: Strategies and Activities*. Palo Alto, Calif.: Mayfield.

Snarey, John. 1985. The cross-cultural universality of sociomoral development: A critical review of Kohlbergian research. *Psychological Bulletin, 97*, 202–32.

Spivack, George, & Shure, Myrna B. 1974. *Social Adjustment of Young Children: A Cognitive Approach to Solving Real-Life Problems*. San Francisco: Jossey-Bass.

Sprung, Barbara. 1975. *Non-sexist Education for Young Children: A Practical Guide*. New York: Citation.

Stack, Carol. 1974. *All Our Kin: Strategies for Survival in a Black Community*. New York: Harper & Row.

Stengel, Susan R. 1982. Moral education for young children. *Young Children, 37*(6), 23–31.

Stephens, William N. 1963. *The Family in Cross-Cultural Perspective*. New York: Holt, Rinehart & Winston.

Stevenson, Harold W., Miller, Leon K., & Hale, Gordon A. 1967. Children's ability to guess the ages of adults. *Psychological Reports, 20*, 1265–66.

Stone, Lawrence J. 1966. A four-year-old views the world. Unpublished manuscript, Vassar College, Poughkeepsie, N.Y.

Strauss, Anselm L. 1952. The development and transformation of monetary meanings of the child. *American Sociological Review, 17*, 275–86.

Suls, Jerry, & Kalle, Robert J. 1978. Intention, damage, and age of transgressor as determinants of children's moral judgments. *Child Development, 49*, 1270–73.

Thompson, Spencer K. 1975. Gender labels and early sex role development. *Child Development, 46,* 339–47.

Thurman, S. K., & Lewis, M. 1979. Children's responses to differences: Some possible implications for mainstreaming. *Exceptional Children, 45,* 468–70.

Tucker, J. 1979. The concepts of and attitudes toward work and play in children. Unpublished doctoral dissertation, University of Denver.

Turiel, Elliot. 1975. The development of social concepts: Mores, customs and conventions. In D. J. DePalma and J. M. Foley (Eds.), *Contemporary Issues in Moral Development.* Potomac, Md.: Lawrence Erlbaum Associates.

———. 1978. The development of concepts of social structure: Social-convention. In J. Glick and A. Clarke-Stewart (Eds.), *Personality and Social Development.* New York: Gardner.

———. 1983. *The Development of Social Knowledge: Morality and Convention.* Cambridge, England: Cambridge University.

Turiel, Elliot, & Smetana, Judith G. 1984. Social knowledge and action: The coordination of domains. In W. M. Kurtines and J. L. Gewirtz (Eds.), *Morality, Moral Behavior, and Moral Development.* New York: John Wiley.

Ullian, Dora. 1976. The development of conceptions of masculinity and femininity. In B. Lloyd & J. Archer (Eds.), *Exploring Sex Differences.* New York: Academic.

———. 1984. Why girls are good: A constructivist view. *American Journal of Orthopsychiatry, 54,* 71–82.

Wadsworth, Barry J. 1978. *Piaget for the Classroom Teacher.* New York: Longman.

Walsh, Huber M. 1980. *Introducing the Young Child to the Social World.* New York: Macmillan.

Watson, Malcolm W., & Amgott-Kwan, Terry. 1983. Transitions in children's understanding of parental roles. *Developmental Psychology, 19,* 659–66.

Wehren, Aileen, & De Lisi, Richard. 1983. Judgments and explanations. *Child Development, 54,* 1568–78.

Weinraub, Marsha, Clemens, Lynda P., Sockloff, Alan, Ethridge, Teresa, Gracely, Edward, & Myers, Barbara. 1984. The development of sex role stereotypes in the third year: Relationships to gender labeling, gender identity, sex-typed toy preference, and family characteristics. *Child Development, 55,* 1493–1503.

Weinstein, Eugene A. 1957. Development of the concept of flag and the sense of national identity. *Child Development, 28,* 167–74.

Weisner, Thomas S., & Gallimore, R. 1977. My brother's keeper: Child and sibling caretaking. *Current Anthropology, 18,* 169–90.

Werner, Emmy E. 1984. *Child Care: Kith, Kin, and Hired Hands.* Baltimore: University Park Press.

White, Edward, Elsom, Bill, & Prawat, Richard. 1978. Children's conceptions of death. *Child Development, 49,* 307–10.

Whiting, Beatrice B., & Edwards, Carolyn P. 1973. A cross-cultural analysis of sex differences in the behavior of children aged 3–11. *Journal of Social Psychology, 91*, 171–88.

Whiting, Beatrice B., & Whiting, John W. M. 1975. *Children of Six Cultures: A Psychocultural Analysis*. Cambridge, Mass: Harvard University Press.

Whiting, John W. M., Chasdi, E. H., Antonovsky, H. F., & Ayres, B. C. 1966. The learning of values. In E. Z. Vogt & E. M. Albert (Eds.), *People of Rimrock: A Study of Values in Five Cultures*. Cambridge, Mass.: Harvard University Press.

Williams, J. E., & Morland, J. K. 1976. *Race, Color, and the Young Child*. Chapel Hill: Univ. of North Carolina Press.

Williams, Thomas Rhys. 1983. *Socialization*. Englewood Cliffs, N.J.: Prentice-Hall.

Wong, David B. 1984. *Moral Relativity*. Berkeley: University of California Press.

Youniss, James. 1975. Another perspective on social cognition. In A. Pick (Ed.), *Minnesota Symposium on Child Psychology, Volume 9*. Minneapolis: University of Minnesota Press.

———. 1980. *Parents and Peers in Social Development: A Sullivan-Piaget Perspective*. Chicago: University of Chicago Press.

———. 1983. Understanding differences within friendship. In R. L. Leahy (Ed.), *The Child's Construction of Social Inequality*. New York: Academic.

About the Authors

CAROLYN POPE EDWARDS is an associate professor of education and Director of the Early Childhood Laboratory School at the University of Massachusetts, Amherst. She previously taught at Vassar College and was a research associate at the University of Nairobi, Kenya. A graduate of Radcliffe College, where she majored in anthropology, Dr. Edwards received her doctorate in human development from Harvard University. Her special interests are teacher education, children's social and moral development, and infant daycare. In addition to her work in the United States, she has conducted fieldwork in Mexico, Kenya, and Italy. She is the author of numerous journal articles and contributed chapters on child development, particularly as seen from a cross-cultural perspective.

PATRICIA G. RAMSEY is an assistant professor of psychology and education and Director of Gorse Child Study Center at Mount Holyoke College in South Hadley, Massachusetts. Formerly, she taught in the Early Childhood Departments at Wheelock College, Indiana University, and the University of Massachusetts. She holds a masters degree from California State University in San Francisco and a doctorate in early childhood education from the University of Massachusetts in Amherst. She is a former preschool and kindergarten teacher.

Index

Acceleration of competence, 16–18
Adoption, 109
Adult role models, 70
Affective perspective taking, 152
Age group categories, 37–57, 182
  behavioral roles and, 49–51
  of children, 45–55
  classroom activities on, 42–44, 51–55
  development of understanding of, 38–44
  suggested books for children, 55–57
Age roles, 49–51
Authority, respect for, 163–64, 174, 184–85
Axline, Virginia M., 153

Baldwin, James Mark, 14–15
Behavioral roles, age group and, 49–51
Behaviorist psychology, 6
Berti, Anna E., 128–29, 131, 133, 136
Beuf, Ann, 68
Blaine, Marge, 71
Bombi, Anna S., 128–29, 133, 136
Books
  on age-group categories, 55–57
  on cultural identity, 97–101
  on economic concepts, 145–47
  on the family, 122–24
  on friendship, 124–25
  on gender identity, 75–77
  on morality, 177–79
  on occupational concepts, 145–47
  on racial identity, 97–101
  sex-role stereotypes in, 70–72, 73
Brooks, Jeanne, 38
Brooks-Gunn, Jeanne, 15, 59
Brucken, Laura, 66
Bullock, Daniel, 6

Cause-and-effect reasoning, 154–55
Clarification in thinking games, 28–29
Classroom activities
  on age-groups, 51–55
  on aging and age differences, 42–44
  on cultural identity, 91–96
  on economic concepts, 133–38
  on friendship, 119–22
  on gender identity, 62–66
  on kinship and family, 113–16
  on moral judging, 170–76
  on occupational concepts, 141–45
  on racial identity, 84–90
  on sex roles, 72–75
  for social interpretation skills, 155–60
Cognitive development
  as aim of education, 15–16
  knowledge of self and others in, 14–15
  organization of knowledge in, 11–12
  role of child-environment interaction in, 12–14
  stages or levels in, 8–11
  See also Piaget, Jean
Complementary relationships, 138
Connell, R. W., 127
Constructive play, 18. See also Thinking games
Conventional rules, 167
Cordua, Glenn D., 68
Cultural identity, 78–79, 90–96
  classroom activities on, 91–96
  language in, 90–91, 93–96
  social conventions in, 90, 92
  stereotypes and overgeneralizations in, 96–97
  suggested books for children, 97–101
Curriculum
  impact of Piaget on, 7

Curriculum (*continued*)
    thinking games as part of, 22, 25
Customs, 167

Damon, William, 9-10, 73, 163, 164, 166,
    171, 174, 184
Davidson, Emily S., 71
DeFrain, John D., 17
Democratic standards, 15-16
Deutsch, Werner, 115
DeVries, Rheta, 12
Discussions
    on gender identity, 64-66
    moral, 170-71, 174-76
    See also Thinking games
Divorce, 110-13
Drabman, Ronald S., 68
Duckworth, Eleanor, 18
Dyk, Walter, 48

Economic concepts, 127-38
    classroom activities on, 133-38
    ownership and management of
        economic resources, 130-31
    production-to-consumption
        transactions, 129-30
    social inequality, 131-33
    suggested books for children, 145-47
    use and value of money, 127-29
Edelbrock, Craig, 70
Education
    constructive experience in, 18
    development as aim of, 15-16
    as elaboration and extension of
        competence, 16-18
Edwards, Carolyn P., 29, 45, 48, 50, 51,
    168
Egocentrism, 14
Ein, P. L., 69
Eisenberg, Nancy, 66
Empathy, 152-53
Empirical abstraction, 12-13
Erwin, Joan, 140, 155

Families (Tax), 108
Family, 102-16, 183
    age roles in, 50-51
    classroom activities on, 113-16
    development of concept of, 104-10

divorce and, 110-13
kinship systems and, 109-10
nature of, 103-4
suggested books for children, 122-24
Fassler, Joan, 178
Feiring, Candice, 37
Fidler, Dorothy S., 71
Field, Tiffany, 38
Fischer, Kurt W., 6, 10, 11-12, 60, 154,
    183
Flavell, J. H., 158
Flerx, Vickie, 71
Fogel, Alan, 38
Forman, George E., 18
Friendship, 102-4, 116-25, 183
    classroom activities on, 119-22
    development of concept of, 116-22
    nature of, 103-4
    suggested books for children, 124-25
Furth, Hans G., 37, 140

Garrett, C. S., 69
Gender identity, 182
    age group categories versus, 46, 48-49
    behavior differences and, 48-49
    classroom activities on, 62-66
    defined, 59
    development of, 60-62
    principles to guide teachers, 59
    suggested books for children, 75-77
Genetic epistemology, 6
Gewirth, Alan, 149
Ginott, Haim, 153

Halverson, Charles F., 71
Handicapped children, 153-54
Hanline, Mary Francis, 153
Hill, Fleet, 18
Hite, Tina, 66
Hoffman, Martin L., 152
Hooper, Frank H., 17

Interpersonal moral rules, 167
Interviews as thinking games, 22-23, 62-
    63. *See also* Thinking games

Jahoda, Gustav, 127
Janis, Marjorie G., 178

Justice, understanding of, 164–67, 171, 185

Kamii, Constance, 12
Katz, Lillian G., 150, 166
Katz, Phillis A., 79
Kinship. *See* Family
Klineberg, O., 90
Kohlberg, Lawrence, 11, 15, 162–63, 167
Krogh, Suzanne L., 178
Kropp, Jerri Jandon, 71
Kuhn, Deanna, 66, 140, 155
Kuschner, David S., 18

Lamb, Michael E., 70
Lambert, W. E., 90
Lamme, Linda L., 178
Language, 90–91, 93–96
Levels of development, 10
Lewis, Michael L., 15, 37, 38, 47, 50, 51, 78, 153
Liebow, Elliot, 104
Lis, Adriana, 136
Logue, Mary Ellin, 29, 111

Maccoby, Eleanor, 68
Madsen, William, 105
Matthews, Wendy S., 59
McGraw, Kenneth O., 68
Meyer, Rochelle, 15
Moore, Shirley, 7
Morality, 148–79
    classroom activities on, 155–60, 170–76
    defining, 149
    distinguishing right and wrong, 160–74
    in interpreting a social situation, 151–60
    sample moral discussion, 174–76
    suggested books for children, 177–79
    teacher's role in, 19–22, 149–51
Moral perspective taking, 152
Morland, J. K., 79, 83
Moustakas, Clark, 153
Much, Nancy C., 167, 169
Murray, Edward, 66

Nash, Sharon Churnin, 66
Nucci, Larry P., 167, 168

Occupational concepts, 138–47
    classroom activities on, 141–45
    job selection, 139–40
    social division of labor, 140–41
    suggested books for children, 145–47

Paley, Virginia G., 48
Peer role models, 70
Personal examples in thinking games, 28
Perspective taking, 151–54
Phenice, Lillian, 41
Piaget, Jean, 5–8, 9, 130, 155, 162, 163, 167, 183
    clinical method of, 19–20
    cognitive structure and, 14
    stages of development of, 9
    structure of knowledge and, 11
Porter, J. D., 83

Questions, in thinking games
    follow-up, 28–29
    guidelines for formulating and using, 29–31
    initial strategies, 26–28

Racial identity, 78–90, 182
    classroom activities on, 84–90
    cross-racial recognition, 83–84
    perceptual salience of differences, 79–81
    permanence of, 81–82, 86–87
    racially related preferences, 82–83, 89
    stereotypes and overgeneralizations in, 96–97
    suggested books for children, 97–101
Ramsey, Patricia G., 78–101
Reflexive abstraction, 13–14
Regulations, 167
Reinforcement in thinking games, 32–33
Relational concepts
    of the family, 106–9
    of friendship, 116–19
Representational competence, 17–18
Rest, James, 151
Rogers, Ronald W., 71
Role models, 70
Roopnarine, Jaipaul L., 70
Rudman, Marsha K., 178

74251

Rule domains, 167–70
Russell, Anna S., 29

Sapon-Shevin, Mara, 153
Scientific standards, 15–16
Selman, Robert L., 155
Sex-role identity
    acquiring, 66–72
    classroom activities on, 72–75
    defined, 59
    differences between boys and girls in,
        69–72
    principles to guide teachers, 59
Sexual identity, defined, 59
Shantz, Carolyn U., 5
Shure, Myrna B., 158
Shweder, Richard A., 167, 169
Sigel, Irving E., 17, 20
Size categories, age and, 38–42, 43, 48–49
Skills
    development of, 11–12
    levels of, 10
Skits as thinking games, 22–23
    on age and size, 43–44
    on gender identity, 63–64
    See also Thinking games
Smetana, Judith G., 167
Smith, Charles A., 156, 157
Social cognition
    assumptions underlying, 8–15
    described, 4–5
    importance of, 3–5
    teacher as guide in discussing, 19–22
    work of Piaget in, 5–8
Social conventions
    in cultural identity, 90, 92
    sex roles as, 67–69
Social perspective taking, 152
Socioeconomic status
    development of awareness of, 131–33
    representational competence and, 17
Spatial perspective taking, 151–52
Spivack, George, 158
Stack, Carol, 104
Stages of development, 9
Stengel, Susan R., 169
Stereotypes

in cultural or racial identity, 96–97
    sex-role, 70–72, 73
Stone, Lawrence J., 39
Sugawara, Alan I., 70

Tax, Meredith, 108
Teachers
    as adult role models, 70
    behaviorist psychology and, 6
    role in assisting children's gender
        awareness, 58–59
    A in promoting personality, 19–22,
        149–51
    role in social cognition, 3, 5, 7–8
Thinking games, 21–33
    acting out story-situation in, 25–26
    on age-group categories, 43, 44, 53–55
    conclusion of, 32
    on cultural identity, 92–93, 95
    developing ideas for, 24
    on economic concepts, 136–38
    follow-up activities for, 32–33
    on friendship, 121–22
    on gender identity, 63–64
    on kinship concepts, 114–16
    moderating discussion in, 31–32
    on morality, 158–60, 171–74
    preparation for, 25
    questions in, 26–31
    on racial identity, 86–90
    requirements of, 25
    on sex roles, 73–75
    types of, 22–24
Thurman, S. K., 78, 153
Tower, Alan, 71
Tremaine, L., 69
Turiel, Elliot, 11, 69, 163, 167

Walsh, Huber M., 134
Ward, Evangeline H., 150
Weinstein, Eugene A., 127
Williams, J. E., 79, 83
Williams, Thomas Rhys, 104
Work. See Occupational concepts

Yasuna, Amy, 71
Youniss, James, 54